When Marx Mattered

When Marx Mattered

An Intellectual Odyssey

HAROLD J. BERSHADY

Routledge
Taylor & Francis Group
LONDON AND NEW YORK

First published 2014 by Transaction Publishers

2 Park Square, Milton Park, Abingdon, Oxfordshire OX14 4RN
711 Third Avenue, New York, NY 10017

Routledge is an imprint of the Taylor & Francis Group, an informa business

First issued in paperback 2017

Copyright © 2014 Taylor & Francis

All rights reserved. No part of this book may be reprinted or reproduced or utilised in any form or by any electronic, mechanical, or other means, now known or hereafter invented, including photocopying and recording, or in any information storage or retrieval system, without permission in writing from the publishers.

Notice:
Product or corporate names may be trademarks or registered trademarks, and are used only for identification and explanation without intent to infringe.

Library of Congress Catalog Number: 2013037534

Library of Congress Cataloging-in-Publication Data

Bershady, Harold J.
   When Marx mattered : an intellectual odyssey / Harold J. Bershady.
     pages cm
   ISBN 978-1-4128-5369-9 (cloth : alk. paper)
   1. Bershady, Harold J. 2. Sociologists--United States--Biography. 3. College teachers--United States--Biography. 4. Jews--United States--Biography. 5. Socialism--United States--History. I. Title.
   HM479.B477A3 2014
   301.092--dc23
   [B]
                                                                        2013037534

ISBN 13: 978-1-4128-5369-9 (hbk)
ISBN 13: 978-1-138-51790-5 (pbk)

To my son, Matthew, and grandson, Isaac, who continue

Contents

Introduction ix

1. Personal Background and Setting 1
2. Theory and Hope 25
3. Theory and Practice 39
4. Illusion and Reality 63
5. McCarthy, Philosophy, and the Jewish Question 77
6. Other Discoveries 97
7. Mannheim, Morality, and Neo-Marxism 111
8. The New Left 121
9. Penn Sociology in the Age of Aquarius: 1960–1965 137
10. Pot and Protest 161
11. Negation of the Negation 175
12. Emanations 181
13. Der Alter Goy 195
14. The More Things Change . . . 217

| 15 | We Happy Few | 233 |

Afterword — 247

Acknowledgments — 251

Index — 253

Introduction

This book is an intellectual autobiography that explores three loosely related questions. The first question is: why were so many of the Marxists and socialists of various kinds I knew when I was in college, graduate school, and for a couple of decades thereafter Jewish Americans? Why, for that matter, had I, also a Jewish American, become a Marxist socialist when I was in my teens? The second question is: what were the influences, persons, and experiences that redirected most of these people, including me, away from Marxism toward a broader, more qualified, generally liberal outlook? And the third question is: what were the experiences that contributed to the making of someone like me and several of my colleagues, not all of whom are Jewish or were ever Marxists, into becoming sociological theorists?

A few general observations on each question might be useful in framing the story of the book.

On the first question: almost the first thing many of the radicals themselves noted in their fleeting and often discounted self-reflections is that virtually every one of them was a first- or just-barely-second-generation descendent of immigrant Jews from Eastern Europe. This observation occurred in the mid-1940s. Many of the parents of the radicals were themselves radicals, having become radical in Europe or soon after arriving in the United States. Most still spoke Yiddish and did not speak English well. Almost none was religious, yet they were fiercely proud of being Jewish, and all saw in Soviet Russia and Communism the promise of an end to social afflictions and injustices of many kinds. The idea of Communism was a passion for the radicals I knew, as well as for their parents. It was not a fantasy to be enjoyed at one's leisure, as one would a romance that leads after many adventures to an inevitably successful conclusion, but as a fervently desired destiny to be strived for and achieved.

Most of the parents of the radicals I knew worked at various jobs either in the textile industry, as municipal workers, or in the factories that had started up again during the Second World War. A few had become accountants or teachers, some were salesmen, others were merchants and had developed small businesses. All the parents saw themselves as being working class, and all wanted their children to be educated. Indeed, the radicals I met as an undergraduate, almost all of whom were WWII veterans and eight to ten years older than I, were becoming educated, pursuing studies that would lead to professional positions—most in social work and teaching, a smaller number in accounting and law, and a few in medicine. Some part of the reason that many Jewish students, radical or otherwise, in the mid- and late 1940s did not even make an effort to go to medical school (despite the half-true cliché of their mothers' clamoring for their sons to become doctors) was depressingly clear: although loosened during the war, the quota system permitting only a small trickle of Jews and other minorities into medical schools was still in effect. But for the radical students and for their parents in particular there was, I think, an additional reason.

Becoming a doctor would for many effectively remove them from the precincts of the working class. Being educated was one thing. Being educated and rich, as it was assumed a doctor would become, was another. And this is indeed the source of the ambivalence of how a career as a doctor was viewed by many of the radicals I knew. My father, who had an authentic radical pedigree, used to praise my scholarly accomplishments and in the next breath say with a joking irony touched with wistfulness, "But if you were a *real* doctor, Harold, the money would come rolling in." Yes, and the trouble is I might roll even farther away from my parents and their lives and class and values than being a mere professor had taken me.

Political radicals, of course, desired financial and worldly successes, whether they were Jews or not. Radicals are not self-abnegating saints. Nor are they immune to the all-too-common sour grapes from those who did not achieve such successes. Radicals are as petty, mean-spirited, and envious as anyone else. The problem with financial and worldly successes is the temptations to which they often give rise.

The Jewish and few non-Jewish radicals I knew in the late 1940s up to the early 1960s held these attitudes, and at times expressed them openly and passionately. However, they were not as commonly held, I believe, among non-Jewish radicals. My friend and colleague

Introduction

Digby Baltzell, perhaps best known as the author of *The Protestant Establishment—Aristocracy and Class in America*,[1] used to say half-jokingly but also half-seriously that he never met a Communist who wasn't a millionaire. But he was an upper-class Protestant speaking of other upper-class Protestants he knew who were Communists and whose families over several generations in the United States had become rich and well established. The bulk of the radical Jews, who were from Eastern Europe, were relative newcomers with poor to modest resources at best. (See Mike Gold, *Jews without Money*.[2]) It would take another two generations for Jewish radicals to appear whose families had money. But these families were no longer "new money," and their sons and daughters were less at risk at being seduced by the dazzle of money and possessions.

For the Jewish radicals, the trouble with riches was that they might divert them from their radical aims, as they had for others. Expressed in contemporary ideological terms, these aims were, generally, not new; they were a historicized version of ancient Hebrew eschatological prophecies of a messianic age, an "end of days," in which Jews as a people would rescue all humankind from wars and suffering. The hope generated by these prophecies of salvation flared many times over the millennia in Europe, in the Middle Ages, again in the seventeenth century that ushered in the Hasidic movement, and then in the nineteenth century, inspiring Zionism. For religious Jews it flared again during the terrible years of the Nazi Holocaust, when there was nothing left but hope. But for a great many Jews, the modern, worldly idea of salvation rose powerfully in the nineteenth century and has not been extinguished since.

However much they have joked and felt uncomfortable about it, denied it, fled it, Jews have felt different from and "other than" non-Jews: smarter, special—even, allow me to say, chosen. Chosen and therefore obliged to teach the ignorant, help the poor, cure the ill, protect and defend the innocent—that is, provide a modicum of salvation to those who need it. These are the pursuits proper for Jews, and as soon as the doors of the professional schools were opened, an extraordinary proportion of Jews flocked into teaching, law, medicine, and social work—the helping professions. Rich Jews are looked on by other Jews with wonder and envy and are allowed a certain degree of prestige—and if they contribute to worthy causes are also given approval and respect. But it is the Jews in the learning and helping professions who are viewed with respect, pride, and satisfaction. I have sometimes wondered what

Marx, the nineteenth-century prophet of hope for greater justice, would have made of the fact that so many Jews in the United States had by 1960—nearly a century after his death—become social workers rather than the bankers and money handlers he alleged many Jews had degenerated into becoming in Europe. Would he have characterized social work as the American solution to "the Jewish question"?

For some radical, intellectual Jews of the nineteenth and early twentieth centuries, such as Moses Hess (*Communist Confession of Faith*[3]), Ernst Bloch *(The Principle of Hope*[4]), and Georg Lukács in the explicit acknowledgment of his messianism (*History and Class Consciousness*, second preface[5]), Marxism was expressed as a modern, achievable version of the ancient prophecy. Hope for salvation through messianic deliverance is hardly the kind of stray, short-lived spark given off by the churning materialist wheels of history, however dialectically driven. Yet this ancient "spark" ignited the passions of the early modern radical thinkers, as it continues to do for Jews today, whether they are radical, meliorist, or even, in some cases, conservative.

The radicals I first met were all a-religious, even antireligious, yet all, since they were males, had experienced the rite of passage of the bar mitzvah. This fact in itself may not mean much, since the bar mitzvah was often a pro forma affair and equally often achieved in a rote manner. Yet, undergoing a bar mitzvah does imply that their predominantly secular but still often Yiddish-speaking parents' households retained remnants of Hebrew-Yiddish culture. Yiddish culture is not simply a matter of cuisine—bagels, lox, matzo, potato pancakes, and so on; this soul food provides emblematic tokens that reflect a more comprehensive culture and its history. Songs, stories, jokes, tales of hardship and persecution, of bravery, of sacrifice and rescue are threaded into the language and outlook of Eastern European Jews at every turn and re-expressed in English. Shades of Moses and Aaron, of David and Goliath, of Sarah and Esther and Joseph and Abraham and Judah Maccabee still inhabit Jewish households, with sometimes pale to near invisibility, almost unnoticed, but hovering, and to some degree heard and felt.

It is not surprising that growing up in households and communities in which strands of this salvationary culture are not expressed religiously but nonetheless held and communicated affected the outlook of the younger generation. In addition to a few becoming radical and a few becoming conservative, there are two other effects on political views. Some of the children of parents who had developed small businesses tend to adopt an outlook that is fiscally conservative but socially

Introduction

liberal. This can be seen in programs sponsored or endorsed by Jews who hold political office, such as former Senator Joseph Lieberman, former Governor Ed Rendell, or Congresswoman Allyson Schwartz. The largest effect, however, is that Jews in the United States have been predominantly liberal in their outlook and political affiliations. Liberal social programs aim to help people. As all the polling data continue to show, Jews vote overwhelmingly for the liberal programs of Democratic candidates. But in addition to the small and frequently fluctuating numbers of Jews who become radicals, there is another, perhaps smaller and also fluctuating number of Jews, some of whom were once radical but are now politically and to some extent even socially conservative. A few observations on these apparently very different kinds of Jews may serve to distinguish them more clearly from Jews who were once radical but have become liberals.

One fairly obvious reason for Jews to become or appear to become conservative is the role of the professional association. If Jewish or non-Jewish doctors want to practice medicine in a city in which the local medical society is well-known to be dominated by Republicans, they might facilitate their professional careers by joining the Republican Party. How they vote is another matter. For external purposes they are Republicans and counted as such. This situation is even more pertinent to lawyers, whose practice may impinge on political domains. Some may sincerely endorse conservative programs. But for others, the phenomenon of being one thing on the outside another on the inside is not new to Jews—nor does it apply only to them, of course. The presentation of self in everyday life, as Erving Goffman has shown, is never a straightforward affair. For this reason, the number of genuine conservatives among Jews and other groups who are professionals is unclear. The same considerations apply to the greater number of Jews and others who are or appear to be liberals. There are, however, less ambiguous instances of genuine conservatism among Jews and non-Jews alike.

All of us identify with others—parents, older siblings, relatives, teachers, and friends. It is not surprising, then, that conservative families are likely to produce conservative children, liberal families liberal children. "Likely," however, is the operative word in the preceding sentence. The interesting case is when a son or daughter adopts a political attitude opposite that of his or her family and early community. Norman Podhoretz, the former editor of *Commentary* magazine, a national journal focusing on Jewish and contemporary affairs, describes this situation in his two memoirs, *Making It*[6] and *Breaking Rank*[7] He grew up in a poor, Eastern European Jewish section of Brownsville in Brooklyn. Most of the people he knew as a child, including family members, were political leftists of some sort. The turning point for him was when a teacher, recognizing his intellectual and literary abilities, set about ridding him of the language and mannerisms of the street in the belief that these would be impediments to his wider recognition and success. The tutoring and not least the solicitous attention he received from this politically conservative teacher, even in matters unrelated to academic subjects, were, in their ways, a fulfillment of the high values the family placed on education and, perhaps despite some latent ambivalence, on success. This combination of instruction and attention continued for the newly well-spoken and conventionally well-mannered Podhoretz through college and graduate school, where some of his admired teachers were liberal, while others were critical of the left and sympathetic to or in support of conservative programs. What is also interesting are some of the choices Podhoretz made. He very much kept his Jewish identity but coupled this for several years with liberal, even radical views and then with the conservative positions he began to adopt in reaction to the growing rowdyism of the left and their spokesmen, some of whom were also Jews. A large part of the story of the two memoirs is of a young Jewish man who wishes to enter into and be recognized by the larger non-Jewish society while still openly being a Jew. This attitude is akin to that of many liberal Jews as well but quite opposite to that of many Jewish radicals who wish to change society and also seek in their universalist quests to distance themselves from being overtly Jewish.

Podhoretz and I are of the same generation and have had partially similar experiences but have come to develop contrary political and social views. There are other members of our generation, however, who, unlike Podhoretz, first passed through a consistent and rigorous radical mill before becoming conservative. Their disaffection from radicalism was in part intellectual and in part moral. They saw radical thinking and analysis to be too irreparably faulty both to grasp the complexities of society and to serve as a chart of the means to gain socialist ends. And radical practices, namely those of the American Communist Party and Soviet Russia, were increasingly revealed to be deeply corrupt. Perhaps worst of all was the growing understanding of the Holocaust perpetrated by the Soviets in the name of socialism. The move to political and social conservatism seemed for some disillusioned radicals to be assuming the sharpest opposition to these radical faults.

For my father's generation, there was a single, more focused and indeed overwhelming reason that some radical Jews and non-Jews became conservative. (My father, however, never went farther than becoming a liberal.) And that reason was, simply, the loss of the enormous hopes they had put in the Soviet Union when it became clear that the murderous and totalitarian practices of the Soviets, mixed with implacable anti-Semitism and xenophobia, were twins to those of Nazi Germany. All faith in the Soviet project collapsed. And for many liberal Russians caught in the vortex of the Soviet horrors—the mounting executions and imprisonments of those who deviated from what was acceptable to the Soviet powers in politics, literature, art, philosophy, law, science—*Hope against* Hope,[8] the response in the first years, gave way to *Hope Abandoned*[9] as Nadehzda Mandelstam unforgettably recorded in her two great books. In the United Sates, conservatives declared that radicals and liberals had been duped by the Soviets all along, that the masks of justice and freedom the Soviets donned were flimsy camouflages for a regime that was even more repressive and aggrandizing than that of the czar. "The truth" about the Soviets had been clear from the very start, they said, but liberals and radicals had remained willfully blind to it. As we know from their own accounts, the phenomenon some psychologists call a "gestalt switch" occurred to some of these deeply disillusioned radicals (see *The God that Failed*[10]). Some not only became politically conservative but turned back to religion as well. It is a painful story of disappointment and grief, and often lasting bitterness.

Although some radicals reacted with visceral revulsion to the practices of the Soviets and turned to conservatism, other radicals, with no less revulsion, turned toward a modified social democratic liberalism. Some of the conservative ex-radicals are better known since they have published essays and books describing their disillusion and consequent adoption of profoundly different views and political causes. But those who became liberals are, I believe, more numerous, if not as well recognized. It is to their experiences in the evolution of outlook and commitments that the second question of this book is addressed and many of its pages attempt to explore. A few prefatory comments may help set the stage for the chapters that will follow.

Most of the radicals I knew in college, almost all of whom were first-generation Jews, became my friends as well as friends with each other.

While in college, we discovered many of the inadequacies of Marxist thought together. We also discovered some of the profound misunderstandings of American society that guided the American Communist Party as well as the rigidity of the party and their occasional attempts to be intimidating to their adherents. Far from least, we learned of and discussed the terrible corruption of the Soviets. Some of these understandings occurred more slowly than others, but they occurred in common. Through the process of arriving at this common understanding and friendship, our ultimate hopes and desires for a more just society were not abandoned but altered and sustained in perhaps more realistic terms.

Most of these friends dispersed after college to enter different graduate schools and eventually settle in different communities, marry, raise families, and practice their new careers—as social workers, grade school or high school teachers, managers in city agencies, professors, and lawyers. Many remained in touch with each other for several years. This community of friends, having arrived at understandings through cooperative effort, and not least in their later engagement in the sometimes arduous day-to-day work in which they were able to better the lives of clients, patients, citizens, and students, turned even more to liberal programs as the realistic avenues of achieving some part of their still deeply felt hopes.

The radicals that I met and became friends with in graduate school during the early 1960s had somewhat parallel experiences. A few more of them than my earlier radical friends were second-generation Jews. Most became professors after completing graduate work in history, English literature, sociology, or law. A few became journalists; one or two became community organizers. Many had learned a great deal about American society from their study with notable professors, some of whom were exemplary in the unyielding liberal attitudes that, given the Cold War hysteria of the time, they maintained in the face of occasionally strong public criticism. The views of many of these radical students shifted toward liberalism partly as a result of their studies, partly because of identification with admired professors, and also in response to the more extreme and destructive forms of radicalism that emerged in the late 1960s. Some of them remained in diminishing contact with each other for many years. For many, the understanding of American society and of where they are in it has become similar to that of a friend and colleague of mine, a professor of American history who was radical as a student but is now liberal. As he has come to understand, he told me a few years ago, Americans eventually return, after a time of excess, "to the middle." There are always extremes to the right or the left, he said, and hierarchies of many kinds exist, but sooner or later they are increasingly, if not always totally, absorbed into the great maw of the middle in politics, culture, and social class that is American society. This is rather a Tocquevillian view, he acknowledged, but Tocqueville had a surer and deeper insight into America than any of the Marxists. This professor is highly respected in his profession and an influential teacher. His earlier radicalism attracted and influenced students. His more recent, thoughtful liberalism will also be attractive and influential to students.

Study, identification with exemplary liberal professors and with other radicals who have moderated their views, work experiences, reflection, and reinforcing friendships—all contributed to the modification in the views of many of the radicals I know. The radicals who emerged in the mid- and late 1970s, many of whom are second- and even third-generation Jews, have, from what I can tell, largely retained their radical views, but these views are mainly bookish and express a Marxist-inspired interpretation of many subjects. Their research often concentrates on social practices that are unjust or that serve dominant class interests. Few are, or have had the opportunity to be, engaged in political or social activity, but some have been active in providing assistance to impoverished communities. And although lacking a follow-up agenda—oddly out of keeping with earlier radical protests—some may have been involved in the Occupy Wall Street demonstrations. Their academic influence has waned, and by the late 1990s their voices had become faint. I do not know how many or whether any of them have altered their views, how many have gone to the right or how many have remained on the left. But it is likely, I think, that my historian friend's observation will be borne out for some in this younger group as well.

The third question this book explores is: why did some of my colleagues and I become sociological theorists? Although this may appear to be the easiest question of the three, it is in fact the most difficult since it requires that I become an object to myself. Nevertheless, a few comments on this may prepare the reader for some of the materials of the first chapters:

Aspects of social life were both puzzling and somewhat frightening to me as a child. The Nazis, anti-Semitism, my family's flight from Europe, the Depression were not only incomprehensible but menacing. They were like puzzles made of very sharp, spiky metallic parts whose edges needed to be put together with other parts and the whole enclosed by a safe, solid border in order to be made harmless. These puzzling social storms were clearly threatening to my family. Although threatening to me, too, they were physically intangible, expressed only in the worried conversations of parents and family. However, my family's welfare meant a great deal to me, and I very much wanted to help them and make them safe. As we entered the Second World War and our initial losses in the Pacific and the Atlantic theaters mounted, a glum anxiety seemed to settle over the nation and my family as well. Two of my beloved uncles were in the army, and one was soon sent into a dangerous war zone. The poor, contradictory explanations given for the causes of the war were inadequate even for a curious boy. The puzzles loomed, made me more anxious, and I needed to understand and solve them. I very much wanted to fight and overcome the enemies of America and my family but of course was much too young. My unexpected introduction to Marx's theories when I was in my early teens seemed to provide the solution to the whole range of questions that had so bothered me. The political and moral sides of Marx's thought were there, entwined in much of what he wrote, but they were initially second to my own moral concerns. The synoptic perspective Marx had created seemed to make much-needed sense of a confusing world. A bit later I also saw in his theory a hope for greater justice and ultimate peace. Not until society became less threatening to me, however, which is another way of saying not until I became more self-confident, did the social world become an object of genuine curiosity, one of increasing fascination that I was comfortable in wanting to study.

A few of the sociological theorists of my generation may have experienced something similar. All of them, however, whether they are of the same generation or younger, were and continue to be curious about the origins, nature, make-up, and directions of either the entirety of the social world or of one of its critical parts. For some, the curiosity was kindled early, and sociology was a natural subject to study in college. For others, the curiosity remained latent until aroused, often serendipitously, by a compelling teacher. Some sociological theorists began their studies in history or economics or philosophy or religion, but discovered in a sociology course ideas that were closer to what they were looking for.

One course in sociology is never enough. One has to enter and then permit oneself to be steadily immersed in the great sea of ideas produced by Marx, Tocqueville, Dilthey, Weber, Durkheim, Simmel,

Introduction

Mannheim, Freud, Mead, Schutz, Parsons, Levi-Strauss, Geertz, Goffman, and Bellah, among many others. And one has to learn fairly soon thereafter how to swim in this sea that is constantly being fed and stirred by other theories. In nonmetaphorical terms, one has to learn that he or she is able to think abstractly for considerable periods of time. Ability is not enough, however. One also has to have a taste for this sort of thing, so that despite the difficulties and frustrations involved in working with theories, one finds pleasure in trying to construct or assess or alter them. Not least and perhaps even most difficult, one has to learn what a "good" theory is all about. This last point, sometimes the subject of a two-semester methodological course, requires a few more words in this book.

It is often said and, indeed, often confirmed that many ideas are not changed, or at least not often changed, simply by rational argument. Ideas are deeply invested with moral convictions and affect, which is another way of saying that ideas are affected with biases of some sort. "Only a dead man," as my epigrammatic friend Digby Baltzell used to say, "is without bias." There is nothing intrinsically wrong with bias, however. One cannot be and look everywhere. Bias means that one has values and interests that direct one to select some things to think about and examine over others. In a general sense, this book is about biases, about values and interests that have been durable or more recently acquired or have turned out to be short-lived. For scholars in the natural and social sciences and humanities there is often (unfortunately not often enough) an investment as well in assaying "that most difficult and ambiguous and perhaps nonexistent thing called the truth" of a viewpoint or proposition or interpretation, as my old philosophy professor used to say. If there is "evidence" (itself a tricky idea) that contradicts a proposition, or if the proposition is seen, upon analysis, to involve inconsistent implications, it is then judged to be at least inadequate and must be altered or discarded.

This programmatic statement for evaluating propositions is widely subscribed to, but it is difficult to follow consistently. One needs a strong ego to acknowledge he or she is "wrong," and being at least occasionally wrong is, alas, part of the intellectual life. Other than this potential personal pitfall, one needs to become aware of and evaluate the limits of one's biases. The problem is that biases are often deeply implicit and unconscious. A conscious effort has to be made to search for the case that might contradict the proposition of interest. I have discovered, sometimes quite by accident and with an unhappy shock, that propositions I held about aspects of social life that I thought were indubitable were either flatly wrong or overstated. How could I have let this proposition stay in my mind so long without examining it carefully? But of course, I hadn't recognized my own biases. For this reason, constant, responsible, rational criticism is always needed. An idea or proposition is issued by a person. But one doesn't accept or reject the idea because one likes or dislikes the person. Impersonal standards are an essential part of intellectual work. Understanding and upholding these standards is every scholar's ethical duty. There are several examples of biased work in this book, some consciously and even willfully held without examination, some recognized as having been held until assessed and discarded, and some that have remained unassessed but assumed to be vindicated—none of the latter by me, I hope. These stories too are parts of the book.

Much of what follows, from the first chapter on, focuses on the trajectory of my messianic/utopian attitudes from their origins in childhood through their development in Marxism, their tempering through study and work experiences, and their departure as I began more fully to appreciate the destructive potential of unbridled utopianism. That is the crux of the book. But it is also, I think, a generation story, and, notwithstanding differences in detail, many members of my as well as a younger generation will find in the outline of my story an outline of theirs.

We have all lived though many things. We understand more, tried to act responsibly, and by and large have done the right things and done well. Our children are grown and they too, thank goodness, are doing the right things and doing well. Our grandchildren are coming up, and they may be curious about us, about the generations described in this book, some of whose members when they convene mention odd things and then sometimes laugh or sometimes shrug. They may find in the following pages some explanation of what the laughing and shrugging are all about. And they will soon turn, as we have and our children have, to find work that they love and that will help others find their way. Need for salvation and hope will continue, will always continue.

Notes

1. Random House, New York, 1964.
2. International Publishers, New York, 1930.
3. London, 1846. This pamphlet, written with Friederich Engels, was a precursor of *The Communist Manifesto*, which appeared in 1848. For a fuller discussion, see Shlomo Avineri, *Moses Hess: Prophet of Communism and Zionism*, New York University Press, 1987.

Introduction

4. MIT Press, Cambridge, 1995.
5. MIT Press, Cambridge, 1971.
6. Random House, New York, 1967.
7. Harper and Row, New York, 1979.
8. Atheneum, New York, 1970.
9. Atheneum, New York, 1974.
10. Harper and Bros., New York, 1949.

1

Personal Background and Setting

Several entangled influences of personal and family history and local, national, and international events drew me to Marx. I was born in Toronto, Canada in 1929. All the adults and children I knew until I was about five years old and started kindergarten spoke Yiddish. I was called Hershl or varieties of that name (Hershele, Hersh, Heshie, and Hesh) rather than Harold. One or two family members and friends still call me Hershl or Heshie today. Many of the people I knew also spoke English, and I was bilingual until I was about eight or nine years old, when thinking and speaking in English had become spontaneous and primary. With one exception, my Yiddish today is approximately that of an eight-year-old. The exception is that my knowledge of adult Yiddish curses and profanity—the part of a language overheard that is taboo and therefore always remembered best—remains quite good.

In Toronto, my mother and father rented two rooms in a house on Palmerston Avenue, one of several streets in a neighborhood of Jewish immigrants. (I went back to visit this neighborhood a few years ago. It is now a Portuguese neighborhood, and the houses are painted much more colorfully.) My family and the owners of this house became good friends, and we celebrated Jewish holidays with them. I still remember the pleasure of sitting in a little straw hut put up next to the house and eating a meal. This was, I discovered some years later, to celebrate Sukkot, the harvest festival.

All of my relatives, including my parents, had immigrated from small villages, *shtetls*, near Kiev in Ukraine. My mother's family, however, had come to the New World first. They had managed to get to Buffalo, New York, in 1922, before the laws establishing strict quotas for immigrants were passed. Their host family was my grandmother's sister, my great aunt. She and her husband had settled in Buffalo twelve to fifteen years earlier where he had begun a construction business that in the post–World War I boom was thriving.

My father and his family took a different route. They had gone in 1921 from Kiev to Odessa to Bucharest. In Bucharest he met my mother, and they were betrothed. But he and his family did not have an American host. After my mother left for the United States, he, his parents, two younger sisters, and a younger brother managed to get to Paris. There he found work as a cutter in the garment trades. After four years he was able to immigrate to Toronto, where my mother joined him, and they were married.

In Toronto, my father worked as a pattern maker and cutter of ladies' coats for Simpsons' Department Store. He did well at Simpsons, but the depression that shook the world in 1929 also shook Canada. With the retail clothing business in sharp decline by 1935, and his job soon ending, my parents decided to move to Buffalo, where, with the help of the larger extended family, he might find some work. My parents had become Canadian citizens, and there was no quota restriction for them.

I didn't want to leave Toronto. I had good friends in first grade and loved my first-grade teacher, whose name I still remember, Miss James. Besides, I was loyal to the king, not to somebody called a president. I had been to Buffalo several times to visit my grandparents and uncles and aunts. I loved them and enjoyed visiting them, but we always went back to Toronto. I had also gone with my parents a couple of times in a sleeping car to New York City to visit relatives, and still have wisps of memory of gently rocking in the berth and hearing the clacking of the train wheels on the tracks. The promise of more such rides did not change my mind, nor was the promise of getting a genuine hockey stick and puck when we got to Buffalo any better. I would stay in Toronto, I declared, and live where we'd always lived, with our friends on Palmerston Avenue. *They*—my parents—could go to Buffalo. I have seen photographs of myself taken during this time. And although I can remember something of the feelings I had then, I cannot connect myself today to that chubby, smiling little boy in the photographs who had those feelings. Time has constantly altered my appearance, but my stubborn essence has remained.

My sister, Marilyn, was born a month after we moved to Buffalo. Another calamity! The four of us plus my three uncles, an aunt, and my two grandparents all lived during our first year in Buffalo in my grandparents' three-and-a-half-bedroom, one-bathroom flat. This occupied the entire first floor of a two-story house my grandfather had built in the 1920s.

My grandfather was a "plasterer." I put his occupation in quotes because I discovered later that his plastering, which was genuine, was also a general term he used to describe repairs he performed or oversaw to the several houses he owned and rented out. He must have had some money with him when they arrived in Buffalo. My great aunt reminisced many years later that her brother-in-law, my grandfather, had owned several properties in his Ukrainian shtetl, and was considered to have been a prosperous man. None of this was apparent to me as a child. He wore work clothes much of the time and kept tools and a wheelbarrow, which I particularly remember, in a shed in back of the house. When he didn't leave to do work, he sat at a little table in his bedroom and read or studied what I later understood to be portions of the Talmud.

Judging from the two-family houses and small lawns in the neighborhood in which my grandfather had built his house, the neighborhood had once been at the more modest end of the middle class. When we moved in it had become primarily working class. Many rooms were rented, and more than two families lived in several of the two-family houses. About a third of the people who lived there were immigrant Jews, another third German and Irish, and a third black. There were a few corner shops whose owners lived above their stores and also a few modest, genteel families down on their luck. The women of these families would show themselves occasionally en route to a store—thin and drawn looking but always primly dressed, always with hats and veils and gloves, and always holding a small purse and a woven shopping basket. They were clearly not Jewish. By 1935 there was much less work for everybody, and times were tight.

Because I am a male and the first born in the New World, my family treated me with special favor. Although not intended as such, this went a long way to compensate me for having been unwillingly dragged across the border from Canada to Buffalo. I would often bring my grandmother a cup of tea with a cube or two of hard sugar and sit with her and talk. Sometimes she asked me to comb her long, wavy, gray and gold hair, and while I was doing this she would tell me stories of her life in Ukraine. Those stories transported me to that little village near Kiev where she had lived, was married, and bore her children. Almost all the inhabitants of the village, called Sokolievke, were Jews. I learned the villagers' names, habits, occupations, and the kinds of clothes they wore, and could refer to them almost as familiarly as she did. I never tired of hearing her stories of their doings and descriptions of what they looked like. "Jack the goat" (Yankel tsop) was one of my favorites. He had a small beard like a goat and scampered about his and his wife's crowded millinery shop spilling buttons, misplacing needles, thimbles, thread, and creating general havoc. Village life, as my grandmother described it, was tranquil and orderly, sometimes comic, and, with the exception of an occasional miscreant, benign. I felt as comfortable imagining myself walking on its unpaved dirt roads as I did when actually walking on the concrete sidewalks of what had become my own neighborhood in Buffalo, New York.

When my grandmother and I were talking together on her front porch during the summer, a fellow villager or two who had also immigrated to Buffalo might walk by. Like all larger American cities by the 1920s and 1930s, Buffalo was made up of ethnic neighborhoods in which people from the same countries in Europe, Asia, and Central and South America had settled. My grandmother greeted her landsmen as they walked past and occasionally would turn to me and say something about them. I remember one of her comments in particular because it was not only startling and funny to my seven-year-old ears, but also because many years later I found its sense repeated in more general terms by Sigmund Freud. A bald-headed, red-faced man, thick in body and coarse in manner came lumbering by. He was known in the neighborhood as an ill-mannered, loud-mouthed boor, the sort of person my family called a "bol-agole," a wagon driver. My grandmother said of him as he passed, "A ferd geyt ariber di velt un blaybt a ferd" (a horse goes around the world and remains a horse). Neither the perils of his escape from Ukraine nor any of the hardships he was facing in the New World had modified him. He was still the ill-mannered, loud-mouthed boor he had been in Sokolievke. Character is fate is the way Freud put it.

So the village might have remained had it not been for the ever more frequent pillaging of its households and ravaging of its families in the five or six years before my family left in 1921. These brutal acts were the work of those whom my grandmother called "the bandits." Because I was very young, I was spared much description of these raids. Their occurrence, however, was voiced, said quickly, remembered almost unwillingly, and as quickly shuttered away into some memory vault into which I had at the time no access. It was clear to me, even as a child of seven or eight, that the bandit raids were critical to the ending of the story; they were the closing scenes to the tales of pastoral village life my family had known in the "old country." To my questions of why the raids had occurred, my grandmother would sigh and say with a resigned nod, "They hated the Jews"—an answer that left me with the disturbing puzzle of why Jews were hated.

In tandem with my grandmother's afternoon village tales were my father's bedtime Bible stories. The stories he chose were often of the Jews' captivity in Egypt and of their perilous rescue by Moses. I imagined and worried about Moses as a baby hidden in the bulrushes, was fearful of the test put to him by the pharaoh, surprised but also relieved by the angel who magically moved his hand from the gold to the burning coals; I shuddered at the pain he must have felt when he picked up the coals and put them to his mouth, understood why and was sorry that he could speak only in a slurred manner thereafter, was startled by the burning bush he encountered, heard God's instructions and command to remove his sandals when in the presence of the Lord, tried to imagine—unsuccessfully—what the Being that spoke in the bush might actually look like, was grateful Jewish households were marked and spared the fearful plagues, thought of myself running with the Jews as they fled from Egypt, watched in wonder and delight as the waters were parted, was sickened but also thankful to see the pharaoh's approaching soldiers drown, entered the desert with fear but also as an adventure, stared in apprehension as he brought the tablets down and chastised the idolaters, ate the unleavened bread, sorrowed at his death, and with the rest of the Jews, looked to the Promised Land.

Although they had occurred in ancient times, the Bible stories of enslavement, of testing, and of near death and escape were nonetheless thrilling. And since I was born about the same time that Passover occurs, the ritual reenactment of the Jewish flight through the desert became my favorite holiday. I identified with Moses. Moses may never have seen God, even on the mountain, but he had spoken with him. He was God's special emissary, had saved the Jews, given them rules to live by, and led them to the borders of the land of milk and honey. This utopian dream of a land of abundance and peace won through great and dangerous effort was sown in me while still a child.

The structure and many of the rudiments of the Mosaic story were recapitulated in the unlikely adventures of the superheroes of the comic books. I had begun to read children's books about age four but discovered the more exciting fare of comic books soon thereafter and must have read many hundreds until other books supplanted them. Superman in particular had many quasi-Mosaic qualities: he was very young when separated from his parents; lived as a secret alien in his host society; was endowed with great powers and became tireless in their use against evildoers; had an unshakeable moral sense; never wavered in coming to the aid of the oppressed; and however mighty his deeds, was—like Moses, who did not reach the Promised Land—always the giver rather than the recipient of aid. All the other superheroes had similar qualities; they frequently faced great danger to themselves in their fight against evil, but they too turned out to be invincible in the end. I am quite sure Moses and Superman fused in my boy's mind. Moses was the Superman of the Jews; Superman was the Moses of everyone. It was not until much later, sometime in my forties, that I read about the creators of Superman and learned, not to my surprise, that they were Jews.

The Depression of the 1930s was harrowing to a great many families, my own included. Added to their hardships was a more distant yet rapidly approaching source of worry: the ominous rise of the Nazis and a hatred of Jews erupting all over Europe and beginning to course into America. My parents, uncles, and aunt gathered around the radio to listen to Father Coughlin's diatribes against Jews ("A Kholyera zol im khapn"—"Cholera he should catch," my mother used to say of him) and hear the latest news of the Nazi conquests in Belgium, Poland, and France. My father's parents, my other grandparents, had managed to reach the United States in the mid-1930s and were now living in Pittsburgh. They were cared for by my father's older brother, my Uncle Sam, who had somehow managed to get around the immigration quotas. But his two sisters, a brother, a brother- and sister-in-law, and four nephews were still in Paris, and there was growing apprehension about their safety. I saw my family's faces tense with worry and anger when they listened to the news or read the newspapers. My grandmother, in particular, feared the war was unleashing the hatred of Jews from which they had fled in Europe, and which would now reach our family in its new haven—from which there was no where left to flee. Even as a child I sensed the lingering sorrow my family felt over leaving the old world and the disorientation and anxiety they faced in the new.

Yet, my family was not a psychologically depressed one. I remember joining my family in laughing at the wonderful comedians and stories on the radio—Fred Allen and Jack Benny, *Abie's Irish Rose*, *Fibber McGee and Molly*, "Charlie McCarthy," and others. Woody Allen captured some of this in his movie *Radio Days*. My family had a well-developed sense of humor and irony. The adults enjoyed one another, shouted hair-raising curses when a mishap occurred, sang punning songs of the sexual antics of a rabbi and his wife, which I only began to understand and to laugh at when I grew older, and during the week or on Sundays they would wind up the Victrola to listen in rapture to recordings of Caruso, Galli-Curci, and the famous cantors Pinchik and Yoselle Rosenblatt or the violinist Mischa Elman. My mother had a good alto voice. Soon after arriving in the United States she went to New York City to visit her aunt. There she met Pinchik, and during her two-year stay in New York City sang with him. When we listened to his recordings, and if she felt like it, she would sing along. She was rather proud of having had that experience.

Sometimes a record would be put on of Maurice Schwartz, the Ukrainian Jewish actor, telling a story. One that I remember, because I heard it several times and it affected my moral sensibility, was called "A khazn, a shikerr" ("A Drunken Cantor"). It is a tale of a cantor too poor to pay for medicines for his devoted, beautiful, talented, gentle, thoughtful, loving, delicate, graceful daughter, who is slowly wasting away. No one will help him. His daughter gradually grows frailer and paler. He beseeches one person after another for a kopek, just one kopek, to buy medicine for his adjectivally endowed daughter, but his pleas go unanswered. His daughter becomes feebler, her eyes grow wider, her skin becomes translucent, and with a last whispered word she calls for her beloved father and dies. In sorrow and despair the cantor takes to drink and tells the tale. It was certified 100 percent pure, genuine, unadulterated schmaltz, but heartrending, and our hearts were rent. Schwartz's performance was a marvel of the actor's art, as his voice lurched in places as though in a drunken stagger, or lapsed into snatches of cantorial melody, or into tenderness, and always punctuated with sighs and sobs. The story made me sad, but I was filled with unbelief and anger that no one would help the poor cantor. It was wrong! No matter how often the record was played, everyone cried a little when hearing it. I have no doubt this story helped shape my social conscience. It occurred to me years later to wonder how the poor cantor managed to get money for the drink in which he drowned his sorrows, but I never raised the question. The stories, music, and Yiddish wordplay and curses were legacies that have stayed with me my entire life.

Everyone in my family worked. My aunt was a salesperson in a department store. Her salary was based entirely on commissions, which made her become adept at assaying and persuading the few potential customers to buy. My oldest uncle, Dave, helped my grandfather and also sold life insurance—also a commission-based income. My father and another uncle, Max, started a small manufacturing business making ladies' coats to sell wholesale to the local women's haberdasheries. The business sputtered along until World War II began. My youngest uncle, Ed, eleven years older than I, worked as a clerk in a drug store during the day and went to business school at night to study accounting. My mother and grandmother cooked and sewed, repaired clothes, cleaned the house, and cared for my baby sister and me and everyone else. My family's household economy was of necessity an austere one. But by pooling and husbanding their slender resources, they managed to stay marginally above other, smaller families we knew who had to rely on public aid.

From time to time I still wanted to go back to Canada. But other than that and one other unfulfilled yearning, I never experienced any lacks. I had books and toys and clothes and, judging from old photographs, plenty of food. But I also wanted to have piano lessons. My grandmother had a small upright piano in the living room. When my aunt Dorothy came home from work she would often kick off her shoes, sit down at the piano for a half-hour or so, and belt out and sing the latest songs, mainly those made popular by Bing Crosby. I found this great fun. She said she played by ear, but I saw both her hands going all over the keys. I liked the fuller sounds of the piano; its sonorities were much richer than the singing of Mischa Elman's violin. My aunt showed me what she did with her hands—these instructions were, in effect, lessons—and I mimicked her as best I could. I listened to the radio and transcribed the melodies I remembered onto the piano. They were clumsy and childish efforts, and there was much thumping with my left hand as I beat out the rhythms, but I held back in asking my parents for the piano lessons that might improve my music making. I saw how hard they worked, how financially pinched we were, and assumed, without really knowing, that piano lessons would cost more than they could afford. I settled on noodling my way around the keyboard of my grandmother's piano, and actually developed a fairly good sense of how to make a variety of sounds with this instrument.

I have one particularly vivid memory of my contribution to the family's well-being, and that is of helping my grandmother to darn socks. She would put a small glass under the hole in the sock, pull the sock taut so that the hole would be centered over the open end of the glass, and begin to darn the sock. She would stitch back and forth many times in one direction then turn the sock ninety degrees to stitch back and forth in the other. I threaded the needles for her and so took a certain proprietary interest in the finished product. And the finished product was indeed a small miracle of stitching: even, delicate, and stronger than the original. I don't know how many people today still darn their socks, probably not many, but I'm sure the sock industry would not be happy to see a sock-darning craze spring up.

The fact they were a bit better off than some other families did not give my family license to indulge in snobbery of any kind. If I were to tout some little accomplishment—which I sometimes did—such as a high grade on an exam, as though it were out of the ordinary, they would deflate me by congratulating me and then telling me to go stand on my head. This was equivalent to the mocking "Big deal!" But they could be much more severe. They detested and mocked snobbery and braggadocio all the more when so many people were in great need. The comparison to others that is intrinsic to snobbish acts achieves its self-elevating intention by diminishing those others yet further and adding to the pain they already feel.

An example of my family's attitude toward snobbery that remains etched in my memory and doubtless contributed to my personal makeup as well as to my social views occurred when I was about seven or eight years old. One of my mother's older cousins, Molly—whose original name in Ukraine was Malke—finally snared and married a dentist and forthwith changed her name to Mildred. With her newfound riches she bought a small convertible coupe with a rumble seat (into which I once surreptitiously crept) and flounced about town in new clothes and her new car, a lady of leisure. (Fancy-shmancy, one of my aunts said.) She spent much of her day visiting her elderly relatives, including my grandmother, for afternoon teas. She referred to her husband only as "the doctor"—I don't think any of us ever knew his first name. My grandmother found these weekly visits burdensome but was happy her niece had finally found and married a man.

As I look back now, I see that my grandmother was aware of her niece's unhappiness and did not mock or begrudge her good fortune. But the members of the extended family were not so mature or so kind. They hooted in derision at this affectation of gentility and status, dubbing her "Mildrick," converting the last syllable of her name to sound almost like the Yiddish/German word for offal.

I absorbed the antagonism to snobbery and affectation, which was directed to everyone who manifested them, not only to Jews. As I came to understand many years later, snobbery and affectation are forms of conspicuous display; underlying them is an anxious attempt to shore up one's achievements and status—things that are always in danger of being surpassed or lost. Poor Malke.

In my twenties, when I entered the fictional world of Isaac Bashevis Singer, I discovered other currents that had contributed to my family's attitude toward snobbery—and toward modesty. One was fear of the evil eye. A snobbish act, or any act that called attention to one, might summon the evil eye and thus invite misfortune. My father did not hold with such "small village foolishness," as he put it, but many of my relatives, including my mother, did. Another factor, this one more realistic, was the concern that Jews who became particularly visible were more likely to be noticed by Jew-hating gentiles, which might have dire consequences. The result of all this was to invest snobbery and display with considerable negative affect, and modesty with approval—both attitudes that seem to have become less pervasive among Jews and non-Jews alike in 2012 than they were in 1936.

In 1936, after having lived in my grandparents' house for almost a year, we found a small second-floor flat two blocks away. I could still visit my grandmother easily, which I did almost every day. I loved being with her and my aunt and uncles. Our flat had two bedrooms. My baby sister and I had one; a boarder rented the other. My parents slept on a foldout couch in the living room.

A hot water tank heated the bathroom. It shook and hissed and seemed to threaten to explode any moment, which prompted me not to dally there. The major heat in the flat came from a potbellied coal stove in the living room that glowed red from the burning coals. Since the living room was the warmest place in the flat, and winters were long and cold (this is Buffalo I am talking about), we spent a lot of time there reading and playing with our toys. We were warned to keep a safe distance from the stove, which was another source of anxiety.

One good thing about this upstairs flat was the porch. I had simply to step out the door of my bedroom to be on it. It was shaded in summer by the tall chestnut tree in front of the house, and gave me a good view of the street and the work being done in the mattress factory next door. We spent a lot of time on that porch during the summer, teaching my sister how to talk and walk, eating lunch, reading, and playing with friends.

Summers were often hot, and the windows of the factory next door would be kept open. At times, the men in the factory would ask me what

I was reading, and I would go over to the end of the porch nearest the factory and talk to them over the noise of the machines. I wasn't sure if they were teasing me or actually interested, but I told them about some of the books—by Clarence Buddington Kelland, Zane Grey, and Louisa May Alcott. We liked talking to each other. I think I read the complete works of these authors over the three summers we spent on the porch. And I also think I gave pretty good accounts of them to the men.

I remember being upset by one of the books I was reading, Zane Grey's *The Vanishing* American.[1] I reread the book about twenty years ago. It's not at the literary level of Theodore Dreiser or Sinclair Lewis, two of Grey's near contemporaries. The characters are a bit one-dimensional. But the book is moving and morally courageous for its time. It was published in the 1920s and is about the deracination of an American Indian boy, a Navaho, who is kidnapped by whites. Forced to assimilate to white ways, the boy finds as he grows up he is not accepted either by the Navahos or, with the exception of a young white woman, by whites. The Navaho tribe is portrayed as having been rendered helpless by the whites, no longer able to defend against white plundering, being treated with contempt by missionaries, and increasingly decimated by diseases the Europeans had brought.

I argued about this book with my fourth-grade teacher, Miss Ziegler. She asked the class in the beginning of the term what books we'd been reading over the summer. I told her I'd read *The Vanishing American* and said it is a great book. I was then not yet nine years old; she seemed not quite a hundred—probably somewhere between forty-five and fifty years old. She disagreed with me, dismissed the novel as a piece of trash that misrepresented religion and advocated objectionable practices. She never said what those practices were exactly. But a few years later it occurred to me she probably meant the love between the Navaho man and the white woman. We argued about the merits of this book for a while. I thought she was totally wrong, but she had the power, and after a short while I simply shut up. I still think she was wrong.

I liked everything I had read or heard about American Indians and didn't want them to be hurt. The Iroquois Indian tribe lived on a reservation near Buffalo, and the Natural History museum, to which I went many times, had several dioramas of Indian life. Some of the clay-sculpted faces meant to represent Indians looked like they could have been my relatives—high cheekbones, slightly aquiline noses, dark hair—and I wondered whether the American Indians might actually be the ten lost tribes. Many years later, when I told a cousin of my visit to one of the sites of the Anasazi Indians, she immediately said, "Oh yes. Anasaazi-Ashkenazy." So! I wasn't the only one who had wondered about the connection between Indians and Jews.

I so much liked what I saw at the Natural History museum that I joined an American Indian club, Woodcrafters, when I was about ten years old. This club, and others like it, was started by the chief naturalist of the museum, Ellsworth Jaeger, and sponsored by the Buffalo Jewish Community Center. We learned something of the beliefs, songs, dances, and ways of life of many Native American tribes. I danced one of these, the dance devised by the Indians of the Pacific Northwest to represent fish, for my grandmother. She got red in the face laughing—dangerous for her high blood pressure—as I wiggled and made rapid back-and-forth scissors-like motions with my feet. I taught my son how to do this dance and could probably still do it today, but I'd have to lean against a wall. Old fish don't wiggle too well.

We also learned how to identify a couple of dozen different kinds of trees by examining their bark and leaves—a knowledge I have since largely forgotten. Many of the Indian tribes were peaceful and portrayed as living in harmony with nature. Much of what was important to their way of life had been destroyed or taken from them by European settlers—a painful history that made me angry and sad. The analogy I drew between the hurt the Indians suffered from the Europeans and the hurt my family suffered from the bandits in Ukraine doubtless became one of the springs that fed my later radicalism.

Sometimes, if I were on the porch of our flat early in the morning, I would also see the owner of the factory drive up and park in his large, gleaming, new De Soto. As with all the other boys, I could identify every car and model that was made. The owner would step out. I could see his shiny shoes. He was a small, round man, always in a suit and tie, and no matter how warm the weather, always wearing a hat. As he walked the few steps to the front door of the factory, he would pull his keys out of his jacket pocket, unlock the door, and go inside. If I were playing on the street at the end of the day, I would sometimes see him leave. He would lock the door, pull on it to test whether it was locked, walk to his car, see me, smile, nod, and drive off. The men called him by his name, Mr. Fink, and I would occasionally say, "Good-bye, Mr. Fink" as he drove off. This would get an especially large smile from him. The men I saw who worked for him were bigger. They wore dungarees or work pants and work shirts. Their sleeves were rolled up. They never wore hats except in the winter, and then it was mainly caps. And most of them came and went by bus and streetcar. None of the men ever unlocked and locked the doors of the factory; they didn't have the keys. I grasped some of the external indicators of class and property ownership very early.

Another good thing about this flat was that it was our place, at least for the few years we lived there, and we did not have to be quite as careful as when we lived with my grandparents. My grandparents were orthodox and pious Jews. My parents were considerably fallen away, but they still kept a kosher household and observed the rituals of many of the holidays. This meant, among other things, that on Saturday mornings when I didn't go to the synagogue with my grandfather I could listen to the children's radio programs without skulking. I could even turn the radio up loud enough to hear comfortably. My father smilingly said we were acting like Reform Jews. I realized he was making a joke, but didn't understand it. He explained that Reform Jews were more modern. No, we weren't Reform Jews, but we were more modern than the Orthodox Jews. These sectarian differences, to which Reconstructionist was soon added, were arcane and baffling then, but became clearer to me many years later.

I did learn that the most important, perhaps only, Reform Rabbi in the city at the time was named Rabbi Fink. He gave a radio address every Sunday to which my parents occasionally listened. It occurred to me that Mr. Fink, the owner of the mattress factory, and Rabbi Fink might be related. I was told they weren't. Since both men were Jews and highly regarded, the Jewish question became even more puzzling.

To my intermittent yet insistent questioning as to why Jews were hated, I received no clear answers. My parents murmured that Christians could not forgive Jews for not recognizing Christ. But I had many school friends who were Christians, and I never experienced in the small orbit in which I lived even a hint of being unforgiven or of anti-Jewish sentiment from them or from anyone else.

Buffalo, in the 1930s, was a largely working-class city of about four hundred thousand people. About half of the population was Catholic, of which about half were Polish in origin, with Italian, German, and Irish making up most of the remainder. There were also sizeable numbers of African Americans and white Anglo Saxon Protestants, a handful of Chinese and Native Americans, and about thirty-five thousand Jews, mostly from Eastern Europe. Jews were the smallest of the ethnic groups from Europe.

The German Bund in Buffalo was also small, but before the Second World War it fervently advocated the Nazi cause. I only learned of the Bund's existence and activities as an adult, and cannot recall ever as a child having encountered either its pro-Nazi or anti-Semitic slogans. Most of the German population was Catholic, as were the Bund members, but considering the Nazi treatment of Poland, it is doubtful the Bund was accorded much sympathy by their co-religionists in the much larger Polish community. Nor were the Italians and Irish particularly anti-Semitic. In any event, the hair-raising charge I heard or read somewhere (from a scrawl on a building wall? from one of Father Coughlin's broadcasts?) that the Jews had killed Jesus Christ spurred me to further questioning.

I had learned of Christ from the songs and pageants of the Christmas season, a holiday my family did not observe, though many of my friends did, and one that I enjoyed. My parents denied the charge against Jews, said Christ's crucifixion was a punishment typical of the Romans, and added that the allegation was an excuse some Christians used to attack Jews. This left the reasons for the attacks on Jews unclear. But the issue of Jewish culpability in Christ's death still weighed on me. Were my parents absolutely right? They weren't Christian, after all. Was there even a shred of truth to the allegation?

I asked two of my closest Christian friends whether they thought Jews had in fact killed Christ. As Christians they should know. They assured me, as my parents had, that this had not been done by the Jews, but by the Romans. I was relieved. I don't know what I would have done had the answer been in the affirmative. I don't think they were just being kind. We knew we were of different faiths because we celebrated different holidays. But our religious differences were for the most part an abstraction that had nothing to do with our many everyday, ongoing acts of friendship.

Once, when I was about eight or nine years old, a friend of mine unexpectedly rushed the two of us to the nearby Catholic Church. We had been dawdling on our way home from school, then were noticed and began to be chased by a gang of marauding older boys who were reputed to seek, capture, tease, and hurt younger kids. The church to which my friend's family belonged was a half-block away, and its doors were open. We got there just in time. I didn't know what to do and was uneasy about being in this strange, taboo building, but also curious. Following my friend's lead and whispered encouragement, I dipped my hands into what he called "holy water" and lit a candle. The gory crucifixes stared down at me and made me more anxious. Would my parents object to where I was? Had I committed a terrible

Personal Background and Setting

transgression of some terms of the Jewish faith? Nothing untoward happened, however. No punishing bolt descended from on high. My parents were never overtly anti-Christian, and they weren't disapproving when I told them of my escape and the ritual acts I had performed in the church. This experience, and the calm, matter-of-fact quality of my parents' response, likely helped weaken the taboo against churches for me that many Jews feel, and I was able to enter churches thereafter with friends or to listen to a service with little discomfort.

The Christians my parents had known in Ukraine and Romania where they had initially fled were either Russian Orthodox or Catholic, and they were wary of them, to be sure. The Christians they knew in Buffalo, including the near-frothing Bund, seemed not too dissimilar from many of those they had known earlier and thus viewed as a potential danger. Although all my parents' close friends were Jews, they were able to establish friendly relations with Christians whom they considered trustworthy and decent. All of the people who worked for my father were Polish, yet they and my father—indeed they and we, my mother, sister, and I—were on very amicable terms. This was helped perhaps by the fact that my father could speak Polish fluently; but also, I think, it was because he honored their holidays and their families as well. We gave each other gifts and showed one another family photographs. Nevertheless, while I might have Christian friends, my parents assumed my relationships with these friends would also be civil and amicable, but not close. This was a taken for granted part of the family outlook and never stated outright. My family's attitude went counter to my feelings for my Christian friends, however. One consequence of the difference in our attitudes was that while I never brought any of my Christian friends over to our house, I sometimes did go to their houses. These imbalances began to move me slightly away from an unquestioned acceptance of my family's view.

By the age of ten or eleven, I understood that although the intensity and extent of the hatred of Jews varied over the millennia, the hatred was always present. The Jews I knew or thought I knew—my family and their friends, the people in my grandmother's village, my school friends—all of whom were, so far as I knew, blameless of any wrongdoing, made the hatred incomprehensible. It became clear to me that Jews were innocent victims of a kind of madness that possessed people at different times, including the one I was living in. But why the Jews? And why was this madness flaring now? These were mysterious and troubling questions I very much wanted to have answered.

In September 1939, when I was ten years old, Germany and England went to war. My mother had sent me to the grocery store to buy bread, and there I heard the excited announcer on the store radio. I felt intensely alert and frightened. I still had a few shreds of allegiance for Canada, and by extension for "the mother country," England. As the news continued, knots of still unemployed men as well as people who did not have a radio of their own gathered in the doorways of neighborhood stores and bars, where every radio that could be found was turned on and blaring. The men were listening intently. Some began to say we would be in the war too, perhaps within a year. Others scoffed—we were thousands of miles away; we were safe. I ran home, no longer quite so frightened but excited and still alert, hoping we would go to war. I wanted to fight the Nazis.

My parents were somber. Poland too was being invaded. There were large communities of Jews throughout Poland, especially in Warsaw and Krakow, and my parents feared for their lives. The Nazis and Fascists, my father said, aimed to conquer all of Europe. The Germans in particular were going to try to finish this war in the way they wished the First World War had ended, with German victory. But the "Boches," he said, would find stiff resistance from their longstanding adversaries, France and England. The Nazi war machine, however, was huge and ruthless. All of Europe would be involved. And soon enough America too. There would be a great deal of bloodshed, he feared. A very great deal.

In 1941 we did go to war. There were no longer idle men on the streets. A mood of concentration and seriousness had quickly settled on everyone. A public camaraderie soon developed. The rationing that was imposed affected everyone. The air-raid drills bound the city together. Above all, the attack on the nation united us. One could feel all this simply by walking in neighborhoods that before the war had been considered unsafe but in which one now felt secure. During the Second World War, Americans were not attacking one another. I wondered whether I might go to war. It wasn't only because the Nazis were doing horrible things to Jews; they were a scourge upon the earth and destroying everyone in their path. But my fighting days would be at least five or six years in the future. By then, I hoped, the Nazis and the Japanese would have been defeated.

I had started to prepare for my bar mitzvah about a year before we went to war. This consisted mainly in learning how to read and recite the Hebrew prayers from the *Daily Prayer Book*, which in Hebrew Is called a *Siddur*, and also read from the Torah. The bar mitzvah was scheduled to take place when I was thirteen, about a month and a half before graduation from grade school. By early 1941 the two upcoming events were over a year away, but they began to occupy an increasing amount of my attention. The Hebrew teachers concentrated on teaching us to read and recite the prayers in the holy tongue, but did not teach us their meanings. This phonic method neither instilled religious feeling nor yielded much sense of Hebrew as a language. It also must have bored the teachers to distraction. Many of them used to doze off as we students droned on. This gave the pranksters among us opportunities to be creative, which helped us get through it all. Nevertheless, we went through this tedium of learning to make meaningless sounds in the proper way for the sake of family and community, and because we wanted to complete the bar mitzvah.

I managed to get hold of an ancient English-Hebrew version of the Old Testament and the *Daily Prayer Book*. The English was antiquated and not understandable in places, but helpful in indicating the drift of some of the prayers. This made the rituals of the Rite of Passage less of a charade. Whenever a prayer referred to God by name—Adonoi in the Hebrew—as so many of them did, I felt I might invoke Him. I would pause for an instant and then go on. In order to keep up with everyone else, I had to recite the remainder of the prayer at breakneck speed—a facility I managed to acquire.

Learning to read the prayers in Hebrew school was not my first encounter with praying. One of my earliest memories is of my grandmother who, in a hushed and reverential ritual, recited prayers over the lighting of the candles each Friday just before sunset, ushering in the Sabbath eve. On the Sabbath day I sometimes accompanied my grandfather to the large, ornate, domed synagogue, the Jefferson Street Shul, the pride of Buffalo's orthodox Jewish community, to which I also went with my parents on the high holidays. I was enormously pleased to be allowed, even though a child, to sit with my grandfather in the company of the men. The men bowed and swayed from side to side, occasionally tapped their breasts with their fists, sometimes mumbled the prayers quickly, at other times sang them out, and frequently ended a prayer with a resounding o-meyn. Most of the men were as old as my grandfather, had gray beards and furrowed brows, wore glasses, and were bent. Over their dark, worn Sabbath suits they wrapped themselves in prayer shawls almost as large as a cape and donned black scull caps, yarmulkes, some of them shaped like a fez. Their breath smelled stale. They patted my head sometimes and spoke to me in a patois consisting largely of Yiddish and a few Hebrew words mixed with ungrammatical English phrases. My Yiddish was good enough to understand them. I didn't know what they were saying when they prayed, but they were kind and accepting and serious. I kept still and watched and listened.

After my grandfather died, I went two or three times a week for almost a year with my uncles to a different synagogue, small and plain, that had been converted from a one-story cottage. The members of the congregation were my grandfather's landsmen, immigrants from the same shtetl, hardworking and poor. They managed to make a living by a variety of means—peddling household goods and a few articles of cheap clothing from door to door or collecting used newspapers and scrap metal or delivering milk and eggs. One ran a small grocery store. Except for the grocer's plain clothes, all wore shirts and pants of widely differing patterns and styles picked up at used clothing stores, shoes of every kind, including high-top sneakers, and scarves and sweaters, many with holes in the bodies and sleeves. One of the men perpetually wore a bow tie under the collar of whatever kind of shirt he had on, and in later years was dubbed by one of my uncles as Frank Sinatra—an appellation the bow tie wearer smiled at, but seemed unsure of what it meant. These might have been considered stylistic statements in the 1960s and 1970s, but this was in 1937–38, the pit of the Depression. The men here were kind to me. And I liked them and found them lively. Sometimes at the conclusion of the morning prayers, one of the men would pull out a bottle of whisky, which they all called "shnapps," and the grocer would supply a bag of puff pastries called "kikhlekh." Most of the men would down a shot of whisky, say "L'khayim" (to life), and eat a bit of pastry, chat and joke for a few minutes, and then go off to work. This was their breakfast. The camaraderie and communal experience of the ritual of daily prayer was comforting, but did not yield much more for me than an appreciation of its religious and social importance for these men. This was something I wished for but could not give myself over to and thus could not claim for myself.

My father's and uncle's coat manufacturing business grew rapidly after the war began. They soon needed larger quarters and rented about 25,000 square feet on the second floor of a furniture warehouse. Most of the remainder of that floor, also about 2,500 square feet, was separated by a wall. This other section was filled with replicas of the furniture sold by the store downstairs. The new location of my father's and uncle's business was about eight blocks from where we lived.

Personal Background and Setting

Since my father was in charge of the manufacturing end of the business, he designed the layout of the shop. He set up two tables, side by side, each about twenty-five feet long by three-and-a-half feet wide. One was for making coat patterns and cutting linings. The other table, on which sat a large electric cutting machine, was for cutting many layers of cloth. Beyond these tables were eighteen sewing machines. And beyond the sewing machines was the pressing station with its two huge steam-driven machines; nearby was another pressing station used for touch-up work, with two long ironing boards and twenty-pound irons. There were also many racks on which to hang the completed coats. In a section of the shop farthest from the work areas, my father had placed a couple of desks, on one of which was a large, solid Royal typewriter. All of the working areas were close to the front of the shop near the fifty-foot wall of plate glass windows on which my father had had the logo, Fashion Cloak Company, neatly painted.

During the war, domestic cloth production had been curtailed to meet military needs. But through a lucky break, my father and uncle had a huge inventory of cloth. With people working again, and most suppliers unable to meet demand, they hardly needed to sell their coats. Everything they made was bought practically before it was even thought of. The demands on my father's time and energies were enormous. But after years of struggle and near poverty, this was his chance, and he took it.

The janitor's apartment on the same floor as my father's shop had stood vacant for a few years. The janitor, a former railroad man with a magnificent but much-scratched chrome-plated railroad pocketwatch on a chain, had removed himself to a small, private cubbyhole in the basement of the building. I never understood why he had done this. Perhaps his wife had died or left him. But from his basement quarters he attended to his duties and drank quietly and without interruption. He was a nice man, and helpful to my parents and to me, but he smelled like a brewery. It would save my father time and energy, and also be cheaper, if we were to move into the janitor's vacated apartment. And this is what we did. For the two days it took us to move, my sister and I stayed with my grandmother. On the third day we all went to the new apartment. The first room my parents showed me was to be my room. It was large enough to hold my books and model airplanes—and, wondrous to behold, there was an old, beat-up rolltop desk against one wall. I immediately loved that desk. The janitor had supplied the desk from one of the storage bins secreted in the maze of rooms in the basement. My sister had her own spacious room too, as did my parents. There were radiators in each room, and thanks to the janitor of blessed memory, they always worked well.

Fourteen months after we moved another wondrous thing happened, this one far greater than the unexpected appearance of a rolltop desk. It was several months before my twelfth birthday. I came home from school, put my books in my room, and sauntered into the living room/dining room. There, in full splendor sat a large, black, ornately carved upright piano. It might have been a hundred years old, the kind of piano used in local music halls. After the shock and surprise subsided a bit, I tried it out. The keys were very clean—obviously my mother had been at them. The action and resonance of this regal instrument weren't bad: lighter and fuller than my grandmother's piano, but of course it was out of tune. My parents had paid five dollars total to purchase the piano and having it moved.

Later in the week a piano tuner came. And a few days after that a carefully dressed, refined-looking gentleman appeared. He was very clean, spoke with a soft European accent, and had a kindly manner. He was probably about forty-five years old, but seemed older. He was to be my piano teacher! This man was a refugee from Austria. My parents had found him through a local branch of one of the Jewish agencies that helped Jewish refugees to resettle in the United States. His mother had been a concert pianist, and she had given him his first music lessons. His father had played violin in the orchestra of the Staatsoper of Vienna. The few references my teacher made to his parents were always in the past tense, so I assumed they were dead. He never spoke of the causes of their deaths, and I, not wishing to evoke possibly painful memories, did not ask. We did not yet know of the Holocaust, but we knew Jews were being killed throughout Europe. My teacher played both piano and violin, but soon found work as a violinist in the new Buffalo Philharmonic Orchestra. My parents paid him two dollars each week for a one-hour piano lesson.

I loved playing the piano, practiced two to three hours and often more each day, and progressed rapidly. The only drawback was that my piano sat in the combination living room/dining room, and my playing could be intrusive. But about six months later I found another piano deep in the recesses of the warehouse, and I often went there late at night and played with as much abandon as I wanted. My audience, the sofas, easy chairs, and end tables, stacked one on top of the other,

Personal Background and Setting

was always filled to the rafters, but quiet and attentive. No one stirred while I went through my half-hour warm-up exercises of scales, chords, and arpeggios. And if a piece I was practicing called for a *sforzando*, I didn't hold back. My listeners remained in rapt attention. That piano was pretty bad, but one has to put up with all sorts of pianos on tour.

There were, unhappily, also many drawbacks to the apartment. All the windows were translucent, not clear, with chicken wire embedded in the glass. They were encased by steel bars attached to the outer walls. But the windows were large and could open easily, which was a pleasure in the summer. Not one of the walls—all made of a dirty ivory-colored beaverboard—joined the ceilings. Within the gaps between the tops of the walls and the ceilings, a space of about a foot and a half, stretched the sprinkler pipes. These gaps meant that if I kept my light on after other people went to bed, my light would reach into their rooms. I rigged a small, shaded light next to my bed so that I could read, which helped, but the light, although faint, could still be seen everywhere. And of course, the slightest sound was heard throughout the apartment. The floors of the apartment were made of cement—the building was, after all, a warehouse—and the cement had been painted red. My mother got rugs to put on the floors, but they weren't completely covered.

My mother was very self-conscious of the place, and except for immediate family, close friends, my piano teacher, and a couple of the people who worked for my father, she did not want anyone to visit. Although she didn't say so, I knew she would prefer me not to bring my friends over, and I never did. For the same reason I began, after a few months, to go to my piano teacher's house for lessons. I understood her sense of shame and to some extent shared it. Although my father was very busy, I couldn't tell whether we were still poor. We certainly continued to live as though we were poor. As I grew older, I became increasingly angry that we or anyone had to suffer the humiliations of poverty. This is, as I continue to believe today, unconscionable in a society as rich as ours.

As the war progressed and the early calamitous news came in, my anxiety, and that of most other people, rose almost daily. I very much wished for the war to end soon, for us to be victorious. I didn't understand the war and could make no sense of it. Why had it happened? Why did the Japanese attack us? I wanted to beat them all, the Japanese and especially the Nazis, but didn't know how.

My uncles, still waiting for the draft board's call, were able to attend my bar mitzvah. I got through it without mishap, said the prayers, read from the Torah, and gave an impassioned speech on the need for world peace. A month and a half later I graduated from grade school, an occasion that, luckily for me, my uncles were still able to attend.

For a graduation gift, my father gave me several Russian novels and also one that he called "Don Keeshawt," pronouncing *Don Quixote* as a Russian speaker would. He had started reading these books when he was about my age, he said, not too long after his bar mitzvah, and thought I was probably ready for them. Although he had not had much formal schooling—a couple of years in a Russian high school—he set about educating himself over the years and read widely in the Russian and French classics and in modern science up to about 1925.

I wasn't quite ready for these novels, actually, but I loved them nevertheless, loved the jawbreaking names of their characters (e.g., Chichikov, Akaky Akakyevitch) and the emotional power of their stories. They had influenced my father, and I reread each one a few times over the next several years. But even with my partial understanding, I wondered whether I might have a few of the characteristics of Alyosha Karamazov as Dostoyevsky described them. I was at this time going through an intensely religious period.

Several months before my bar mitzvah, I began to try to reach God. I needed to understand what was happening in the world and thought if I could commune directly with God I would get the answer. I had got hold of a book in the school library on world religions. The variety of deities was astonishing, and a little bewildering, but what stood out was the fact there was no place, no people without a deity or deities. The effort at communion I made was entirely personal and devoid of conventions of religious ritual. But I didn't want to overlook any possible name for the deity, and so addressed them all—as many as I could remember. I did not pray in any formal sense. I thought in English a couple of times a day, most often in bed at night. I wanted to traverse the void between the Deity and me, and concentrated intently. This effort continued for about a year and a half. My grandfather used to say that only when every Jew observed all the commandments would the world be saved. And in the next breath he would sigh and say it is a burden to be a Jew. I certainly wasn't holding up my end, and from his point of view was contributing to the world's doom. But perhaps there was no God. I had heard that said before and dismissed it, but began to think it might be true.

In reading what I have just written and thinking back to what I had been attempting, I now realize that the boy I am writing about was both insular and innocent, a frequent combination, and also quite arrogant. I surely was not the only one searching for spiritual illumination and guidance, but I acted as though I, of all the others who were also searching but of whom I was oblivious, might be the one actually to find it! This certainly was *khutzpa*. But it was probably the Moses identification operating as well. However, in concluding, as I did, that since my efforts did not succeed in reaching God, the source of such illumination, God did not exist, presumed great power and authority on my part—also a part of my Moses identification. As I discovered personally and intellectually some years later, the sources of all this were unearthed by Freud with great insight. These presumptions have by now, I hope, diminished somewhat. Or at least they are better disguised.

In 1943 we had been in the war for two years. The Soviets were now our allies. My parents never referred to the Soviet Union as the Soviet Union. To them it was always Russia. Unknown to me at the time, the Communist ferment that had spread throughout Russia in the early part of the twentieth century had also briefly touched them; but they remained doubtful that Russians, though living now in a presumably nonreligious society, would ever rid themselves of their centuries-long hatred of Jews. Nevertheless, they believed that with the Russians as our allies, the tide would turn and we would defeat the Nazis. In my household, the Russians were viewed with cautious optimism, and I was glad to have some connection to this distant land where one of its villages had won so much of my affection.

Two of my beloved uncles, Ed and Max, were now in the army. Ed, the youngest, was stationed in Hawaii; Max had just finished basic training and was waiting to be shipped to Europe. My third uncle, Dave, the oldest of the three, but still well within draft age, had started a small business vital to the defense effort, and would probably not be drafted. I admired him. He was intelligent and courageous. When he was the age I was during the war, he had served as lookout in what had become a lawless and dangerous Ukraine, and helped his family escape into Romania. He and I used to talk together often. Before my parents were able to rent their own flat, my uncle Dave had offered me the use of his tiny room, under the stairs, which had a small table and chair, as a haven in which I could read undisturbed and do my homework.

A V-mail letter came from Uncle Max en route to Europe saying that Italy would be his likely destination. He said this by using Yiddish phrases the military censor would likely miss or let pass. He referred to meals he hoped to be having made of "lokshn," which means noodles or pasta—a word Jews sometimes also used to refer to Italians. This started off another round of anxiety and, on my part, more questions. I asked my uncle Dave what he thought had started the Nazi conquests and killings in the first place. He gave me a bare-bones Marxist answer, the gist of which was the following:

The war, he said, was a result of problems that were built into the make-up of capitalism. Germany had been suffering a severe economic depression, worse even than the one we had just gone through. Their industrialists desperately needed markets to begin production again. In every capitalist country, the industrialists, the capitalists, controlled the government, and when other means failed they set out through warfare to capture new markets. As long as capitalism existed, we could expect this process to repeat itself in one country after another, and there would be no end to wars and destruction and death. Only in a socialist society, in which the fruits of labor would be produced and distributed equably, in accord with human needs, would the necessity of perpetual wars be ended.

This was a totally unexpected answer. I had never thought in this way before, knew nothing about capitalism, and did not understand my uncle's comments very well. But they seemed to promise to answer questions that had bothered me for a long time. I asked whether he thought our ally, Russia—the Union of Soviet Socialist Republics—was the socialist society he was talking about. My knowledge of Russia was garnered mainly from the Russian novels my father had given me to read in English translation. These books had given me a kind of interior view of nineteenth-century Russians. But I knew little of the politics and governance of contemporary Russia other than from the newspapers, which sometimes called Joseph Stalin a dictator. My uncle thought the Russians were trying to be socialist, but had quite a way to go. What could I read that would help me understand socialism and capitalism better? He suggested I start with *The Communist Manifesto*.

Note

1.   Harper Bros, New York, 1925.

2

Theory and Hope

I enjoyed the fierce, ironic, and in places poetic language of *The Communist Manifesto*. And although my initial grasp of the argument was unsure, I found it compelling. After several readings over the next few weeks with the aid of a dictionary and more questioning of my uncle, I got the hang of it, understood the categories Marx used (in 1848) and the basic historical-economic principles of his analysis. During this reading, likely because of it, a shift in my thinking occurred. The victimization as well as the world role of the Jews, themes that had accompanied me through much of my childhood and early adolescence, had been combined with the victimization and world role of the proletariat. The Jews had a universal God; the proletariat was a universal class. The proletariat was, so to speak, the Jews writ large. Victimization became a much more inclusive category. I understood the Jews were not synonymous with the proletariat; but they, as well as others, such as American Indians and Negroes (a 1940s term), were among the capitalist victims. And if capitalist victimization could be overcome, then the victimization of Jews would also be ended. The Jews believed their mission was to save the world; the proletariat would actually do the job. With this equation I became as deeply identified with the victims of oppression as with their messianic saviors.

When I told my father I had been reading the *Manifesto*, he said the essay was important, and he was glad I was reading it; Marx had a definite, and in many ways valuable, view of the world. But, he added, I should also know that Marx was anti-Jewish and this fact, he said, affected the way Jews in Communist countries (i.e., the Soviet Union) were treated. I found both pieces of information distressing. Did this mean that Jews who had somehow managed to survive the pogroms in Russia were now endangered under Soviet rule? And wasn't Marx, according to both my father and my uncle, supposed to be Jewish? Why would he be anti-Jewish? It was not until several years later that I was able to come to some terms with these questions. The relations of Jews to Marxism and of Marx to Judaism are complex, and they concerned me intermittently, and sometimes intensely, for several years.

In an American history class in high school in the year I read the *Manifesto* I wrote a Marxist-inspired essay on the Monroe Doctrine. The Monroe Doctrine, I said, did not only aim to provide "hemispheric protection and solidarity," as that high-sounding phrase would have it. The doctrine, I wrote, was a masked effort by the rising American bourgeoisie to secure a huge potential market without European intervention. After returning the essay with comments, my teacher asked me to see him after class.

I liked this teacher, Joseph Salmon, a great deal and chatted with him fairly often after class. He was very intelligent and tough, graphic in the way he taught history (he once jumped off his desk and observed that "Rome did not fall in a day"), but at bottom he was kind. He had helped found the L'Ouverture Club in the school, the only club whose members were almost all black students. I thought the name of the club was odd, but did not see any significance in this other than that my teacher was decent and trying to help black students feel comfortable in the school. Nevertheless, I was anxious. Had I done something wrong, veered too far from the assigned texts? He asked how I had arrived at this interpretation, which in fact was not found in our high school history texts. After I told him about reading the *Manifesto* and more or less extrapolating from it, he said my interpretation was promising, but needed further development and historical support. He graded my paper A-, which leavened his criticism. Some years later, when I learned of Toussaint L'Ouverture's role in the Haitian uprising against the French, I began to understand more fully my teacher's sympathetic response to the black students and to my essay. He suggested I might find a study group that met every Wednesday afternoon in a nearby library useful in broadening my understanding.

I wrote a letter to my uncle Max in Italy describing the direction my thinking had taken. We had deciphered his earlier letter to us saying he would soon be eating "lokshn" (pasta) correctly. He was in a signal corps unit of General Mark Clark's Fifth Army fighting their way up through the boot of Italy. From what we were learning in reading the newspapers and listening to the radio, the fighting was fierce, and there were heavy casualties on both sides. The signal corps, however, was not a fighting unit, and its members, while still vulnerable to severe injury, stood a better chance of not being killed. This information was not readily accessible to my grandmother, who couldn't read the American papers or much understand the radio announcers. But despite our best efforts to keep this news from her, she was able to infer from our worried responses that the war news was often not good. The American army in Italy, however, was succeeding. And my uncle's letters, invariably cheerful, often contained amusing anecdotes of the different, tasty, nonkosher food he did not succeed in preventing himself from eating (which was acceptable to my grandmother under the circumstances) and comic renderings of efforts to speak with members of the local Italian population. We interpreted his positive letters as efforts to allay our worries—an interpretation we learned to have been correct when he retuned home after the war ended and we heard of some of the dangers he had experienced. But he answered my letter to him with a V-mail letter saying he thought I was "growing up." This commendation cheered me on. Nevertheless, we were all affected with worry and fear generated by the constant barrage of war news, and I continued to wish until the war ended that I could help fight the Nazis and the Japanese.

The study group my teacher recommended met in a small side room of the library. The room had a heavy, very solid-looking oak table in it and six or seven equally solid oak chairs. The group was made up of five men. Except for one who appeared to be in his early eighties, the others seemed to be between the ages of forty-five and seventy. I was fifteen years old and felt uncomfortable joining such a group. The men made no fuss about my youth, however, and simply accepted me as a member. I guessed my teacher must have mentioned me to at least one of the men, and they were alerted I might join them.

Over the course of our weekly meetings I learned two of the men had begun graduate studies a few years before 1929, but the Depression made it impossible for them to continue. I didn't ask, but thought they had part-time jobs. Another of the men told me he had had to drop out of medical school, also because of the Depression. He managed to start a small grocery store that blossomed into a delicatessen and began to do well after the war started. Too late, he said, to go back to medical school. One of the older men spoke with a heavy European accent (perhaps Hungarian); he told me he was a retired engineer. His view of dialectics, on which he once gave a two-second discourse, seemed amusingly absurd even to my fifteen-year-old mind: "Venn ze positif und ze negatif com togezzer, zey go poof!" I didn't learn much of the oldest man's background, but remember his precise diction and the somewhat theatrical quality of his speech.

The texts being discussed during the first month or two I attended were by Daniel De Leon, an American socialist. I assumed, given his name, De Leon was Spanish, possibly even related to the more famous Ponce De Leon. I learned later he was Sephardic, a Jew of Spanish origin.

De Leon was a vigorous proponent of socialism in the late nineteenth to early twentieth centuries. He proposed forming an association that would band together working people of all nations into a single cooperative entity. This was to be done through trade unions and other organizations such as the Industrial Workers of the World, which he had helped found. Although De Leon advocated revolutionary overthrow of capitalism, he was also amenable to peaceful means whenever possible. He ran twice for governor of New York State in the 1890s as a member of the Socialist Labor Party, commonly referred to as the SLP.

In telling us this history, the oldest member of the study group recalled escorting De Leon fifty years earlier as he campaigned for governor in Buffalo. They went into working-class neighborhoods where De Leon, with shirtsleeves rolled up, sat in one packed kitchen after another and discussed with the working men gathered there the socialist programs he would enact as governor. I found the plainspoken and unassuming De Leon of this story attractive. (I since learned that the highly educated and frequently imperious De Leon was anything but unassuming. But such was the gullibility of a youthful believer.) The story, however, also opened up the rich topic of socialism in the United States. I had been unaware this topic existed; many years later I explored it a bit.

When I told my teacher about the discussion group and some of the things I was learning, he suggested I might find Jack London's *Martin Eden*[1] interesting. This suggestion surprised and puzzled me. I had read several of London's novels—*The Sea Wolf*,[2] *Call of the Wild*,[3] *Burning Daylight*,[4] among others, and much enjoyed them. He wrote in a vivid, exciting way, but they were all adventure stories. What did *Martin Eden* have to do with the Monroe Doctrine or *The Communist Manifesto*? I got the book first thing and read it.

Martin Eden is a semi-autobiographical novel. The hero, a poor, ignorant young sailor, has a yearning and, as it turns out, a gift for writing, and sets out to educate himself. He is encouraged in this endeavor by a young bourgeois woman who finds him attractive but wants to "smooth out" the roughness of his manners and outlook. The bourgeoisie he encounters, whether of the petite or grand variety, are beastly and uncaring and dismissive of anyone not a member of their class.

Some of the intellectuals he meets, especially one, an anarchist who is crippled in body but powerful in mind and spirit, teach him things about the world he had never dreamed of. The anarchist is exemplary. He is unafraid to voice and argue his views with anyone, even in the face of dangers to himself. He is an eagle. The passage in the novel in which Eden meets and talks with the anarchist is short, but is like a beacon that shines a light through the remainder of the book. Eden is further educated at Berkeley and becomes a successful writer. But even after his successes, he is rejected by the young bourgeois woman he loves. His novels, like his person, are "too coarse." He despairs, seeks the solace of the sea that had once buoyed him, permits himself to sink below the waves he had ridden in his youth, and drowns.

Gotenyu! (My God!) What did this have to do with me? I identified with the main character, as one always does when the character is presented in a sympathetic way (I identified with some of Anna Karenina's anguish, for example.) But I was a million light years distant from being a Martin Eden type. This was a story that Maurice Schwartz could have recorded. Although written in his usual lively style, London discussed intellectual matters in *Martin Eden* that were absent from his other books. Is this why my teacher had recommended this book? I was almost too embarrassed to ask, for fear I would appear stupid, but I finally did ask. My teacher said that *Martin Eden* was a story of learning and of courage and the faltering of courage in the face of great difficulties. And did I know, he added, that Jack London had been a member of the Socialist Labor Party? He said no more, but I realized, without using this language, that I was getting a kind of moral lesson. I have tried, with uneven success, to keep this lesson in mind over the years.

The SLP published a weekly newspaper, *The People*, which De Leon had once edited. This paper was still available in 1944 in a few newsstands in the city, and I picked up a copy. On its front page was an announcement of an open meeting of the SLP to which all were invited. The meeting was scheduled to take place in two weeks in one of the local hotels. I mentioned this to a high school friend who shared my interests. We decided to go.

About four or five middle-aged men and a few women, plainly and neatly dressed, sat in a small room around a table. Could this be the membership of the SLP? I hoped not. The table had a white cloth on it, several copies of *The People*, a coffee urn, and very white paper cups. Each of the SLP members greeted us individually, introduced themselves by name, identified themselves as the membership committee, and offered us chairs. This was done simply, in much the same straightforward manner as I assumed De Leon had acted a half-century earlier. The man running the meeting had a Greek surname, but I couldn't identify the origins of the others. They all spoke in accented English. All had come to the meeting from their homes in Lackawanna (about which more in a moment). Socialism was not discussed, which disappointed my friend and me. The talk was mainly on getting enough names on a petition to permit SLP candidates to run for offices in the state election scheduled about a year and a half away. In the hope of getting some literature, we asked where their main office was. They gave us an address and phone number in Lackawanna. If we planned on visiting, we should call in advance. Two weeks later, my friend and I took the bus to Lackawanna.

Lackawanna is a working-class suburb of Buffalo that housed the huge, clanging Bethlehem and Republic Steel mills. Most of the people who lived there had their origins in Hungary, Ukraine, Slovakia, and Poland; a smaller number were from Czechoslovakia, Greece, and other Slavic and Baltic countries. Other than local tradesmen, priests, and service people, everyone else in Lackawanna worked in the steel mills, now going twenty-four hours each day, seven days per week, producing metal used in tanks, planes, guns, and ships. The town was noisy, grimy, and poor. Whatever colors the worn frame houses may have been originally, they were now gray, stained, and covered with the coal dust spewed from the steel mills and coal-fired freight trains. The air was hazy from soot year round, and acrid with the odor of burnt coal and burnt metal.

The "headquarters" of the local SLP was the living room of an upstairs flat in a frame house. A tall, spare man, middle-aged and bespectacled, who I assumed owned the house, greeted us cordially and sat us down. He put us at our ease quickly, and we began to talk. He was an accountant, well spoken and largely self-taught. His parents were Polish immigrants; his father had worked in the steel mills, his mother was a laundress. He loved literature, as I did, and had a modest but excellent collection of books. The books were kept in glass-enclosed cases. The cases were necessary, he said, to keep the coal dust out. But even an enclosed case was not enough. The dust seeped into crevices and around windowsills and got into everything—clothes, food, linens, whatever was in the house. To protect his books further, he had put a long cloth cover on all of the books in each shelf. His pride was a complete set of Shakespeare's plays, each bound in a slim, separate volume, and all covered by a protective scarf. The Modern Library published many of the other books on his shelves, as they did of my small but growing collection. We discussed some of the books I also had read, and he made suggestions of novels he thought were good. He gave my friend and me several pamphlet-style essays by De Leon on socialism and unions and a few essays by Marx. We also talked a little about De Leon's work.

The main thing about De Leon I learned at that meeting was he had had contact with Lenin, who thought favorably of him. With his syndicalist views, De Leon might have put the germ of the union of socialist soviets—soviet means council—into Lenin's mind. Before leaving, I promised to help get signatures on the petition to allow SLP candidates to run for office.

Other than the Modern Library edition of Marx's *Capital*, which I had recently bought and begun studying, I wanted to read more of Marx and Lenin's writings. Their shorter works in particular would be more contained and easier to assimilate. When I returned to my library study group, one of the men recommended the International Publishers bookstore, which was located on one of the side streets in the business section of town.

During the summer of 1945, I went door to door in working-class neighborhoods signing up people for the SLP petition. This had enjoyable moments. I helped a little girl with the fingering and rhythmic beat of Chopin's "Minute Waltz" and assured her she didn't have to complete the piece in exactly one minute. Minute also means small, a small waltz, not a super fast one. Her mother promptly signed the petition. But I also became aware that I did not think or talk or have many of the attitudes or characteristics of a "proletarian." I chalked up the uneasiness of this recognition to the fact that I was entering strange neighborhoods and houses and felt like an intruder—all of which was true, but the lesser of the reasons. The SLP got on the ballot. The following year, none of their candidates was elected.

Under the sway of De Leon's writings, I also decided during the summer of 1945 to try to unionize the workers of my father's shop. His manufacturing business had grown geometrically during the war years, and by 1945 he employed eighteen people, sixteen women and two men. The women were sewing machine operators; one of the men was a cutter, the other a presser. My mother also did some of the sewing, but she was not an "employee."

We all knew each other well. My sister would go into the shop from our adjoining apartment to give my father messages from my mother, and I would commandeer my father's typewriter to type his business correspondence. Sometimes, late at night, I would go back into the shop to write my high school papers.

Perhaps three or four times a year, the presser, whose first name was Luke, and his wife would visit us on Sunday afternoons for desert and coffee. They didn't have children of their own and had taken a fancy to my sister and me. Luke made up funny little rhymes for my sister, which she loved, and taught me how to use the giant steam pressing machines, which I much enjoyed doing. For about a year I had the best pressed pants in my high school. Every one of us spoke to each other on a first-name basis. No one called my father "boss"—he was always Irving, however oddly his name was pronounced by his Polish employees. "Ear-vink" is the closest I can come to it.

My father always spoke to his workers in their native language, in which he was fluent. They spoke to me and my sister in broken English, which was good enough to be understood. But there were two exceptions: Italian women who came to work as seamstresses for my father in the spring of 1943. They could barely speak any English. I had learned a litany of Italian swear words from my Italian friends in high school, but this meager linguistic store was totally inadequate, and in every way inappropriate, to use in speaking to anyone in the shop. My father, however, who had a great ear, could speak easily to the Italian women in their own language within a year. *Madonn'!* as my Italian high school friends would have said, wagging their right hand. My father told me that knowing the French and Romanian languages, as he did, made picking up the Italian easy.

I told my father I was going to try to unionize his shop, and he said I should go right ahead. He wasn't being nasty or sarcastic about this. He said he thought it would be interesting for me. He was not opposed to unions, he added, and if the people who worked for him wanted to unionize, they should go right ahead and do so.

Every one of his employees was working on a piecework basis, a practice that had been abolished by the clothing workers' unions decades earlier as an exploitative one. Clothing workers now got a steady wage they could rely on as long as they were employed. The union I thought to approach was the Amalgamated Clothing Workers of America, or ACWA. I'd heard about this union. One of my father's business colleagues had a much larger shop that made men's work clothes—overalls, shirts, jackets. All of his workers belonged to the ACWA. In fact, Luke had once worked in that larger shop, but had switched over to my father's shop soon after my father started in business. Before contacting the union, I thought I should speak to my father's employees to learn whether they'd be interested.

I first approached Luke, the presser, my friend and teacher, master of the steam pressing machines. As I told him what I had in mind, his perpetual unlit cigar stump began to waggle in the corner of his mouth, and he looked at me as though I'd gone mad. After I'd finished my spiel about the benefits of unionizing, he told me approximately the following: a union could be good, he acknowledged. He himself had belonged to one for ten years before he came to work for my father. But he was better off in my father's shop than he had been before. First, Luke said, my father paid very well, better than he could earn in any unionized shop. Second, he didn't have to pay union dues, which would take a chunk out of his pay. Third, my father cared for his employees and helped them, if he could, when they needed it. For example, he told me, when Anna (one of the finishers) needed money for her mother's hospital bills my father had lent her $500 without interest. (I hadn't known this.) My father, Ear-vink, was a good man, Luke told me. He worked harder than anyone else. He was not like a lot of bosses who grow fat sitting at their desks. (My father in fact was lean and compact.) It was good to work here, Luke said. A union would be wrong. We don't need it and we don't want it.

I knew my father worked hard and long. He not only had each of the skills of his employees—he could, and many times did, cut the many layers of cloth and lining that went into the making of the coats, sew the sections up on the machines, do the final stitching, and press the finished garments. Twice a year, summer and winter, he also went to New York to sketch the new styles. When he came back he translated his sketches into patterns that went into the making of the coats, a task that in the larger businesses was the sole work of specialist pattern makers. But following this, he worked out the arrangement of the patterns on the cloth so that there would be the least amount of cloth left over for the scrap bin after the cutting. He had learned how to do all this when he worked in the garment trades in Paris and Toronto. He was quick, strong, well coordinated, and had a good eye and mind. And since my uncle Max was in the army, my father had the added responsibilities of contacting the suppliers of the raw materials that were used (for which I did the requisite typing) as well as the local stores to arrange for delivery of the finished products. He hardly had to sell his coats. In the midst of war shortages he very fortunately had the goods, and people wanted to buy them. Everyone in the shop saw him dash about, doing all these things. And he would fairly often join his workers for lunch, when they would all sit and chatter, tell stories, laugh, vent their views on politics, families, soldiers, Europe, America, and Buffalo for three-quarters of an hour or so before smoking a cigarette and going back to work. My father's shop worked very well. Everyone knew he was "the boss," but he was not a "management" with whom contracts had to be negotiated, as he would have become if a union were to come in. As his business improved he increased the pay of his employees, and he still made money. He and my mother had worked many years for others; they very well knew how difficult it had been and how important it was to make a decent living.

After speaking with Luke, I decided it would be pointless to pursue the unionization of my father's shop any further. It was too small a shop anyway. The remainder of the summer I spent helping my father—typing his letters, labeling and packing up the coats to be sent to the stores—and reading and playing the piano. I overheard Luke speaking to my father. He was talking about me. "He's a good boy," I heard him say. "He'll be all right." I felt I had been totally foolish.

I bought a few collections of Marx's writings from the International Publishers bookstore that summer, several pamphlet-essays by Plekhanov, Stalin, Lenin, and a curious, short essay entitled "Marxism and Poetry" by an author I had not heard of before, George Thomson. (Many years later, I found in an essay by Terry Eagleton in *The New Left Review* reference to a George Thomson who was a professor of classics at Birmingham University in England. *This* Thomson had written an essay on false consciousness in ancient thought—an unambiguously Marxist theme and title—and he could also have been the author of "Marxism and Poetry.") I was particularly struck by the title of Thomson's essay because it had not yet occurred to me that Marxism had anything to do with literature.

I read some of the pamphlets first because they were shorter. This was a serious undertaking, and I studied them with care. Thomson's analysis of poetic rhythms and forms that, he argued, operated in sync with the rhythms of work and production was suggestive, but paid insufficient attention to poetic traditions—poets in 1945 still wrote sonnets, for example—and seemed forced and reductive even to my naïve ears. Several of the other essays were much better. I loaned my history teacher one of Plekhanov's essays, and after reading and discussing it with me he pointed out the humorous and ironic passages I had missed.

There are many things to be found in reading a text, he said, other than understanding its overt meaning. My mind immediately flashed back to *Martin Eden*; I vowed to myself to reread that book soon.

Stalin's essays on the origin of language and historical and dialectical materialism were a disappointment and also odd. They were wooden in style and formulaic in content. But also, Stalin's arguments were presented with an implacable certainty. Each of the "hences" that began his many concluding sentences was like a bolt shot home, shutting out further argument. I learned nothing from them other than that Stalin considered himself or was attempting to be something of a scholar. Perhaps he was following in his predecessor's footsteps. Lenin had first set the quasi-scholarly example.

My grandmother died in March of 1944, a year before the war in Europe ended. We had assured her that the war was going well and that her sons, my uncles, were safe—statements we believed were true. Although she did not have access to the news, she saw the gold stars and flags that began to appear on houses in the neighborhood, talked with other women, and, I'm quite sure, understood the enormity of the conflict and destruction. "So much killing," she would say, "of Jews as well as gentiles. So much grief." Her death left a gap in my life that my memories of her filled somewhat.

The war ended in September 1945, just as I was entering my senior year in high school. My uncles returned home. My history teacher said that not only was the Second World War the most technologically advanced and complex war that had ever been fought, but that for the first time in history the civilian populations learned almost to the minute of the battles fought, of the generals on either side, of the size of the armies, of the defeats and the victories. But it was finally over. We all felt that we could breathe again. The future began to open.

During the fist term of that final school year, a Catholic girl of Italian background and I became good friends. We discovered each other in an English class. We had similar tastes in literature and soon thereafter found we had similar tastes in music as well. This was, if not quite heaven, close to it. When school let out we would go to the local coffee shop, talk, smoke cigarettes, and listen to Dizzy Gillespie, Stan Kenton, Ella Fitzgerald, and other jazz notables. Sometimes after classes we went into the empty school auditorium, which housed a Steinway concert grand, and I would play for her—pieces by Chopin or Mozart or Beethoven or Gershwin and also the Grieg piano concerto that I was working up. There is nothing like the action or the dynamic range one can get from a good concert grand. She liked my playing and made comments that were direct and helpful. My dynamics, she sometimes said, were a bit exaggerated in places, and I also had a tendency to use too much rubato. This was counseling of emotional constraint from an Italian girl! Mama mia! But she was right. My playing was likely an emanation of my Jewish soul or perhaps influenced by an earlier model—my mother's recordings of Mischa Elman. I set about immediately correcting these faults in my taste, and hoped that I succeeded.

As our friendship deepened and turned romantic—how could it not?—the possibility of our getting married occurred to me. If we were to marry, I knew my parents would disapprove. They would not have considered me dead and gone through the yearlong ritual of mourning as I had heard certain Orthodox Jewish parents had done when one of their children married outside the faith. My parents, particularly my mother, would have been wounded at my leaving the fold. They would not reject my wife or me, but be sorrowful and carry the wound to their graves.

About thirty years later, when reading Isaac Bashevis Singer's *The Slave*,[5] a story set in eighteenth-century Poland of the love between a Christian woman and a Jewish man, I was reminded of my high school dilemma. My girlfriend could not, nor would I have wanted or permitted her to, masquerade as a Jewish woman, fearful of being found out, as Bashevis Singer's heroine had done.

By the time I was fifteen years old I had turned away from formal religion and have never since gone back. Nevertheless, I would not then nor will I now give up being a Jew, in particular, a first-generation Jewish American of Eastern European parentage. To give up being a Jew would have meant giving up my family and my memory, which would destroy me. I began to think of myself as a nonbelieving Jew, but, notwithstanding the apparent contradiction in this, an undogmatic nonbeliever with spiritual hankerings and appreciation of the orientation religion can provide and the hold it can have. The Jewish holidays tugged at me then as they continue to do today, but with ever less insistence.

I did not speak of marriage to my girlfriend. I was too confused and uncertain of myself to decide anything. We stayed in a kind of limbo for the remainder of the school year, talking with and enjoying one another for the time being. The phrase "for the time being" is peculiar because it has no clear parameters. I thought we would wait and see where we were after a year of college. The mean age of marriage in early 1946, as I remember discovering, was 19.1 years for males, 18.4 years for females. We had some time before reaching the mean and making a decision.

The socialist texts I was reading, combined with my romantic dilemma, convinced me that the dichotomy—either a Jew or a gentile—was not only false to my experience but also humanly and socially limiting. I was more than just a Jew. I was a human being whose likes and dislikes, loves and hates transcended religious categories. In a socialist society, the question of one's ethnic and religious identity would not take precedence. Socialism was a third way. One could choose to associate with any human being on the basis of personal interests and affinities. There would be no compulsion to associate with others on exclusionary bases, whether of religion, national origins, social position, educational level, gender, ethnicity, or age. So I believed at the time, and despite many years studying how solidarities among people are formed, continue to hope for and see signs of today. Socialists are equal members of society, and as such can choose freely. This vision, in addition to my desire to overcome being a victim, bound me to socialism even more strongly.

Notes

1. Penguin Group USA, New York, 1993.
2. Dover Publications, Mineola, NY, 1999.
3. Dover, Mineola, NY, 1990.
4. CreateSpace Independent Publishing Co., 2013.
5. Farrar, Straus & Giroux, New York, 1988.

3

Theory and Practice

College for me meant the University of Buffalo. There were no college counselors at my public high school in 1946, and there weren't many other nonparochial choices. Harvard, Yale, and Princeton—who hasn't heard of them? But those universities were like foreign countries to me, exclusive and costly principalities whose inhabitants I had never met or knew much about. When President Franklin D. Roosevelt died, the newspapers mentioned he had gone to Harvard. If *he*, with his patrician and class credentials, had gone to Harvard, I couldn't possibly think of Harvard for myself. It would take a few years before the ethnic and class barriers to the exclusive private colleges and universities would be fully struck down. And although every Jew in Buffalo probably knew that Albert Einstein was at the Institute for Advanced Studies at Princeton, which I confused with Princeton University, I wasn't Einstein. I was good at math and believed if I studied I would be able to understand the theory of relativity; but that would take a few years. Princeton was too rarefied. Not least, going to a college out of town would be costly. I believed my father's business was doing well, but I didn't want to take too much from him. No, it was definitely the University of Buffalo for me.

In early spring 1946, my high school informed its seniors that the college entrance exams would be given in two weeks. There was no preparation for them. Nothing existed then like the special classes preparing for the SATs and the year in advance practice runs that many private high schools offer. The exam I took was scheduled for three hours and consisted of true/false and multiple-choice questions, a Miller analogies test, and two on-the-spot short essays. The exam seemed simple; I finished early, confident I had done well. My only worry was my Latin and chemistry grades. It had taken me almost four years to pass two years of Latin. And I disliked the chemistry course, which, like the Latin, was another exercise in rote learning. There were, therefore, a few grades of F on my record. The principal of the high school warned us at the beginning of each year that our records would be permanent and follow us wherever we went for the remainder of our lives. This worried me some, but turned out to be pure twaddle. Another bit of scare tactics to try to get us to work harder. I hated memorizing chemical valences and Latin declensions and cases, but the grinding efforts to do so have left me with an odd legacy of still remembering singular and plural forms for masculine, feminine, and neuter Latin nouns, and formulas for water, carbon dioxide, and sulfuric acid, among a few other compounds. I was accepted into college.

I was eager to start college and signed up for two summer courses, one in history of philosophy, the other in freshman English. Classes would begin two weeks after graduating high school. I had never seen the university, didn't even know quite where it was. It took me a little over an hour by bus and street car to get there. And when I stepped off the streetcar—its last stop—and looked up, I was a bit startled and intimidated. What I saw was totally unlike my three-story stone-and-cement high school building that sat squeezed and alien between small streets and frame houses.

The University of Buffalo was located at the northeastern edge of the city. There it occupied about 125 acres of what once had been farmland. Gently rolling grassy lawns made up a large part of the campus; a small wooded area was at one end, a parking lot at another. Tree-lined walks led to the main buildings. With its stone, ivy-covered buildings, and clock tower in the center of the campus, the university looked like a small, private liberal arts college of the kind one might find in New England. I didn't know yet what a small liberal arts college in New England looked like, but at first glance the University of Buffalo looked pretty classy. Was this the place I was going to go to? Would they really accept me? True, I lived in a warehouse, but my mind was on ancient Greece. And with this conclusion, I walked into my first class.

The philosophy professor was a retired Unitarian minister. And while it was obvious he knew a great deal, he made dreadful efforts to be humorous and was exceptionally dull. Some of the books, however, were not dull. I have used Wilhelm Windelband's *History of Philosophy*[1] as a resource as well as an example of interpretation of ideas ever since. I devoured the books my professor assigned and some that he recommended and realized how much I *didn't* know; but that simply meant I would take a lot more philosophy courses.

The English professor was a wag. He smoked and swore in class and told "dirty," but literary, jokes, which made me feel I was finally in the adult world. He discussed some authors I hadn't already read—Henry James, for instance, who was new to me. I found James' novels somewhat frustrating to read; it seemed forever before he got to the crux of things, but at the same time the route he took was psychologically subtle and illuminating. Several years later when talking to my philosophy professor, Marvin Farber, about the James brothers, he said he thought William was the better writer, Henry the better psychologist. I'm still not sure. Perhaps Henry was better at both.

I explored the campus that summer. I had been naïve when starting high school, and it took almost a year before I began to feel comfortable there. I didn't want to repeat that experience in college. By talking with some of the professors, I learned how important the university was to the life of the city. Though seemingly countrified, it was deceptively large and complex. The university had an evening program for part-time students located in the downtown section of the city, medical, dental, and nursing schools near one of the major hospitals in the center of the city, a law school near the city's courts, and social work and engineering schools housed on the campus proper. Graduates of these schools occupied the majority of professional positions in the city and suburbs.

What was most important to me, however, was what I discovered about the liberal arts program and faculty. The liberal arts college was small, but offered graduate training in several disciplines leading to the doctoral degree. Moreover—and this was the big surprise—the university's faculty was sometimes called a farm school for the Ivy League! This was the first I had even heard of the Ivy League, but I soon found out what the expression stood for. Many of the professors had graduate degrees from Harvard, Yale, and Columbia. Other universities from the East, Midwest, and West were also represented, but their graduates among the faculty were apparently not as numerous, or perhaps not as clearly identified, as the ones from the Ivy League universities. A few of the professors had been trained at Oxford. And in the late 1930s a sprinkling of European refugee scholars from Germany and France was added. Before he was drafted, and even while working with my father, my uncle Max had taken night courses at the University of Buffalo. I read some of the books in his library while he was in the army—mainly the novels of Sinclair Lewis and one or two texts. He much admired Chancellor Capen, the head of the university, and when I started going to the university he told me quite a bit about him. What I learned eased some of my social qualms and made me feel

I was as legitimate a member of the university community as anyone else. Since Capen had a salutary effect on me and my radical friends, I will recapitulate briefly some of the things my uncle told me as well as a few things I found out about him for myself.

From the early 1920s, when he accepted the post as chancellor, until he retired in 1950, Samuel P. Capen made it known that he advocated liberal standards and practices. Against much initial and recurring opposition, he established an admissions policy to all sectors of the university—to the faculty, student body, and administration—based solely on ability. Race, ethnicity, religion, gender, age, and, not openly mentioned but included in practice, sexual orientation were irrelevant to the ability to administer, to teach, and to learn.

By the late 1920s, the university had hired several Jewish as well as a few women faculty. My uncle Max told me that several professors were Jews and highly respected in their professions. These professors were also, of course, highly touted in the Jewish community in Buffalo. I later read in Carey McWilliams' *A Mask for Privilege*[2] (1948) that there were more Jewish and women faculty at the University of Buffalo by 1945 than in other institutions of its kind and size.

By the late 1930s many of the faculty had gained international reputations. Wealthy donors, likely cultivated by Capen and wanting to contribute to and also be associated with the growing prestige of the university, gave substantial sums for book acquisitions and the building of a fine new library and other buildings. With the initiative of English professors and the head of the library, C. D. Abbott, and with Capen's encouragement, the library gathered within its new quarters the most extensive collection of modern English and American poetry manuscripts in the country. This I discovered by myself. The University of Buffalo has a greater Joyce collection than the University of Dublin, thanks to the labors of Joyce specialist Oscar Silverman, and Bloomsday, June 16, is celebrated yearly. And throughout the year the library draws poets and scholarly visitors from the United States and abroad. I took courses from both Abbott and Silverman and enjoyed and learned much from them.

Fewer than four thousand students and faculty were at the university in the 1930s when my uncle Max attended night classes—a little less than 1 percent of the total population of metropolitan Buffalo. But in Catholic, working-class Buffalo, this liberal university was held to be a bastion of immorality and radicalism. "Jew B" some of the most fearful locals called it. Capen was reviled many times, my uncle said, but remained unyielding in advocating liberal standards and open, rational discussion and debate. And for this he was also extolled.

When I entered the University of Buffalo as a full-time freshman in early fall 1946, I was seventeen years old. The university was growing rapidly—it would reach the nine-thousand-student mark within two years—and new buildings and walkways were sprouting up on the campus. My girlfriend did not join me. She had yielded to her parents' insistence, likely motivated by discomfort with the liberalism of the university, to accept the scholarship offered by a local Catholic women's college. Our relationship cooled and came to an end within a few months.

Over half the students in my crowded fall classes were six to twelve years older. My Uncle Ed, eleven years older than I, and several of his friends, all fellow ex-GIs, were at the university at the same time I was. We never took classes together, which might have been fun. They were among the first wave of veterans of the Second World War able to get a college education because the G.I. Bill financed it. Most were from New York state; a few from more distant parts. Several were indelibly marked by the war, had prosthetic devices on limbs, or wore shirts with an empty pinned-up sleeve. Some had furrowed scars on their faces left by slivers of shrapnel. Many wore army-issued clothes—cotton twill pants and shirts in warmer weather, dark, olive green wool in winter. In emulation of the veterans, many younger male students, and I too, began to shop at army-navy stores in search of military-style khaki clothes. I still wear an army-style khaki cloth belt in the summer.

Smoking was permitted in college classrooms in 1946, and many of the veterans chewed and puffed on cigars and cigarettes during lectures or in the student union where they gambled at card games, shot pool, and swore a great deal—all through a haze of tobacco smoke. We younger students looked on, wondering at but loath to ask about their war experiences, and somewhat intimidated by their hardened, savvy style: they were men; we, despite our new khaki clothes, were still boys.

Most of the veterans had a no-nonsense attitude and were intent on completing their undergraduate studies quickly. Too much time had already passed. They aimed to establish themselves in the larger community as soon as they could, marry, raise a family, go into business, become teachers, pharmacists, lawyers, accountants, doctors, psychologists. In this attitude too, they were more mature than many of the younger students for whom the future was as yet distant and indefinite.

Although the veterans were, on the whole, clearer about what they wanted, there were many points of genuine communication between them and the younger students. One such was in a campus organization initially organized by veterans—American Youth for Democracy (AYD)—that soon attracted younger students.

The aim of AYD was to oppose the prejudice and bigotry in American life that had been endemic to the European fascist opponents we had just fought and defeated. Anti-Negro and anti-Jewish attitudes and practices in America were the new enemy; they too had to be defeated. I joined AYD in my first semester in college and became friendly with several of its members—all veterans. After several meetings, one of the members, who was married, invited me to his house where, he said, there would be a discussion with other members I might find interesting.

My new friend, his wife, and six- or seven-month-old son lived in a three-room garret apartment in what was becoming the small bohemian section of Buffalo. Painters, sculptors, writers, and a handful of faculty and students had already begun to move into this neighborhood. Rent was cheap, and there was public transportation to the university, Kleinhans music hall, the Albright (soon to be Albright-Knox) art museum, the Grovesnor reference library, and the large movie houses. Within a year or two a few storefronts, empty since the Depression, were converted into dimly lit coffee shops. In these shops young people gathered, sipped espresso, ate sweet, oily baklava, and listened to local performers sing folk songs and play the guitar. I am not an enthusiast of most folk music but was charmed by it all, especially by the exotic-looking young women with their long hair gathered in ponytails and their legs clad in black stockings.

My friend had invited four other students, all veterans. To my delight, the discussion turned out to be about Marxism. The issue was Marxist ethics, an area I had so far not broached in my reading or thinking. I was taking a second course on the history of philosophy and had read over the summer Aristotle's *Nicomachean Ethics*. Aristotle's work dealt with the question of happiness and did not quite prepare me for the discussion we had that evening. The analytical methods I was learning in the classroom, however, served me well.

Marx and Engels had ethical views, but they were in large part implicit. "What is a just society?" is a general way of initially putting the root ethical question they and others have considered. For Marx and Engels, a just society hinges on several senses in which persons are considered equal and thus equally deserving. But it is obvious that people are not literally equal. Some are smarter, faster, stronger, taller, younger, and so on. There are also many different kinds of equality—political, economic, and social, among others. How would these spheres of equality be defined and related, and how would they be realized in a socialist society?

Moreover, beyond the minimum of air, water, rest, food, and shelter essential to sustain human life, those in different stages of life and in different pursuits have different needs. In these senses too, people are not equal. Needs themselves are socially "derived." How would a socialist society satisfy the variety of human needs, and the disparity in resources required to meet them, fairly and impartially? These were the sorts of questions we discussed that evening and in several meetings thereafter. Discussions of this kind are perhaps common among undergraduates, and the questions are not definitively answerable. But they stirred my heart and sharpened my mind. The occasion is vivid in my memory because it was my first active engagement with student veterans. Above all, I had found a group of like-minded fellow students.

I returned to the library study group a few times, but it was beginning to break up. The old man of the group was ill and attended sporadically. The delicatessen owner's business was demanding more of his time. The engineer talked of moving to another state to live with his daughter and grandchildren. The Depression was over. We had won the war. A new period was beginning.

During the first year of its existence at the University of Buffalo, AYD numbered about thirty-five students, most of whom were sophomores and juniors. A preponderance of the members was Jewish, but there were a few non-Jews—students of Polish, German, and Swedish backgrounds, one of English, another of Greek background, and a few female students. The student of English background seemed somewhat anomalous in this potpourri of students of central, eastern, and southern European ethnic heritages. He was a veteran who had been embittered by the war and become vociferous over the laxity of Americans in not fulfilling American ideals. About three or four couples, male and female students who had paired up before AYD was started, either showed up at meetings together or not at all. There were hardly any black students at the university, and none in AYD.

My new discussion group met separately from AYD, but its five veteran-students, and soon I too, were the chief strategists of AYD's agenda. AYD held biweekly meetings at the student union to discuss current American prejudices, their sources and promulgators, and develop plans of combating them.

Not too often, I would sit down at the grand piano in the student union after an AYD meeting and rattle off something—a Rachmaninoff prelude or Chopin's "Revolutionary Etude," for instance. This latter piece expressed one of my sentiments and is a bit of a showstopper; it not only drew a few AYD friends to the piano but, at least as important, attracted the attention of some female students. This was, I saw after a short while, a kind of showing off that embarrassed me (go stand on your head, Hershl!), and I stopped giving these impromptu recitals after the first semester.

After one of AYD's meetings early in the spring semester, a few of my discussion group friends took me aside and asked whether I had ever considered becoming a Communist. I described my interest in socialism and experiences in the SLP, and they pointed out, quite correctly I thought, that the SLP was never more than a minor group that had lost whatever little vitality it may have once had. The Communist Party, on the other hand, was truly international and growing. American comrades were joined in common cause with comrades in all the major industrial countries of the world, especially the Soviet Union. There would not be socialism in one country, they argued, until there was socialism in all.

Was this last proposition correct? I knew there had been and still were religious communities in the United States that were socialist in tenor. I had read about the kibbutzim (or kvutzot) in Palestine that were also socialist. They were all small communities, relatively homogeneous and agrarian, and able to maintain their integrity by carefully regulating, but not excluding, social and economic relations with the environing society. Although admirable in many ways, they were not the sorts of communities I wanted to live in. I wanted to live in a socialist society that was heterogeneous and urban, a dynamic, vigorous society that was open to the world's peoples and cultures. In an offhand quip, Marx once wrote of "the idiocy of rural life." These dismissive words were written by a city dweller referring to a monochrome round of existence that blinkered one's awareness of the world's riches and deadened the mind. I tended to agree with him. But Marx wrote in the mid-nineteenth century, and I believed one could also find "idiocy" in the assembly lines of every major industrial city in the mid-twentieth century. In Marxist parlance, however, modern capitalist industry led to the "immiseration" and alienation of workers, which is not the same thing as blinkering rural idiocy. Not all instances of mental and material poverty are of the same nature; socialism would transform life in the cities, but do little to alter life in the countryside—so I argued to myself in an attempt to keep Marx's views consistent, however casually made. Casuistry has many faces. Yes, for the kind of socialism I wanted, the proposition seemed correct. Socialism had to be achieved in all countries or it would be achieved in none.

I have never had much taste for the speech-making and behind-the-scenes negotiations and intrigue I assumed were common to political activity, but my desire for socialism was strong. I joined the Communist Party shortly before my eighteenth birthday. I was going to be part of an international movement.

Nothing much happened. I felt slightly furtive because the Cold War was under way, and for the same reason also slightly exhilarated. I was given a card by one of my friends and signed it with a pseudonym. A week or two later, my friends and I visited the local Communist Party headquarters, where I was introduced as a new member.

The headquarters of the Communist Party occupied one or two rooms in back of the International Publishers Bookstore. The room we entered was not very large, perhaps slightly larger than an average-size bedroom. In it were a small desk on which papers were stacked, several open folding chairs in front of the desk, and a file cabinet. A ceiling fixture, as I remember, was the main source of light. One wall held photographs of Marx, Lenin, and Stalin, another had pinned on it a large map of the world.

Four men, all middle-aged, came in and greeted us. No names were used. I was simply introduced as a new member. We were the students; they were the membership committee. We sat down. The "committee" pulled over four chairs and sat in front of us. I didn't say much, but watched and listened. The men were dressed as though they had just returned from a day's work in a factory—which they might have. One of the men acted as the spokesman. The others nodded agreement or smiled as the conversation warranted.

The substance of the spokesman's talk was something like the following: The Soviet Union supports and guides the endeavors of workingmen of all countries to achieve Communism. Communism is inevitable. The Soviet Union is a haven for intellectuals and artists, particularly Negroes, who have grasped the essentially exploitative nature of capitalism and seek to escape capitalist oppression. A famous example is Paul Robeson, the great actor and singer. (I hadn't known this.)

The bourgeoisie are frightened. They see Communism on the horizon, moving ever closer, and they will do everything in their power to prevent it from arriving. One of our tasks is to recruit students and others to the Communist Party. In particular, we students, as mental workers, have the important task of exposing bourgeois ideologies for what they are, doctrines created by the bourgeoisie to blind the working class to its true interests. The sooner the working class discards these ideological blinders, the sooner they will arise and overthrow the capitalist system that enslaves them.

These and other comments along the same lines were not issued as commands, but made in a tone more like a laid-back pep talk. Other than observing ordinary (bourgeois!) civility, there was hardly any conversation and certainly no dialogue between us. I was irritated that, except for what I had learned about Paul Robeson, the monologue to which we had been subjected was hackneyed, tedious, and in many respects patronizing. We hardly needed any of this if we were *mental workers*. Moreover, if socialism is inevitable and moving closer, I muttered petulantly to myself, why not just relax; it'll come soon enough. But well-mannered bourgeois boy that I was, I desisted from making an issue. After an hour or so the meeting came to an end. With the exception of the spokesman, whose name I never learned, but with whom I met once more almost a year later, I never saw any of the men again. The following day it occurred to me the spokesman might also have been bored by the rote-like repetition of a talk he probably had given many times before. And in remembering the sounds he made when he spoke, rather than the actual words he used and their meanings, the cadence of his speech, I thought, resembled the cadence of the daily praying of the men I used to hear in the synagogue. This is what sometimes happens, I supposed, when strings of words are said by rote. But was the spokesman's recitation a kind of praying? I was unsure of that, but I had little doubt that he was *not* Jewish.

Life went on fairly much as it had before. We called our small discussion group the John Reed Club to distinguish us from AYD, and continued to meet and discuss Marx's theories. A few of our discussions are worth mentioning because they led, ultimately, to our dissatisfaction with the intellectual force of Marx's theory.

I had been puzzling over a phrase repeated several times at Communist Party headquarters as though it were fully understood: "bourgeois ideology." Such ideas as private property, the related term ownership, and the myriad protective laws pertaining to both terms seem obviously bourgeois. But are they only bourgeois? Is private property truly theft? Would my super silent royal portable typewriter, a high school graduation gift, become collective property in a socialist society? Then how would I be able to dash to the typewriter at three in the morning, as I sometimes did, which I probably wakened my parents in the process, to type up an idea that had occurred to me? And what of my books? I couldn't very well go to the library at three in the mourning to check a reference. It was much easier to own certain books, a dictionary and some texts that I put to frequent use. I was against bourgeois ideas, but didn't want to lose the few possessions to which I had ready access, used a great deal, and considered my property.

Given our ideology, private property was too fraught an idea to discuss without soon being accused of being bourgeois—an accusation that was leveled at me a few times in a joking but slightly reproving way. Two members of the club were not only opposed to private property in principle, but almost livid at the rich for being rich. They seemed to take it as a personal affront that Ford, Rockefeller, Vanderbilt, and other bankers and "pirates of industry" were so powerful and owned so much—money, land, houses, yachts, cars, jewelry, fancy clothes, among many more things. The *Protocols of the Elders of Zion* put out by Henry Ford a few decades earlier was doubtless one of the provocations for their anger at Ford, but not the only one. In their view, Ford, Rockefeller, et al were evil men who had succeeded in expropriating, or as they sometimes said, stealing, from working people what was rightfully theirs. Private property *is* theft!

The attitude of my fellow John Reed Club members was not uncommon. Caricatures of fat, top-hatted, tuxedo-clad tycoons with long grasping fingers and bared teeth reaching to snatch away the paychecks from workingmen's hands were featured in many radical magazines. Nevertheless, this sounded like vulgar Marxism to me. Marx emphasized the compulsions of the system, not the greedy motives of individual men. Besides, "motives" weren't exactly material entities, were they? That logical point did not endear my eighteen-year-old upstart self to one or two of the twenty-seven-year-old members.

But the truth is, I too was not exempt from being uncomfortable and angry when in the presence of people whom I considered rich. A couple of my new nonveteran friends had invited me a few times to dinner at their parents' many-roomed houses, which, with their large well-kept lawns and comfortable furnishings, seemed to me to be ostentatiously lavish. Actually, as I came to realize later, these houses were no more than middle-class, "petit bourgeois" dwellings. The real or "haut" bourgeois, the bankers and industrialists who had great wealth, had removed themselves from Buffalo at least two or three decades earlier and lived on their "farms"—properties of many acres, some with polo grounds—in the suburbs of East Aurora and Orchard Park. I felt awkward and intimidated in the "rich" settings of my friends' parents' houses. I envied the parents for what they owned, but even more, envied their personal power, the confidence and well-being they exuded, the ability that enabled them to gain their large houses and furniture and rugs and paintings and grand pianos and to live in comparative ease. I was quite a good pianist, but my parents could not afford more than an old, yet quite serviceable upright. I felt dwarfed by it all. But I certainly didn't want to reveal any of these feelings. As their guest, this would have been terribly inappropriate, and perhaps worse, would have betrayed my weakness and insecurity. Rather than thrash about and say and do things that would make me look like a fool or a boor, I adhered to the rules of elementary etiquette with the fidelity of a monk attending a ritual observance.

Although intense, the anger of my John Reed Club friends seemed in comparison to mine more abstract. One of the members, quite bright, would flare into anger at the slightest breach of what he considered to be socialist moral standards. Although I didn't like him much and found it difficult to stand up to him, I managed to counter him from time to time when the issues were important enough. But he was the exception. The other members of the group were also intensely involved in social issues, but were more dispassionate in examining them.

I wasn't actually angry with the Rockefellers and their kind because they were mainly names to me and didn't seem quite real. And the movie versions of rich people were pure, often derogatory fantasy; they were portrayed either as boozing nincompoops, ruthless tycoons, or saintly knights with hefty bankbooks ready to help the needy. But in fact, when I talked of rich people, I too scoffed at them, lessened the value of their accomplishments, made them out to be shallow in morals and intellect. It took several years before I understood the sources of my self-doubt, envy, and anger and was able more or less to overcome them—frequently "more" as I grew in self-confidence. My friends' parents, however, likely thought I was a well-mannered young man, if rather stiff. At least, I hope they did.

A week or so later, I asked a professor of anthropology, Victor Barnouw, whether there was private property in pre-bourgeois tribal societies. He was a lovely man, knew where I was coming from, and answered me directly. He said that in many tribal societies—he didn't know whether in all—people were often buried with their possessions. He also pointed out that "primitive communism" was a loose and overstated idea. No clan within a tribal society was ever totally self-subsistent. Marriage between a man and a woman, for example, was an exchange relationship between clans. Also, material goods of various kinds were made for the express purpose of being exchanged among clans, and at times their possession became, as it were, "private property." Marx's dichotomy of societies into two kinds, a Communist society in which goods are made for use versus a capitalist society in which goods are made for exchange never existed, so far as he knew. Use and exchange, he thought, are always found in every society.

This information relieved my anxiety because it implied there is a particular bourgeois version of private property. And if this implication were correct, then there might be a socialist version of private property too. Five or six years later, I read in Simone Weil's *The Need for Roots*[3] a simple yet profound discussion of the contribution of at least a modicum of private property to the well being of the person and the society. By this time, however, the John Reed Club had long been dissolved.

Learning that exchange and private property were both essential in so-called primitive societies raised the issue of the scope as well as the validity of Marx's theory. The edenic "primitive communism" of which Marx spoke may never have existed! And modern capitalism was not a society predicated purely on exchange. Marx's theory, I began to think, would need reworking to bring it up to date. But this reworking would also require rethinking, and it was uncertain how much of the theory would then remain intellectually viable.

I mentioned some of my reservations to my John Reed Club friends. With one exception, they all seemed interested. The exception was the one member of the club who was prone to anger. He was "baroygess" (constantly angry), as my grandmother would have said, but he didn't express anger at my doubts, just stony silence. He kept a generally low profile on campus, but his comments, when he made them, were often as though etched in acid. He frightened me a little, but I attributed some of his attitude to his war experiences. In any event, I pressed on. And one of the members in particular, the one who had invited me to his apartment to join the discussion group, was rather protective of me and quite encouraging.

As I look back on them now, these early reflections were, I believe, the beginning of my intellectual dissatisfaction with Marx's theory, but not yet with the Communist Party. In later study, it became clearer to me that Marx had concentrated on analyzing the earlier phases of modern, industrial capitalism—from the seventeenth century up to the middle of the nineteenth. Another 160 years of capitalism have since accumulated, and capitalism, with its growing global reach, shows no signs of weakening. The death knells signaling capitalism's demise, which Marx thought would soon be ringing round the world, have yet to be rung. Despite severe economic perturbations, capitalism is more vigorous than ever, and it is perhaps only now that it is beginning to grow into its maturity.

Because of Marx's emphasis, his comments on premodern, agrarian, or feudal societies were few and substantively thin; his conception of postmodern, postcapitalist society hopeful but vague. In 1964, the English historian Eric J. Hobsbawm brought out a short book called *Karl Marx: Pre-Capitalist Economic Formations*,[4] which contains most of Marx's writings on the subject.

Three-quarters of the way through my first year of college I was faced with a dilemma whose resolution would be painful whichever way I turned. After about two and a half years, I could learn little more from my original piano teacher, and so sought and found another one. My second piano teacher was an accomplished pianist and a good musician. When I started college, however, books, studying, discussions, meetings, and new friendships commanded more of my attention, and the time I spent playing and practicing the piano began correspondingly to diminish. My piano teacher soon put the matter to me simply: I could be a good pianist, possibly a very good pianist, but only if I practiced more. To be more than a merely good pianist, he said, which he thought is what I would want to be, meant playing and practicing six to eight hours each day. This also meant going to a music school, playing with a variety of ensembles, studying harmony, learning to read scores with facility, exploring the idiomatic styles of different eras. The Eastman School of Music in Rochester was a possibility, and it was nearby. He said I should think very hard about this and make up my mind soon. As performers go, I had started playing quite late, and it would take a lot of work to catch up.

About a month after my teacher spoke to me I heard Leon Fleisher play at a recital in Buffalo. He was about my age. His playing was beautiful, clear, and singing and with the effortless grace that only a top-flight pianist has. It would require a great deal of work over at least four or more years for me to approximate Fleisher's technical level. Whether my musicianship would ever be on a par with his depended on my sensibility, understanding, and taste, all things that could and no doubt would also be cultivated. I thought I could undergo the rigors of such training. But this meant giving up philosophy. And "for the time being" at least, also giving up working for socialism. I decided to give up the piano. The stupidity of it all was that I made this an either/or choice. But I didn't want to be a merely passable pianist; I wanted to be among the best. And so I gave up a lot of pleasure.

Resolute and pushing all doubts as far back in my mind as I could, I went home and closed the lid of the piano. I returned to playing three times—once, very briefly, shortly before I got married; a second time, even more briefly, when my mother died, and finally for a few weeks in my mid-seventies when my arthritic thumbs could no longer negotiate a simple scale. It sometimes takes a very long time to recognize that one has made a mistake; and then it is sometimes too late to correct it.

Yet, my choice was very far from terrible. Who knows what kind of pianist I might have become, what kind of career I might have had? As it was, I learned a great deal, became a teacher, had some wonderful colleagues and students, wrote books, and came to understand many things. These are important to me, and continue to give me great pleasure.

I'm not sure how to communicate the pleasure and excitement that understanding ideas gives me, but these were experiences I was having in great, frequent gulps during these first years in college, and not least in understanding Marx. Some of the members of our John Reed study group had begun reading the English translation of Marx's *The German Ideology*.[5] In this book, Marx called ideas of almost every kind—philosophical, religious, moral, political, economic, esthetic, and so on—ideological. All ideas, he said, are born in historical context in which a rising class attempts to achieve its rule by mental as well as material means. Each new ruling class expresses its interests in ideas that are "more universal" than those of the preceding ruling class. In "the dustbin of history" as Marx put it, there lay a succession of overthrown ruling ideas alongside the overthrown ruling classes that begot them. Until the present age, the so-called universality of ideologies has been a chimera. Only in the present age has a truly universal class emerged, the proletariat, in whose ranks all of humankind is represented. The proletariat is the class of all classes, and as such can express an ideology that, for the first time in history, is genuinely encompassing of all humankind.

Scientific ideas are exempt from this view of ideology because, although also born in history, their truth is established in practice. Scientific ideas, unlike other ideologies, surpass the historical epoch in which they are born.

This particular book of Marx's became one of the cornerstones of the sociology of knowledge. Although a cousin to the history of ideas, the sociology of knowledge is a separate kind of inquiry, one that I pursued in graduate school and that was the focus of my master's thesis. By the time I was taken up with the issues, however, other cornerstones had been laid that supported different social constructions and intentions than the ones Marx had in mind. *The German Ideology* was an important point of departure for Marxists of the Frankfurt School, some of whose ideas will be discussed in a later chapter.

In later works, Engels pointedly declared his and Marx's theory of socialism to be scientific, not a utopian ideology, as were other versions of socialism based solely on moral critiques of the existing society. The theory of the nature and rise of the proletariat, of the inevitable self-destruction of the capitalist order, of the rise from the capitalist ashes of a universal socialist and Communist humanity heralded and peopled by the proletariat is based, Marx held, on analysis of the historical process. In the Introduction to the first volume of *Capital*, he asked that his theory be judged at the bar of science, its truth to be established in practice.

All the members of the John Reed Club understood the arguments well. Yet, nagging questions remained. Is justice, discussed on earlier occasions, for example, merely a bourgeois idea like the idea of private property? It seemed to some of us that many, if not all, of our socialist ideals had not sprung out of thin air, but differed from those of the bourgeoisie not so much in substance as in extent of application. The idea of justice is not the monopoly of the socialists. But the bourgeoisie meted out justice to the few; whereas we socialists wanted justice for all. Weren't we trying to compel the bourgeoisie to abide by the very same standards they had espoused but were often reluctant or unwilling to observe?

In a course on the history and sociology of cities I took in my sophomore year I came across a historical example of a situation somewhat apposite to the one we socialists were trying to accomplish. It is cited in *The Ancient City* by Fustel de Coulanges and is worth quoting here:

> We greatly deceive ourselves [writes Coulanges] on the nature of man if we suppose a religion [Coulanges is referring to the pre-Christian Roman religion] be established by convention and supported by imposture. Let anyone count in Livy how many times this religion embarrassed the patricians themselves, how many times it stood in the way of the senate and impeded its action, and then decide if this religion was an invention for the convenience of statesmen.[6]

We knew Marx believed religion in every historical age served the interests of the ruling class. Religion, as Marx was so often quoted as saying, is "the opiate of the masses." Much less quoted are the clauses that immediately follow: "[Religion] is the sigh of the oppressed creature, the heart of a heartless world." Could we confidently oppose every religious doctrine and institution and expose them as being merely the facilitators and agents of oppression?

The religious questions also proved too contentious for us to discuss at any length. Most of the members argued that religion had invariably been a backward force. Some mentioned the Inquisition; others that the pope had been hand in glove with the Nazis during the war. All the members had gone through a bar mitzvah and were convinced Orthodox rabbis were politically right wing and Reform rabbis were toadies cozying up to the rich. In the "last analysis," as some of us said, religion promises everything, but only for another world, not for this one. It was the opiate of the masses and had to be opposed. Several years later I met some former radicals who had been so steeped in antireligious sentiment they wouldn't listen to one of the great masterpieces of Western music, Bach's *St Matthew Passion*. They appreciated post-baroque music, but Bach, they said, was "too churchy."

I was uncomfortable with this blanket condemnation of religion. There were, after all, Marx's other clauses. And not least, there were my own religious experiences that (other than Hebrew School) were not all politically or in other ways negative. Religion had helped sustain the men I had known in the synagogue. This could not and must not be taken from them. And the one Reform rabbi in the city I knew, Rabbi Fink, who had come to visit my Orthodox, very-far-from-rich grandmother when my grandfather died, was very kind.

I decided to discuss the religious question with a friend a few years older. He was a socialist too, but in the sense Henry Miller was a socialist. He would share anything he had with another person in need. And, like the author of the famous *Tropics*, smuggled copies of which we had read, my friend was comfortable with almost everyone.

My friend was assistant curator of the poetry manuscripts collection of the university, which by 1947 had achieved international renown. He was widely read, well versed in the Marxist canon, and highly intelligent. He was also the one who had recommended Henry Miller's books to me. Miller, he said, despite a degree of gaseousness in his views and in his prose, was a genuine proletarian writer. His books were totally unlike the sentimental stuff, essentially false, that passed for this genre purveyed by other writers.

After I had laid out the religious-ideological issue to him, he brought up Ignazio Silone's *Bread and Wine*.[7] In this novel, he said, a priest at great risk to himself opens the doors of his church to give refuge to a revolutionary fleeing from the Italian fascists. The relationship between the two men is respectful and caring, but of greater import, my friend observed, they hold many of the same moral and social views. It would be a serious misunderstanding, he believed, to posit a sharp divide between the Judeo-Christian religions and Marx's socialist views. There are, of course, important differences, and these too should not be overlooked. And also, he acknowledged, Silone's novel is a fiction, but a fiction that has a ring of truth, and there is little doubt that things of the sort Silone described had actually occurred in Italy and many other countries in Europe during the Nazi-Fascist period. My friend's account of Silone's novel moved me to take the book out of the library later that afternoon. I read it in one sitting. In its directness and emotional honesty, the novel is magnificent.

At a later meeting of the John Reed Club I brought up and described Silone's novel. One of the members knew Silone was an Italian Communist—a fact I did not know, which made the novel all the more impressive. (But unknown to me and likely to the other members, Silone was also among the contributors to *The God That Failed*,[8] the book that was published a decade after *Bread and Wine*.) In the discussion that followed, it was generally acknowledged that churches and religious doctrines were of many kinds. None of the religions is of one piece; there are many variants in each. One of the members pointed out that the pope does not exercise complete control over all Catholics, and mentioned the radicalism of the Catholic Worker Movement as evidence. This was the first time I had heard of this group, which I later explored. There were good priests and good pastors as well as bad ones. A general condemnation would not only be inaccurate but also not serve our interests. It would probably be best to limit our criticism to individual instances, church by church, priest by priest, pastor by pastor. We generally agreed with this argument, but I felt not all of us fully accepted it.

A related question, one that was personally and morally troubling, is that of art—bourgeois or socialist. The question boiled down to the issue of censorship, of what I should and shouldn't read, look at, and listen to. The issue bothered me a great deal but didn't excite as much concern as I thought it might among my fellow John Reed Club members. I discussed this mainly with the poetry curator, with whom I had become quite good friends.

Essays in some of the radical magazines, such as *Masses and Mainstream*, declared certain kinds of "late bourgeois" art to be decadent. James Joyce's *Ulysses*, the poetry of T. S. Eliot and Ezra Pound, the novels of Ernest Hemingway, William Faulkner, and Franz Kafka were frequently singled out as "subjectivist" and for this reason dismissed as politically retrograde and of negative value. To be subjectivist is to ignore the collective, to turn one's eyes and mind away from the larger society to inner concerns and leave the prevailing order untouched.

The more modest interpretation of this kind of criticism is that writers who challenge particular political (or religious or moral) views should not be read. The more extreme interpretation has led to the removal or banning of books and music and paintings from public access. Joyce's *Ulysses and* Miller's *Tropics* were prominent recent examples of the latter in the United States for many years. Darwin's *Origin of Species* and *The Descent of Man* were taboo in Tennessee.

I despised this kind of criticism. I did not want to be told what I should and shouldn't read, nor did I want any art works kept from me. There is of course a political element of some sort in most literature, but politics is hardly all. I liked and was much moved by the works of most of the authors cited. Horror of horrors, I thought *Hunger*[9] and *Growth of the Soil*[10] by Knut Hamsun, which I had recently read, were great books—even though Hamsun supported the Nazis. Should I not have read them? Should they have been burned? Hamsun's Nazi sympathies were absolutely wrong-headed, but his novels have a depth of understanding and an intensity of expression that are rare. This kind of appreciation did not deter socialists with similar tastes as mine, nor did it obviously deter me, from being critical of bourgeois society. Indeed, Leon Trotsky, whose radical credentials must surely be considered impeccable even by Communists, was not so dismayed by Louis Ferdinand Celine's Nazi sentiments as not to acknowledge his achievements! With *Journey to the End of the Night*[11] and *Death on the Installment Plan*,[12] in Trotsky's view, Celine entered world literature. One cannot find more ferocious descriptions of degradation and poverty than in Celine's books. I reread Hamsun's books many years later and found them even more resonant than I had originally thought them to be. Celine's two early books continue to blaze as great works.

The social-esthetic criticism was applied to music, painting, movies—to every kind of "ideational" product high or low. (In later years I overheard older ex-leftists continue to dismiss such movies as *The Court Jester* with Danny Kaye or *Bananas* with Woody Allen as 'frivolous and without social content,' and thus to be avoided. *Narishkeit* [foolishness], as my father would have said.) Most of my John Reed Club friends as well as my curator friend and I ignored such criticisms. Still, some of my friends, I thought, had reservations. They seemed slightly uneasy and made feeble jokes when I showed up carrying a book by Ezra Pound, for example. I wasn't making a statement; I was taking a course in modern poetry.

I was sure the radical critics had gone off on a simplistic tack and were morally and politically wrong. Actually, what I found troubling in some of the subjectivist writers who I thought were also fine artists was their anti-Semitism. But even in this there were often ambiguities. Eliot and Pound were known to give a writer of talent, regardless of ethnicity, religion, color, or gender, any help they could. And Eliot was an admirer of Groucho Marx. He did not pick his Marx on the basis of ethnicity.

When I raised the issue of their anti-Semitism to my poetry professor, Lysander Kemp, who was himself a poet and had recently visited Pound in St. Elizabeth's Hospital in Washington, DC, he said that in his view Eliot, particularly in "The Wasteland," was voicing a historical attitude, not a personal one. I found this explanation unsatisfactory. Eliot was a great poet. Could he not have found a way of showing this was not his attitude by, for example, putting quotation marks around the offending phrases? This hardly would have affected the free-verse metric.

Pound, on the other hand, was more complex. Pound's anti-Semitism seemed bound up with his own unique blend of agrarian economic and proto-fascist doctrines. He was living in Italy during the Second World War, and there gave frequent radio broadcasts and wrote articles critical of American policies, and the "usurious" practices of American bankers. The latter charge of course smacked of anti-Semitism. At the conclusion of the war the American government indicted him for treason. The judge who ruled on the indictment declared Pound mentally unbalanced and unfit for trial. This ruling undoubtedly saved Pound's life. He was then placed in a separate room at St. Elizabeth's Hospital in Washington, DC, where he was allowed to have visitors. Given his fame and influence as a poet, other poets and scholars began to visit him in a fairly steady stream.

There was something oddly personal in Pound's attitude toward Jews, said Kemp, that he did not understand. Pound looked like the stereotype of a Jew—dark hair, aquiline nose, pointy beard, sharp eyes. Perhaps, suggested Kemp, there was some self-hatred there that Pound was projecting. I was unhappy that Pound was anti-Semitic, but nevertheless admired much of what he had done as a poet and as a mentor of poets.

I fretted over the social critics, but my curator friend simply dismissed their judgments as foolish and without merit. He urged me to ignore them. He was of course right, but I wanted to answer them rationally. The substantive counter-argument I was able to make some years later is, to put it most briefly, that human life is more than the "collective." It is made up of many things, each one distinct yet actively influencing and providing vital energies to all the others, and to ignore the contributions of any one is to warp our understanding of them all. The more we understand and appreciate these parts and their interrelations, the more we can act responsibly and to greater effect. "Nothing human is alien to me," said Marx. It is a sentiment with which I fully concur.

I had become friendly with several fellow students in addition to my John Reed Club friends, but the assistant curator of the library's poetry collection soon became my closest friend. We discussed just about everything, double dated a few times, occasionally drank beer together, and went to concerts and lectures. He had read much more literature than I, and his support of my interest contributed to my lifelong reading of world literature. He was of German background and spoke German at about the same eight-year-old level as I spoke Yiddish. We never tried to talk together in this overlap of argots. I met his mother, a small, shy, sweet-tempered woman who spoke with a soft, very pronounced German accent. He did not have a father. I assumed he had already graduated college and was perhaps aiming to become a librarian. To my surprise, I discovered he had barely had more than an undergraduate course or two. His wide-ranging knowledge, especially of modern literature, achieved through his own efforts, got him the job at the university. This was still a time when applicants for jobs at the university were sometimes evaluated more on their substantive responses to questions rather than on formal credentials. He was quite poor, but his job at the university permitted him to take a course each semester without paying tuition. He planned to take as many courses as he could until he graduated.

With the permission of the other members, and at my urging, I persuaded my friend to attend a meeting of the John Reed Club. Among the more serious issues of ideology for us were the political/moral ones. We discussed the "hypothetical" case where there are several groups each contending to be the next ruling class and each with an ideology shaped to its interests. Would we then declare the ideology of the winning group as the true and just one, the one that had proved itself in practice and therefore the more universal one, the others limited and false? If there were no trans-historical ethical and moral standards of any kind, wouldn't this mean in effect that "might makes right?" Then, what if the Nazis had won? Should their new, ruling ideology be considered the more universal one? And what would we have said then, if any of us were still alive to say it, of the fate of the Jews?

We pursued these kinds of questions over the next few meetings, with uneven results. My curator friend was taken with the liveliness and content of the discussions and continued to join us. The John Reed Club, he said, was like another university, a kind of Shadow University. Our discussions were like a set of courses that the regular university didn't offer. But I thought this is what a university is all about, bringing together people who want to understand ideas and more of the world.

The discussions made apparent to us that Marx was operating with a nineteenth-century notion of linear historical progress, and more under the sway of Hegel than he realized. For many eighteenth- and nineteenth-century thinkers and certain of their twentieth-century descendants, history was a record of steady progress in human freedom and achievement. Societal retrogressions were of course acknowledged, but in historical terms they were considered short-lived, and the upward march soon reasserted itself.

Was this an accurate understanding of the historical record? There were, it may be recalled, some of us said, the Dark Ages, which were not exactly short-lived. And from the little we knew, the Chinese empire had existed for centuries without much, if any, forward movement, or movement of any kind. Well and good to say there will eventually be progress. But "eventually" may last for millennia. The view of historical progress Marx held was more utopian than scientific. This conclusion made assertions of historical inevitability specious.

The Marxist conception of ideology seemed to some of us more of a grab bag of many different elements, some clearer, some better argued, some with potential for development, but on the whole not "scientific." When taken together, these elements seemed somewhat akin to but not identical with several of the things anthropologists considered when they spoke of culture. I thought I would return to the topic of ideology in the future—which I did in graduate studies in philosophy and sociology.

After my curator friend had attended and participated in several meetings, some of the members of the John Reed Club suggested I approach him about joining the Communist Party. I did. He declined. But he asked whether he might still come to our meetings. He thought the discussions were valuable; he was learning much, and he would like to continue to participate in them. The members liked him and consented to his request. My curator friend never joined the Communist Party, but he became for a few months a "fellow traveler," and joined us in AYD's ventures.

Before breaking up at the end of the semester, AYD made plans to invite Dashiell Hammett, the famous mystery writer and outspoken social critic, to speak at the university in early fall. AYD had the funds to pay for his airfare and provide a small stipend. We planned to follow up a week or two later by holding a public rally denouncing the latest examples of bigotry by Senator Theodore Bilbo. Thus ended my first year in college. It had been a wonderful year of intellectual ferment and growth for me and, I believe, for the other John Reed club members as well.

Notes

1. Macmillan, New York, 1926.
2. Little, Brown, Boston, 1948.
3. Octagon Books, New York, 1979.
4. International Publishers, New York, 1965.
5. Prometheus Books, Amherst, NY, 1998.

6. Doubleday Anchor, New York, 1956, p. 213.
7. Signet Classics, New York, 1986.
8. MIT Press, Cambridge, 1971.
9. Farrar, Straus & Giroux, New York, 2008.
10. Penguin Books, New York, 2007.
11. New Directions, New York, 1983.
12. New Directions, New York, 1971.

4

Illusion and Reality

When I told my father a few weeks after the school year ended that I had joined the Communist Party, he sat me down and told me a story about his young manhood that I had never heard before. My father had joined the Bolshevik army as a young man of eighteen or nineteen. Like many Jews of his generation in Poland, Ukraine, Russia, and the Slavic and Baltic countries, the Haskalah—the so-called Jewish Enlightenment, which blossomed in the nineteenth century—had affected him. He did not have much formal education, but read many of the great Russian and European writers and novelists, many of whose books were being translated into Yiddish, and had been gripped by a secular vision of a just world in which people of all kinds and faiths could live in amity, free from the social, religious, and economic barriers that had impeded and more often prevented their self-realization. He was not a Communist; he did not hold to the doctrine of the leveling of classes. But he saw in the socialist program of the Soviets an opportunity to fight for and achieve his universalist aspirations.

My father encountered many minor instances of anti-Semitism among ordinary soldiers. These he attributed to lingering sentiments that would diminish and eventually be extinguished as a new generation, schooled in socialist principles, emerged. Near the middle of his second year in the army, however, a particularly ugly incident involving officers shattered his confidence. He had just returned from a difficult mission to one of the front lines where he had been helping install a signal system from headquarters. As he was getting off his bike—the main means of transport the signal corps used—a group of officers approached. "You, Jew," one of them commanded, "what are you doing with that bicycle?" This officer knew who my father was, but my father, assuming they were drunk, explained what he had been doing and where he'd come from. The officer, however, began cursing and shouted that he must be addressed in the proper way. Stepping forward, he struck my father, knocking him down. The other officers laughed. "A Jew with a bike," my father remembered one of them saying. "He stole it and now tries to sell it." They laughed and sauntered off. As he told me the story, his face reddened with remembered humiliation and anger. The officers were members of the educated elite who had joined the Soviet cause. But in his view, whether or not they were drunk made little difference. Drunk or sober, the leaders always set an example for the followers. And, he observed, these leaders were as unjust and prejudiced now as they had been before the revolution. He decided to quit the army and leave the country. He managed to slip away, and after rejoining his family crossed with them quietly over the border into Romania. Then began his many-years trek through Europe, France, Canada, and finally the United States.

I knew my father was born and raised in Ukraine, had lived in several European countries, and could understand and converse easily in many languages, including English. Now, however, it became clearer to me why, even when the Soviets were our allies, he was wary of the Russians and said their attitudes could not be changed overnight, if ever. He urged me to read about the history of the USSR, about the practices Stalin had instigated. He was quick to add he was not condemning all Russians. Many individual Russians were good people. We both knew Russia had produced wonderful writers and musicians. He was referring to a feature of the society as a whole, to what, he said to me with gentle irony, you call "Russian culture . . . It was this culture, this society, which after deposing the old czar had installed a new one. The Russians knew no other way. And it was as a czar, unimpeachable, secretive, absolute, and Jew-hating, that Stalin ruled. Despite the new ideology, the destruction of the aristocracy, the attempt to stamp out religion, rule in Russia would not soon change its dictatorial and prejudicial ways. *Plus ca change, plus c'est la meme chose*," he added with a thin smile.

By 1947, the literature on Soviet Russia since the revolution of 1919–20—books, essays, newspaper articles, specialized monographs, memoirs, and novels—had grown to voluminous and bewildering proportions. Given the hundreds of specialized studies, it is doubtful any one scholar, let alone a beginning college sophomore, could get very far with all this material. There were, however, more general accounts—histories and journal articles mainly—and these were more accessible. But they were no less bewildering. Well over half were negative in their appraisal, a smaller portion was positive, and a third, perhaps the smallest, was largely factual and purportedly impartial. How to evaluate their veracity? After a few weeks of sampling, I decided to concentrate on finding agreement on facts while ignoring interpretations as much as possible.

My father must have known at least some of what I would find, but perhaps not all. The Soviets had attempted to do several good things in the face of enormous obstacles. The efforts to extend health care and education to the entire society are examples of noteworthy social programs. But given the paucity of teachers, physicians, nurses, hospitals, clinics, material and training institutions, these programs continued to fall far short of the mark after many decades. The effort to build a modern industrial plant as quickly as possible on the back of an agrarian, semi-feudal economy was staggeringly difficult, and in 1947, twenty-seven years after the conclusion of the revolution, not yet achieved (nor yet quite fully in 2013, for that matter). The five-year plans were virtually self-defeating for several reasons, not least because of the ignorance and shortsightedness of both the dogmatic agricultural science and the social engineering intrinsic to their planning.

But against the positive efforts must be placed at least the following: the installation of a far-reaching (but no one knows how far) secret police; the destruction of the Kulaks; the murderous treatment of the peasants; the suppression of clerics and ethnic minorities; the "temporary" suspension of the principle of Soviet government—representative councils—justified on grounds of expediency and need for haste; the installation by the Politburo of commissars empowered to decree "proper" political, civic, legal, scientific, and artistic standards; the elimination of Stalin's rivals through expulsion from high positions, exile from the country, imprisonment, or assassination—except for Leon Trotsky, who for almost a decade after the revolution had too much support to be touched; the building of and incarceration into prisons and labor camps as well as "mental hospitals" of those charged with being a "parasite," dissident, or oppositional; the purges—executions—of hundreds of thousands, more likely millions, of people considered retrograde or bourgeois, and hence, as Stalin would say with grim finality, dangerous to the revolution and the Soviet Union; the assassination in 1940 of Stalin's chief rival, Leon Trotsky, reaching from Moscow to his refuge in exile in Mexico.

My father was right. This was not the peaceful, open, socialist society that had been trumpeted by the forerunners of the revolution and its contemporary apologists. This was a nightmare of blood and destruction. Paul Robeson must have willfully blinded himself or been duped.

Didn't the men I had met at Communist Party headquarters know any of this? One of the differences between Russia under Stalin and Russia under the czar was that Stalin's state apparatus, building upon the traditions left by the czar, was more efficient and far-reaching. The result was a barbaric wrath that descended upon anyone who did not shift with the changing Soviet winds. Arthur Koestler's *Darkness at Noon*,[1] which I also read that summer, gave me an unforgettable portrait of the anguish of incarcerated intellectuals facing certain execution. But while still holding to the goals of the revolution, they were attempting to bring their "deviationist" views into alignment with the current Soviet position. (Yet some artists who deviated from the decreed line somehow escaped the Soviet axe, for example, the writer Mikhail Bulgakov and composer Dimitri Shostakovich.)

Later that summer, I met with a friend I had made through AYD. He was four years older, a senior, not a veteran, and a psychology major. Without preamble, I asked whether he knew much about Soviet Russia. I recall the pensive look he gave me before answering. Yes, he said, he had been reading about the Soviets earlier in the summer. The purges? Yes. The forced confessions? Yes. The secret police? The prison camps? Yes. Yes. He had spoken of this with his father, a lawyer, thoughtful, and well read, whom I had met a few times when I had been invited to dinner. My initial uneasiness in this man's presence had soon given way to liking; he was friendly and intelligent and expressed himself laconically, but with good humor.

My friend's father had been following the events in Russia since the revolution. His father, my friend's grandfather, had emigrated from Ukraine. My friend's father, older by ten years than my father, and I were therefore of the same first-born generation, an odd congruence that amused both of us. Russia, he thought, like many countries, was a mixed bag of great cruelty but also great beauty. He wondered whether one gave rise to the other. But whatever the case, Soviet cruelty was on a scale, he thought, similar to that of the Nazis. My friend and I carried this thought with us into the beginning of the fall semester.

Dashiell Hammett had agreed to speak at the university in mid-September. He was famous, had the reputation of being a strong and clear social critic, and we were eager to hear him. We also hoped some of his luster would rub off onto AYD and help increase our membership.

Two members of the executive committee of AYD and I went to pick him up. I had read several of Hammet's stories and liked his style. He wrote in a seemingly colloquial manner, yet it was not prolix as colloquial speech often is. The strong, clean quality of his language reminded me a bit of Hemingway, but I doubt either writer had influenced the other.

Hammet greeted us at the door of his hotel room. He was perhaps in his early fifties, a tall man, thin, red in the face, with a shock of white, bristly hair cut military style. He was drunk, but managed to get into his trench coat. September was still warm, but this was part of his persona. He continued drinking all the way to the university, asking us to stop at five or six bars en route. At each bar he pulled out a fistful of ten-dollar bills, invited us to join him, and ordered a double scotch. We declined, but urged him to make haste or we would be late. We had started out with plenty of time, but at this rate we might not get there. By the time we arrived at the university, he must have downed at least a pint of scotch on top of what he had already had in his hotel room. An audience of about a hundred curious students and faculty awaited him. He managed, stiff-legged, to get to the lectern, and spoke for about twenty minutes. None of what he said made sense. Many people left before it was over. At the end, we whisked him back to his hotel. We were worried this fiasco would hurt AYD, which it of course did. Later, one of the assistant professors in the English department surmised that Hammet had left out every other word in his talk. The missing words, he suggested, might have rendered his talk coherent. An amusing example of lit-crit, I supposed. I was angry and disappointed, but wondered what had made Hammett need to get so pickled. I learned he had been a boozer for years. Wonderful. We had picked just the right kind of person, a *shikker* (drunkard) to help us recruit our fellow college students. I later read his entire oeuvre. He did have talent, but it was dissipated rather quickly.

Over the summer I had decided to do a double major in philosophy and sociology and take as many courses as I could in English and psychology.

The head of the sociology department, Nathaniel Cantor, was highly educated in all the social sciences and a leading figure in his field. He was widely esteemed as a man of principle and as a teacher. He had hired three young instructors, all trained at Columbia, to meet the ballooning postwar student demand that had swollen classes to quadruple their prewar size. I took courses from alt three of the new instructors, Alvin W. Gouldner, Norman Miller, and Jeremiah Wolpert, as well as the older members of the department, Llewellyn Gross and Milt Albrecht, and learned a great deal from each. One of the young instructors, Gouldner, was a particularly forceful lecturer, and in addition to the required fare gave such courses as the sociology of fascism and the sociology of racism. Although there was a well of anger in this man that lay just below the surface and erupted at times, I was drawn by the intensity and what seemed to me the depth of his thinking. It was in his courses that I was introduced to the writings of Max Weber, Emile Durkheim, and Talcott Parsons. These thinkers enriched my understanding immeasurably and eventually changed my life.

After a class on the sociology of fascism, I asked Gouldner as we were walking to get a cup of coffee what sense he made of the Russian purges. He paused a moment, then said the purges were like growing pains. Growing pains of what, I thought to my self, a Behemoth? He explained that the Soviets were attempting to become a socialist society, but had to cope with many internal as well as external threats. Until they became strong both at home and internationally, until they had increased their productivity, educated their people, and rid themselves of ideological as well as literal saboteurs, they would remain vulnerable and unable to grow in the way they hoped. This might take a very long time, I said. He agreed, but observed that revolutions may be made in a day; societies take quite a bit longer. My father might have asked what had been overthrown in this revolution and what had been retained. Although this conversation and his simplistic homily made me wary of Gouldner (I had learned more from my high school history teacher!), I continued to take courses from him. He taught some of the required courses in sociology, which as a major I had to take, and gave me the opportunity to do hands-on social research, which was not only a pleasure to do but continues to be useful to me in appraising the research of others. He was explicit in acknowledging Marx's importance to him, but I couldn't tell from this, nor did I ever know, whether he was a member of the Communist Party. Like many other radicals I have known, he was patronizing of working people, and in his writings characterized them as being dependent and needing protection—similar in these respects to children. He was too ready with anger or ridicule when intellectually challenged or faced with authority, and these qualities impaired his teaching and scholarship. In graduate school, when I undertook a more thorough study of Marx's theory, it seemed to me in retrospect that Gouldner's understanding of Marx was skewed toward the revolutionary side of Marx's thinking, to issues of domination and struggles for power. The systematic nature of Marx's theory, the respect in which Marx was endeavoring to construct an argument based on reason and evidence, not merely on rhetoric—a feature of Marx's work that Joseph Schumpeter, for example, noted in a number of books, perhaps most notably in *Capitalism, Socialism and Democracy*—was absent in Gouldner's teaching or writings. Yet Marx held intellectual values dear and sought to promote them as well.

A month after Hammet's performance, AYD held a rally on the library steps. We had rigged up an effigy of Senator Bilbo. Over an eight-foot pole attached to a Christmas tree stand we draped a sheet with Bilbo's name written in large black letters. Underneath the name we had drawn a skull and crossbones and printed the letters KKK. We put a few pieces of tinder around the stand and doused the sheet with charcoal lighter fluid.

It was a cool, cloudy, late afternoon in mid-October, with gusts coming off Lake Erie portending colder weather on the way. Some ten or twelve AYD members stood nearby. Two Trotskyists—members of the smaller radical group on campus—came by. I knew them from my classes. They were friendly and I liked them. They too were veterans and had many of the same values, but we were rivals and had limited contact. A handful of other students walking to the student union after class stopped and watched. About three or four students wearing fraternity letters on their jackets joined the growing crowd. Another two or three students who looked like athletes—perhaps members of the football team—stood next to the fraternity men. Two AYD members, holding megaphones, were at either side of the effigy.

The speakers began, but were soon interrupted by shouts. There were no racial epithets, probably because Leroy Jones, one of the stars of the football team—indeed of the university—was an African American student who had recently been elected to Phi Beta Kappa. He was an extraordinary student in every respect, and everyone liked him. But I wondered whether the opposition to us might have had some underlying racial animus (Bilbo was an overt racist), and this added to my anger at our being interrupted. In any event, the shouters demanded that we get off the stairs and stop blocking entrance to the library. But we were not blocking the library. The stone stairs were at least twenty-five to thirty feet wide, and we stood well to one side, taking up about seven to eight feet. Many students, in fact (a bit to our chagrin), passed by us on their way in and out of the library. We shouted back, advised our hecklers to walk around us and discover what the inside of the library looked like.

Other members of the crowd joined in the shouting. More students began to gather. I became apprehensive, as I'm sure others did. This might develop into a fistfight! Within a few moments after the commotion had started, a distinguished-looking older man could be seen approaching the library. He walked steadily and deliberately toward us. The man was slender and erect, had a well-trimmed van Dyke beard and gray hair. It was Chancellor Capen. He came directly to where the speakers were standing, held up his hand for attention, and addressed the crowd, which now numbered perhaps thirty students. "I disagree with these students," he said, gesturing slightly toward us, "but they have a right to speak, and I defend that right." He stepped back. There was a low sighing from the crowd as though it were deflating, and then one student after another began drifting away. Chancellor Capen had already turned and was walking back to his office. We lit the effigy; it burned quickly, but before it was fully consumed few students were any longer there to see it. Through quiet yet firm authority, Capen had averted what could have become a nasty situation. I admired him. And although it took a few days to understand, I learned something important about the meaning of integrity from all this.

I puzzled over Capen's disagreement with us. He was well known as a supporter of liberal causes, and we were certainly espousing a liberal cause. And then, as usually happens with insights, within a day or two the answer suddenly came. In burning our effigy, we were doing symbolically to Bilbo what the Ku Klux Klan had been doing actually to African Americans. We were expressing hatred and rage, not providing a strong moral argument, and in this sense were not much better than the Klan. Wasn't this one of the reasons the Nazis and the Soviets were so horrific? Of course, one had to use force to defend oneself when physically attacked. But we weren't being physically attacked. We were trying to curb Bilbo, sway public opinion, and put an end to the Klan. But the way we were going about this was wrong and might have the opposite effect of what we intended. This was a lesson I relearned many times. I look back with increasing respect and affection for Chancellor Capen.

With its thirty-plus members, AYD was the largest radical group on campus. However, I don't think it was ever very persuasive, and its fortunes and membership began to drop steeply after the effigy burning. The other radical groups seemed to have been similarly affected; none of them stepped forward to replace us. We had no further plans for the remainder of the fall semester and were not much in the mood to plan for the spring. It was in this humor that we saw a poster announcing a talk soon to be given in Buffalo by Max Shachtman.

Shachtman had been a close associate of Leon Trotsky but had broken with Trotsky and the Socialist Workers Party (SWP) some years back. He was now a chief theorist and spokesman of the Workers Party (WP), a new group he had formed with about 40 percent of the membership of the SWP. Shachtman had the reputation of being a fiery speaker and trenchant debater, and a few of us decided to attend his talk.

Shachtman lived up to his reputation. He was a lively speaker, had an agile mind, considerable learning and wit, and put on quite a show. Short and vigorous, whenever he got excited, which was often, he stood on his toes and poked his arms in the air for emphasis. However, when he pronounced a word with a "p" or "b" in it—proletarian, bourgeois, people, party, Politburo, Pravda—he emitted a fine spray that, after an hour or so, drenched listeners in the first two rows. Sitting in the third row, I got a bit of this, which doubtless dampened my reaction to his talk. In any event, his criticisms of the Soviet Union and Stalin were the most incisive and damning I had ever heard or read, and my own negative views were reinforced and deepened by him. But his insistence on the proletariat as being of cardinal significance in contemporary as well as future societies was not something with which I could fully concur.

A recent newspaper article reported almost a half-million veterans had enrolled in colleges and universities across the country since the end of the war. A ten- to twelve-fold increase in numbers of college-educated people was projected to occur within a generation. If this projection were accurate (which it turned out to be; by 1978 there were actually over twelve million students in colleges, and more than twelve million had graduated in the intervening years), the size of the proletariat would likely diminish; that in the professions would rise. And even though many professionals earn wages—one of the two parts of Marx's definition of a worker—they are not merely "mental workers." Scientists, engineers, doctors, accountants, pharmacists, lawyers, and teachers have greater autonomy than nonprofessional workers in the way they exercise their duties. There have been and doubtless will continue to be many attempts of employers to infringe upon professional autonomy (which have at times been successful), but generally the professional and the professional organization, not the employer, determine and control the standards of professional work. But numbers are not everything. Whether the proletariat is large or small, to be an effective political force it needs to be organized. And this will require its members to recognize one another as a distinct and solidary entity, a class with specific interests. Marx as well as many contemporary

Marxist writers stressed the importance of class-consciousness as the other integral part of the conception of class. Without consciousness of being part of a class and having common interests, workers are only an empirical/statistical category; they are wage earners, not a class. Only a small segment of workers in the United States has achieved such consciousness at any one time—the Wobblies, for instance—but as for the whole or even a politically viable portion of the labor force, such consciousness does not exist. The International Workers of the World (IWW) that De Leon had helped found was soon riven by internal conflicts, and the Wobblies were quickly defeated. The phrase "working class" in its Marxist sense is presently a fiction, a possible future occurrence, but for the moment a shorthand term for people who work in a particular range of occupations and have a similar lifestyle.

Marx had postulated a contradiction between the collective organization of production and the individual ownership of the means of production. As a consequence, he held, workers have no control over their work or the use to which the wealth they produce is put. Workers are, as it were, "wage slaves." But this contradiction, Marx believed, which is crucial to capitalist production, will eventually spur workers to recognize who and what they are as distinct from the bourgeoisie. Workers will then define themselves as a class and see that wealth collectively produced should be collectively controlled. So defined, and with a surer grasp of their own interests, workers will set about as a class to seize control of the means of production and turn them to collective use.

But how will workers reach this understanding? Will that spur of contradiction dig deep enough to provoke a massive shift in the mentality of working people? The only circumstance I could envision that might prompt working people to band together would be a severe, sustained threat of some sort. Economic depressions are examples of such a threat. But even then, workers might just as well disperse and flee. Both things happened in Southern Europe near the end of the nineteenth century and again at the time of the revolution in Russia after the First World War.

In his *Theses on Feuerbach*,[2] Marx asserted that an object, reality, is not known through abstract contemplation but only through practical, sensuous activity. Yet, Marx's conception of the vast division and coordination of work, which is a social object, was that of a theorist, an abstract understanding quite distinct from the lived, practical, sensuous reality of his or anyone's work life. Not one of the working people

I knew or had interviewed had the slightest sense of the "contradiction" or of the "true proletarian interests" of which Marx spoke. They wanted a secure job. They wanted to stay healthy so they could work. They wanted to like and be on good terms with their fellow employees *and* their bosses. They wanted to make life better for themselves and their families—to assure their parents were cared for in old age and their children educated and healthy as they grew up. They wanted a decent pension. Some wanted a slightly longer vacation, a larger house, a newer car, perhaps a boat. When these things were threatened, they were moved to organize and sometimes to strike. Very few aspired to, or could imagine themselves, owning or even managing the plants and businesses in which they worked. My information was, of course, based on a limited sample—the couple of dozen workingmen I had known in summer laboring jobs, my father's employees, the handful of neighbors whose backyard conversations I had overheard over the years, and the couple of hundred people I had interviewed for my professor's research projects. These people would work and scrabble at just about anything to make ends meet, as they had a decade earlier during the Depression. They did not envision revolution for themselves. Nor were they ever eager to go out on strike. Perhaps they all had "false consciousness," as Engels put it. But this consciousness was false only if one accepted Marx's philosophy of history.

There was indeed a sense of belonging and common purpose among people of all kinds in the United States during the Second World War. This was not class consciousness, however, it was nation consciousness. No less important, ethnic and religious "consciousness" could often take precedence over other kinds. My father's experience in the Bolshevik army was proof of that. No, the idea of the proletariat as a class seemed to me to be too simple, perhaps premature, but presently inadequate. Despite my doubts of much of what he said, I did agree with Shachtman on one general point: given Marx's repeated emphasis upon consciousness—which is not a material but an ideational entity—Marx can hardly be said to have been an economic determinist. I left the lecture appreciating Shachtman's vitality and integrity, but not persuaded by a significant part of his argument.

Over the Christmas break, my friend, whose father had spoken of the parallel between the Nazis and the Soviets, called me. We had become good friends. I had begun dating his sister, and we saw each other frequently. He needed to speak, he said, on a confidential matter. After several minutes of brooding discomfort, he burst out with: "Did you know I'm a member of the Communist Party?" Of course I did not know and was astonished. He had joined two years earlier, had refused to be part of a cell, but had contributed several hundred dollars to party coffers. I told him of my affiliation, which did not surprise him. He did not know of the John Reed Club, but suspected something of the sort existed. As his understanding of the Soviets and their relation to the American Communist Party grew, so too did his apprehension and doubts. He had become convinced the Soviets had corrupted both the idea and the practice of socialism. And, he stressed, the American Communist Party, which took its orders from Moscow, would do the same. As he put it, the leaders of the American CP are basically stooges and follow Soviet orders. The Soviets, moreover, have little understanding of American society and culture; they still operate with a nineteenth-century European model in which class and class relations have been defined for centuries, not only economically but along hereditary lines. As a result, the American CP is not only corrupt but also ignorant and ineffectual. My friend said he was seriously thinking of quitting the Party. He thought it would be futile to try to change it.

In early February of 1948, a month after the spring semester had begun, my friend called again. This time he sounded quite anxious. He had gone to Party Headquarters and told them he wanted to resign. He spoke with a person who, from his description, I was almost certain was the spokesman I had met about a year earlier. The main reason my friend gave was he had lost interest in communism. And since he would soon be going to graduate school in a different state he thought this was a good time to resign. The spokesman's initial reaction seemed friendly and concerned, but his tone soon changed. He assured my friend one could still be a Communist in a different state—a sarcastic jab that raised my friend's hackles—and asked whether there was perhaps some personal problem. After a bit more of this kind of questioning, to which my friend repeated his reason, the party spokesman said it was a mistake to resign, that my friend needed to learn and understand more of what Communism is. Only in a Communist society, the spokesman emphasized, would my friend's abilities and interests be fulfilled. My friend replied all that might be true if Communism were possible, but he now believed it would never be achieved, certainly not in his lifetime. The spokesman then abruptly reversed course: if you decide to resign now, he warned, we would inform your graduate school you were a member of the Communist Party. My friend was furious at this, told the spokesman he should consider him resigned as of that moment, and stormed out. But he was also frightened. Would they carry through on their threat?

When I heard the story, I became incensed, angrier perhaps than ever before or since. This was a kind of blackmail! The spokesman must be contemptuous of us to think we could so easily be frightened into submission. "A brokh in zayne beyner" ("All his bones should be broken!") as one of my relatives would say. The following day I went to Party Headquarters. The spokesman was in. I told him I'd learned of his threat to my friend. If he carried out this threat, I warned, I would go straight to the F.B.I. and turn them all in. (This was of course an idle threat, since to carry it out I would ipso facto have informed on myself. And also, I hadn't the slightest idea where the F.B.I. was located.) Whereupon I took out my card, tore it up, and left. I had been a member of the Communist Party for about a year, from just before I turned eighteen to before I was nineteen. Thus ended my short career as a member of the American Communist Party. I remembered later I had signed the card with a pseudonym that only I knew, and wondered what the Party might have made of it if they bothered to put the pieces together.

My friends at the John Reed Club were outraged when I told them what had happened. They too had been having doubts about the Soviets and the American CP and were considering quitting the Party. I don't know whether my story tilted the scales, but they all quit within a month.

Since our fall debacle, AYD had ceased functioning and would soon be forgotten. The members of the John Reed Club remained friends, but the club had dissolved. Our political careers at the university were over. Two of the members had taken college courses before the war and anticipated completing their studies and graduating in June. We met a few times socially before the end of the semester. We all went to hear Henry Wallace, the candidate for American presidency of the Progressive Party. We all heard Paul Robeson sing. He did have an extraordinary voice.

Notes

1. Bantam, New York, 1968.
2. Mondial, New York, 2000.

5

McCarthy, Philosophy, and the Jewish Question

By the early 1950s, the radical impulse that had animated students in many universities during the late 1940s had been spent. The Cold War was being waged on many fronts, and casualties were beginning to mount. Each day, or so it seemed, another Soviet agent was ferreted out from some hidden, but sensitive, recess of the State Department. The quickening pace of exposure of real or imaginary Communists by the House Un-American Activities Committee (HUAC), the fear—and sometimes the reality—of job loss by those who had expressed or whose friends had expressed any hint of Communist sympathy, the blacklisting of actors and screenwriters, the Algier Hiss espionage Trial—all this generated a mood of uneasiness and suspicion in the country that served to paralyze radical activity. There was protest that freedom of speech was being abridged, that mere association established guilt, but this was essentially ineffective.

Many students of my generation had turned their interests, as had I, to professional training. The new, incoming undergraduate students did not have veterans as their cohorts and models, and their interests were decidedly apolitical. Some of the faculty as well as many older graduate students who had become teaching assistants bemoaned the quiescence and conventionality of the new generation of students. Others of the faculty found the absence of student political activity a relief. These were matters of taste and disposition, of course, and I had to remind myself that the indisputable should not be disputed.

Nevertheless, the virtues of socialism still meant a great deal to me, and though I write now, in 2012 an emeritus professor with many of the kinds of possessions that used to intimidate me in my friends' parents' houses, I am not so sated by comfort nor disillusioned by experience that I no longer see virtues in socialism. Economics is important, but hardly all. The moral issues are at the root.

My intellectual interests then were, and to a lesser extent still are, in the nature and meaning of knowledge and philosophy of history, followed closely by metaphysics and ethics. The philosophy department at the University of Buffalo, though small, had three members who had been trained in Europe: the chair, Marvin Farber, who was American, and Fritz Kaufmann and Shia Moser, who were European refugees. Both Farber and Kaufmann had studied with Edmund Husserl in Germany, Moser with Alfred Tarski in Poland. There were three other full-time members: William Tuthill Parry, who specialized in logic, Mary Whitman in pragmatism, and William Wolfers in Anglo-American philosophy. Occasional seminars and courses were given by notable scholars in the local community who were semi-retired—a rabbi who gave a seminar every third semester or so on medieval Jewish thought, a Unitarian minister who gave a seminar in alternate semesters on the neo-Platonists.

Through Professor Farber, I was awarded a university fellowship that permitted me to study whatever I wished and provided a small stipend. I obviously decided to do graduate work in philosophy and perhaps not so obviously take a minor in the psychology of perception.

All knowledge is selective, and the bases of selection—how some things are included and remembered and others excluded or forgotten—are of considerable interest to me. I came to realize quite consciously in later years that the source of this interest was an early awareness of and regret for the inevitable and growing gap between the life, language, customs, and outlook of my grandparents and parents and I. Indeed, this book is animated in part by an awareness of many generational gaps, and part of its purpose is to record a few refracted bits of the culture of my generation for the generations that follow mine. The psychology department at the University of Buffalo was large and had faculty expert in the kinds of branches—gestalt, developmental, and Freudian—I thought would be particularly useful in helping me understand some of the perceptual, cognitive, and motivational issues.

The chance to study and immerse myself in philosophy and psychology was one of the joys of my life. The university opened up the world of human culture to me, a world it would have taken several thousand lifetimes to assimilate. "All men," said Aristotle in the opening line of his *Metaphysics*,[1] "desire to know." I didn't know about all men, but this proposition certainly applied to me.

A year before I started graduate studies, my family and I left our warehouse apartment. My parents bought a single-family house in a middle-class neighborhood not far from the university. The house had all the amenities one would expect to find in the quiet, tree-lined, and well-tended street on which it was located. Kempt lawns bordered the house, and a separate garage awaited its occupant. All my parents' old furniture was thrown out and new furniture bought. My father also bought a new car to go with the house and garage—a black, shiny, four-door Buick sedan as large as a boat and, with its well-sprung chassis, riding a bit like a boat rocking on a gentle sea.

I was very pleased for them, but at the same time embarrassed and uneasy. How could I, a socialist, reconcile myself to living like a petit bourgeois? The new street we lived on was named Blantyre Road, and some of my radical friends instantly rechristened it Bourgyre Road. I did not have the courage to counter this petty nastiness, but went along with it. They called my parents' car a "Jewick"—expressing self-hatred more than socialist qualms. I'm ashamed of myself and of them in retrospect. My parents hadn't gouged anyone to buy this house, nor were they "lording it" over anyone now that they had it. The Buick was a low-end model, quite common, but of course it was not a "proletarian" Ford or Chevrolet. Didn't my parents deserve whatever small comforts they had worked so hard for? I don't think I would succumb to this sour-grapes pettiness today.

I was uneasy for yet other reasons, however. In responding to my mother's shame of living in the straitened circumstances of the warehouse apartment, I began to feel something of the same shame myself. Although I had an address, a number on a street in a poor but clean and safe part of the city, I never brought any of my friends to that address. With its dirty, streaked walls that did not reach the ceiling, its sprinkler system and cement floors, the apartment was among the poorest of the living quarters I had seen, and I had seen many. But now, although having moved into a perfectly pleasant middle-class house and neighborhood, where everything in my immediate environment betokened the acme of respectability, I felt uncomfortable. I felt illegitimate, that I didn't belong and had no right to be there. This was not a feeling induced by ideological misgivings. Perhaps, I thought, it was because we were Jews in a neighborhood of relatively few (but soon to be growing numbers of) Jewish families. Or perhaps it was because my parents did not belong to anything, to a synagogue or a club, had relatively few friends nearby, and thus seemed unanchored. I felt, in any event, uncomfortable, and even avoided as much as possible having to greet a passerby while walking the couple of blocks to the bus stop.

For reasons I did not understand then, one of the consequences of this feeling was a growing internal anger that was increasingly difficult to control. My major recourse was to flee into my books, into philosophy, psychology, and literature. My minor recourse was to reverse the normal order of living, to read and study as much as possible during the night and sleep during the day. I rationalized this by thinking of myself as a Dostoyevskian intellectual *sans* tea.

Although my parents offered to buy a baby grand piano for me, I refused. I had made a decision and, however painful, was going to stick to it. My new bedroom had a lovely built-in bookcase and a new desk, and this is where I would try to make whatever intellectual music I could. I lived in this pleasant house for the remainder of my undergraduate days and the first years of graduate school.

Not by intention, but because it was part of the standard graduate curriculum, I spent four years of intensive study of many of the same ancient and modern philosophers Marx had studied. His intellectual achievement was far greater than I had realized. He had a command of German, French, and English philosophical schools dominant in his time. He also had assimilated the leading political and economic ideas of the French and English Enlightenment. He was a gifted mathematician, could speak, read, and write in several ancient and modern languages, and had read many of the histories of Europe, India, and the United States current in his time. All this would have been enough to describe him as a polymath. But he had also attempted the daunting task of synthesizing these schools of thought into a single, coherent theory. Although his theory was inadequate, he was a genius. I do not use the term "genius" in the loose way many people today dub anyone with some talent a genius. Archimedes, Aristotle, and Plato were geniuses; Leonardo, Shakespeare, Goethe, Galileo, Michelangelo, Bernini, Newton, Rembrandt, Kant, Bach, Mozart, Beethoven, Marx, Einstein, and Freud were geniuses; and there are others of course. In all cases, geniuses are rare, original, and their work is of the highest order. The comprehensive aspiration of Marx's thought, seeming to illuminate all parts of the social world, was a large part of what had attracted me to his ideas in the first place. I wanted to understand more clearly how he went about constructing his theory, and where and in what respects it was lacking. These concerns were a kind of leitmotif to my philosophy studies.

One of the surprises of graduate school was the dearth of female graduate students. This was in the early 1950s. Twenty-five years later, almost half the students doing graduate work in the humanities and social sciences were women; thirty years later women had begun pursuing advanced degrees in engineering and the physical sciences. In my generation, most women who continued their education after receiving their B.A. degree enrolled in schools of education or social work. At the University of Buffalo, there were no women graduate students in philosophy, perhaps three or four in sociology and history, and two in English. Of the latter, one continually waved her left hand to display her engagement ring; the other was of indeterminate gender. All this was something of a disappointment. But since graduate and undergraduate students mixed often and amicably, my initial discontent was soon dissipated. It was at a social gathering of such students a few years after I had begun graduate studies that I met a young woman who was to become my wife. All was not lost.

In my second year of graduate studies, Senator Joseph McCarthy and his henchmen invaded Buffalo, New York. The head of the teachers' union (who had been my high school Latin teacher) was singled out as a Communist bent on subverting high school students. (Perhaps McCarthy considered Caesar's *Commentaries* a handbook of instructions on how to invade and conquer.) This allegation was not proved, but caused his temporary suspension (with pay) until the matter was clarified. Other mischief took place at the university.

McCarthy claimed to have "evidence" that several members of the faculty were "card-carrying" members of the Communist Party. In one case, that of my logic professor, Professor Parry, the evidence consisted of a so-called report from a witness (never identified) that, as a graduate student at Harvard in the late 1930s, he had sold the *Daily Worker* on Harvard Square. McCarthy claimed this professor was a Soviet agent intent on indoctrinating his students.

I had never had the smallest hint my professor was even sympathetic to Communism, and, given my proclivities, the fact that he passed unnoticed by my antennae made me skeptical that any part of McCarthy's charge had merit. My professor was a logician, born and raised in the east and educated in New England, regions of the country sometimes treated by McCarthy as though they were Soviet outposts. His language consisted of variations of "If P, then Q." Rarely did he supply a concrete instance of P or Q or their implicative variations, and when he did the examples were so utterly prosaic as to be comic ("If he gave her a potato, she would either accept it or refuse it." This became known among his students as the potato alternative.) He was a shy man who had difficulty looking directly at students and lectured to the blackboard or while looking out the window. It was not credible to envisage him hawking or even reading the *Daily Worker*. His love of logic was palpable, his lectures were intense and clear (and sometimes unwittingly funny), and his students respected and liked him. And not least, students learned some principles of logic from him.

Capen had retired. While not running amok, McCarthy was likely given a freer hand than he would have had if Capen were still chancellor. A small number of graduate students protested. Some members of the faculty were vociferously opposed to McCarthy's interference at the university, but others, believing Soviet Russia was a real danger to the United States, were equally vociferous in supporting McCarthy's efforts. The furor McCarthy's visit generated was confined mainly to the faculty and a handful of graduate students and lasted about a year. I doubt undergraduate students were much aware of this. Neither I nor any of the radical students I had known came to McCarthy's attention. My John Reed Club friends were, in any event, no longer at the university. Even my curator friend was no longer in Buffalo. He had won a scholarship to Brandeis and was now studying English literature (and I'm sure was more knowledgeable than his professors). Classes continued on schedule throughout, but some of the graduate students and many of the faculty were a bit jittery. After many meetings of the administration and faculty, compromises both acceptable and shameful were finally reached. My professor, who had tenure, was frozen in his position. He continued to teach and write, conducting himself with dignity. (I learned later that after ten years and a new administration he was promoted and awarded retroactive compensation.) A few professors were reported to have resigned and gone elsewhere.

The charged feelings caused by McCarthy's intrusion subsided soon enough, but with lingering disrespect of many faculty and graduate students for the university administration that had been so feckless. Notwithstanding these feelings, which I shared, the return to a kind of pre-McCarthy quiescence was also a blessing for me because I was able to devote my full attention to studying philosophy.

My father's comment about Marx's anti-Semitism remained as an irritant in a recess of my mind that I had learned by and large to ignore. But it was nevertheless there, and I felt its jab again when, by accident, the issue of Marx's anti-Semitism reappeared. In one of my readings I found a striking Jewish inspired analogy by Moses Hess between Marx's view of history and the Old Testament account of Genesis. Hess, a philosopher in his own right and a forerunner of Zionism, was one of Marx's nineteenth-century colleagues who advocated the formation of a Jewish state. Man makes his own history, said Hess and Marx. And then, said Hess, like God who rested on the seventh day after he had created the world, socialism, which is the completion of the historical process, is the Sabbath of History.

Hess' many-layered analogy would seem at first glance to be idiosyncratic, if not absurd, in light of Marx's scathing criticism of what he considered despicable Jewish attitudes and practices. I read Marx's essay "On the Jewish Question"[2] shortly after encountering Hess' writings. The title of the essay alone evoked images of the Holocaust and the "final solution." I tried very hard to bracket these associations before analyzing what Marx had to say on the subject a hundred years earlier, but I feared my father had been right. The essay did provide painful evidence that Marx was anti-Jewish.

Although Marx's father had converted to Protestantism three years before Marx was born—a condition that enabled him to practice law—each of his parents came from a long line of rabbis. If his anti-Jewish attitude was more than adolescent rebelliousness, this was a puzzle I had to try to solve. At this point in my life my responses soon became dispassionate and analytical. I reread the essay several times and came to the following conclusions. I believe he was ambivalent toward Jews. He wrote the essay in 1843 when he was twenty-five years old—no longer an adolescent—and championed a universal conception of humankind, a belief in which he did not waver until the day of his death forty years later, in 1883. He chastised the Jews who, he claimed, had perverted their metaphysical and salvationary universalism—a single, creator God—into the profane form of the universal solvent, money. Money had become, as it were, the new idol.

Marx's charge was incredible. He surely saw in his own immediate experiences—one of his uncles of whom he was fond, for example, was a rabbi, Hess himself was a self-identified Jew, and many bankers and bourgeoisie who dealt with money were *not* Jews—that this blanket condemnation was false. And he, the soon-to-be-economist, must also have had some knowledge of the very limited role of moneylender available to Jews in the economies of earlier times. He may have been dismayed by the "impurity" of money-lending Jews—this is, of course, conjecture—and, like the outcast Nabi prophets of old who railed against the Jews for having converted the nation of Israel into an idol, was denouncing these practices and warning of eventual disaster: Capitalism, aided and abetted by the errant and idolatrous universalism into which Jews had fallen, would erode the human spirit. If there is any truth in this conjecture, then he must have tacitly placed the enormous burden of human salvation back upon the Jews! But whatever may have been the actual reasons for his misplaced scorn, there is no doubt that in his very language he was also simultaneously praising the salvationary universalism of the Jews. In further consideration, Hess' analogy may be seen to have tapped deep, resonant aspects of Marx's thought.

Most of the people I knew who were attracted to Marx's ideas were Jewish. In some part, socialism for them, and no doubt for me as well, had been prefigured by the Jewish eschatology of the end of days. In some part too, Jews considered themselves a messianic people, and socialism was believed to be the way to save all of humankind. But I knew from my reading that Marx appealed to a great many Christians as well.

In later studying, I found what I believe is an analogy between Marx's idea of the universality of the proletariat and Pauline Christianity. Paul's epistles sought to broaden the social basis of Christianity beyond national boundaries. One could be a Christian, he urged, and remain a member of this or that nation. In Marx's view, the proletariat is also a transnational entity and increasingly made up of members of all capitalist social strata—rentiers, bourgeoisie, petit bourgeoisie, and peasants. All increasingly fall into the proletariat and become wage earners. In their social makeup, both proletarians and Christians are catholic—universal. *The Communist Manifesto* is itself a kind of epistle. Addressed initially to British laborers, it ends with a call, not solely to British laborers, but to "workers of the world." Like Paul's epistles, the *Manifesto* has been translated into every major language. Alasdair MacIntyre, in *Marxism and Christianity*[3] (1968), has explored yet other affinities.

Marx was not flat-out anti-Jewish or flat-out anti-Christian. It became even clearer to me after considering the issues that, however distant from them they may seem, many of Marx's moral and social views as well as his eschatology were touched with Judaic and Christian thought. Like each of us, Marx was subject to the influences and limitations of his time and place. When I discussed my interpretation with my father, he said he thought I was smarter than the Bolsheviks. But of course, he didn't like the Bolsheviks.

I took seminars from each of the faculty. Three seminars were particularly attractive, and what I learned—and didn't learn—in them has continued to resonate in my own work ever since.

Like Nathaniel Cantor, Marvin Farber was one of the stars of the university. He was a noted teacher, respected in his profession, and one of the esteemed sons of the Buffalo Jewish community. He taught undergraduate and graduate courses. At the graduate level he regularly gave two seminars, one on theories of value, the other on philosophy of science. In both, we read works from the ancients up to contemporary American and European philosophers.

While studying with Husserl in Germany, Farber had met several other leading philosophers of the time—Martin Heidegger, Karl Mannheim, Georg Lukács, and Max Scheler. He detested Heidegger for his Nazi sympathies—evident, apparently, even as early as his philosophical writings of the 1920s—but said little of the other three. I knew Lukács was a Marxist and Mannheim a liberal. I had read somewhere that Scheler, who had a complicated religious and political history, came round after initial resistance to supporting Walter Rathenau and the Weimar Republic. The four represented the political and intellectual spectrum of Germany and Europe in the 1920s, and had become famous in European intellectual circles. I was hoping to learn more of them.

Although Farber did not often lecture or venture an explicit critique of the materials, his reputation and manner commanded attention and respect. Mainly, he served as a Socratic-like questioner in discussions that frequently included faculty from other departments. Since the values seminar dealt mainly with recent discussions of "the good," it was assumed, by and large correctly, that students had taken earlier courses in the history of ethics. As an undergraduate, I had had a two-semester survey course on ethical thought from the Greeks, the Middle Ages, and the modern English utilitarian thinkers up to and including Immanuel Kant.

Above all others, it was Kant's moral writings that gave voice to some of my deepest feelings. Treat each man as an end in himself, said Kant, not as a means. This sentence has since become a cliché for some members of the educated public and treated too often with a "yes, yes, of course" attitude, which in effect dismisses it. But there is a powerful sentiment being expressed in the sentence. It is more of a commandment than a cliché. Ever since I was a teenager and could think of such things, I had believed it would be degrading to manipulate or exploit anyone. Now, in graduate school, it occurred to me that this teaching too must have influenced Marx and drawn me to many of Marx's ideas. Wasn't Marx's characterization of the exploitation of the proletariat in modern societies another way of saying the proletariat was being used as a means for capitalist ends? And wasn't the project of socialism a design of the conditions that would promote treatment of persons as ends in themselves?

Of course, I knew that we frequently manipulate and use others in order to gain some end. And I do not exclude myself. But if there were a fair exchange involved, and we were open about this, the potential for exploiting the other would be mitigated, perhaps nullified. This was my reasoning. It was not too far from Kant's.

Another of Kant's maxims, which I also believed expressed one of the highest ethical principles, gave me considerable trouble. To paraphrase Kant's language, the maxim enjoins us to act in such a way that a universal moral law is guiding our conduct.

Kant's ethical maxims were sweeping and absolute; they pertained to all of humanity. They were predicated on the assumption that each person is of value, which we must always respect and in our actions endeavor to uphold. Even a "little white lie," given these ideas, is impermissible in Kant's view since this would treat the other instrumentally and break our communion with him or her. How different this is from the utilitarian ethical calculus! A Kantian when told a tale by a friend that brings in bits of gossip, memories, seemingly unrelated incidents, associations that appear culled from thin air, might respond when asked what he, the Kantian, thought of the tale by saying that it goes on too long and its many details and asides make it difficult to follow. When pressed to declare whether the tale was at least interesting, the Kantian might reply, regretfully, that it was boring. The other might be offended, most likely hurt, and communion between the two would likely be broken. A Utilitarian, on the other hand, seeking to maximize everyone's pleasure and minimize everyone's pain, might have interrupted the storyteller soon after he or she began to wander in associations by excusing himself on the grounds of another pressing appointment (white lie #1) and reassuring the teller they would meet again soon (likely white lie #2). No one's feelings would have been hurt, but there would have been an end to whatever communion there had been between the two.

In some respects I was, and still am, utilitarian in my relationships. To be a strict Kantian requires a somewhat saintly attitude and steely nerves! But the intellectual-moral problem I had with Kant's principles was that I wanted to understand whether they could actually ever be universal and compelling. They were the formulations of a great eighteenth-century thinker, a late product of the Western Enlightenment. But could a Confucian subscribe to them? Could an Inuit?

Discussions in the values seminar were lively but did not go as far as I wished. Farber was kind to me but in other respects circumspect. We did not venture into the views of such existentialist or theological thinkers as Kierkegaard or Tillich, for example, nor such probing contemporary European authors as Cioran, who asked whether there was any point to values. These and other writers I read by myself over the years. Of the philosophers we discussed, existence was not a temptation, as it was for Cioran, but simply a precondition for realization of "the good." This meant that life "itself" is simply a category; only its modalities have value. I thought there was a problem in conceiving "life" this way, as though it were merely a logical premise. The values constructed on such a premise were bound to be "rationalist"; their force logical. Ethical principles, however, needed to be compelling on other, deeper grounds. And unless logical, rational arguments are themselves considered to have value, they could simply be ignored. Of the philosophers I read, only Cioran seemed to recognize the issue.

Although the specter of Communism might be haunting Europe and the House Un-American Activities Committee, the specter of relativism continued to haunt me. The good was rarely defined, but I could not see, from everything we were studying, how to mitigate the threat of a Babel of irreconcilable proclamations of 'the good." We touched on Kant as a historical figure but did not discuss the grounds of his ethics. And there was no discussion whatsoever of Marx's moral views—not exactly surprising since Marx had never bothered to set them down. More important, Marx was being widely portrayed as the dark anti-Christ guiding the evil Soviet empire. We were not about to have intercourse of any kind with an anti-Christ.

However removed and secure the university might have once believed itself to be, we had recently learned that it was vulnerable, not really a bastion of learning in which every idea could be dispassionately discussed. Its walls had been too easily breached, and some of its defenders too quickly surrendered. Opportunistic apostles of the pure and the true had in many cases succeeded in driving out and stilling anyone who uttered even one word of Marx.

The several years of self-imposed silence on Marxist thought, I believed, distorted the American understanding of its opponents and negatively affected America's role in the world. Marxism is more than a set of oppositions. It is also a set of affirmations. It is impossible to understand the enormous appeal Marxist thought had (and in some quarters in 2012 still has) unless one appreciates the moral force of

Marx's ideas. This, I believed, was going unrecognized by practically everyone in our society—by the professors and students in the universities, the experts—or at least the spokesmen—in the Foreign Service and State Departments, the Congress and most of all the general public.

I talked with my father and uncle about this. They both thought there was agreement in basic moral views between the Marxist socialists they had known in Europe and us. Justice, fairness, equality, human fulfillment—we all want this. They could not speak of China or other parts of the world; perhaps there was agreement there too. But they pointed out that socialist or Communist ideas—it hardly mattered which kinds—had become so deeply entwined in the public mind with the Soviet Union that to mention one would automatically bring up the other. As a result, socialism of any kind, however independent of the views and actions promulgated by the Soviet Union, would be eclipsed and likely remain unrecognized even after the Soviet Union had been defeated. The latter prospect, they thought, might occur in my lifetime, not in theirs. They both foresaw a long struggle between the Soviets and us, likely bloody at times, but one that we, with our far more advanced resources, would ultimately win.

As it turned out, the first cultural exchanges between the United States and Soviet Russia, and with these a jot of hope that each of us might see something in the other besides our political differences, began after 1953, when Stalin died. Although Isaac Stern quipped that "they sent us their Jews from Odessa, we sent them our Jews from Odessa," the superb pianists and violinists with whom the exchanges began were not all Jewish! Above all, the exchanges showed that we shared a musical culture. But this was hardly all of it. Not too long later, the poetry of Yevgeny Yevtushenko and novels of Alexander Solzenitsin also showed us with the graphic particularity of the artist just how barbaric the Soviet Union under Stalin's rule had been. And this also showed us that in common with the literary artists and their many followers we shared a moral culture as well. There was little expediency in Stalin's edicts, only fear, hatred, and boundless cruelty. Nothing I had read in the writings of Marx would have justified the monstrous acts described by Yevtushenko and Solzenitsin. All the more reason, it seemed to me, we and particularly the Soviets needed to know what Marx's ethical-moral views were. Then we could separate Marx from the Soviet Union, as I had already done several years ago.

The overt intellectual study of Marx's thought had to await the 1960s when several scholars commented on Marx's moral-ethical views—Jean Paul Sartre and Erich Fromm among them. A more thorough examination is in Eugene Kamenka's *The Ethical Foundations of Marxism*[4] (1962).

I took the values seminar in fall of 1952, just as the Stevenson-Eisenhower presidential campaign was getting under way. Everyone I knew was for Stevenson. He supported liberal causes and spoke fluently and with insight and wit—an unbeatable combination for academics. We feared Eisenhower would amplify the military and continue the draft. The draft, we had been told twelve years earlier, would last for the duration of the Second World War. But some of my friends, fearing the taste for having a strong military force had whetted the nation's appetite, thought "the duration" would last longer than the war. It wasn't only Eisenhower's military disposition and political conservatism that troubled us; his style too, his verbal flubs and grammatical gaffs, put us off. How could this barely articulate man be president? It was a miracle he managed to lead the armed forces. The Korean War was causing great distress for me and all of my fellow students. We didn't fear being drafted since we would likely get deferments. It was the fact of the war. We had just finished a gigantic war and now were in another one that followed almost seamlessly. Was there any genuine provocation? Would we go to war against China next? Would there be an end to the killing? Eisenhower promised to bring the Korean War to an end. Would he? Could he? The daily news reports of the war and its casualties made it difficult to put the war out of my mind for long. Although it was not called that, several commentators thought the war was a "preemptive" action by the United States. The fear that Mao's China would join with Soviet Russia and together with their satellites, including a Communist Korea, form a monolithic Communist empire spanning more than half the globe loomed large in American policy and in American minds—as it continued to do for another twenty-five years.

From the little I knew of the cultural and historical differences between China and Russia, and between Mao and Stalin, this fear did not seem warranted. It could have been to our advantage to see Korea unified, friendly to us, and perhaps serving as a bulwark on the border of China. Diplomacy was needed, and collaboration.

It was along such lines that my friends and I hoped Stevenson might take us were he to be elected president. Most Americans, however, were responding in ignorance and fear. We had bedded down with a warrior, Generalissimo Chang Kai-shek. We guessed another warrior, Eisenhower, would likely be the next president.

Some of the older acquaintances I had known as an undergraduate were now fighting in Korea. A few had been reported killed. Once, while walking up a tree-lined path in the university during a clear, cool morning in early fall, the birds still flitting about and chirping, the air bright and clean and fresh, the thought of the killing taking place in Korea, of some men and faces I knew now dead and gone forever while I was in this safe, beautiful, calm place flashed through my mind, and I had to stop for a few minutes to collect myself.

Studying philosophy was a much-needed diversion and respite from these worries. The hope I had held since adolescence, however, that a substantive, nonrelative standard could be found that would allow objective evaluations among values was not realized in the values seminar or since. But even if such a standard could be found, I no longer believed it would make much, if any, difference in our conduct.

Although the presidential campaign and the passions it aroused occupied much of the attention of students and faculty, it is uncertain how classes and seminars were affected. The values seminar would seem an obvious place for the issues of the campaign to intrude, but so far as I could tell, they never did. The materials of the seminar were too abstract, and Farber was a disciplined scholar-teacher.

Farber had a mannerism that was misleading to almost all students and colleagues. After careful watching I decoded it. When he disagreed with someone, his lips would barely purse and his head would move slightly up and down as though saying, "You see what idiocy I have to put up with?" When he agreed, his head would wag slightly from side to side as though saying, "Yes, this is good!" (I'm sure I too have ambiguous gestures of which I am unaware, and that some of my students also have decoded them. There is a certain continuity between the academic generations, informal as well as formal.) I tried to alert my fellow students to the meaning of these counterintuitive gestures, but it was amusing to think of him in conversation with unknowing colleagues who, upon leaving, would either feel pleased or a bit uncertain, neither of which would have been warranted.

The philosophy of science seminar was, I think, the one Farber found more congenial. Again, we briefly reviewed earlier views from the Greek atomists on up, but it was in the contemporary materials, post Hume and post Kant, that discussions became livelier. The three major forms of knowledge—analytical, interpretive, and causal—and certain of their combinations, occupied the bulk of seminar discussions. Farber gave a few lectures on phenomenology that I initially found baffling, but that nevertheless aroused my curiosity. This subject too I pursued in later study.

My main interest was in the kinds of knowledge yielded by the social sciences. In one of my presentations, I described an unresolved tension in social science between two kinds of knowledge—the interpretational and the causal. Interpretational analysis concentrates on uncovering the meanings of past events, documents, and utterances by exploring the contexts in which they have occurred. Causal analysis concentrates on formulating the relationships of abstracted qualities of things into strong statements, causal laws, such as $F = MA$. When applying these laws to actual things under specified conditions, causal analysis tells us what will likely be or what likely has been. I gave a few examples of these from anthropology (interpretational) and Skinnerian psychology (quasi-causal), but, mustering a bit of courage, used as my main example the explanatory tensions in Marx's theory. In a nutshell, they are the causal analysis of the economy versus the intentional interpretation of ideologies. In later reading, I discovered this dichotomy precisely differentiates the emphases on interpretation of the German Frankfurt School Marxists from the emphases on causation of the French structuralist Marxists. The seminar members were interested by my Marx example and made useful comments; and Farber, wagging his head from side to side, thought my analysis was promising. These early insights proved to be useful in my later work in social theory.

Mary Whitman, a young assistant professor, gave a seminar devoted mainly to John Dewey and secondarily to George H. Mead and Charles Peirce. William James was given scant attention. I had heard of Dewey and the other writers, but not previously read any of their works. I found them a revelation. Their understanding of the complexity of the act, of the many moral, cognitive, and existential tensions in each of the constantly shifting ("problematic," as Dewey called them) situations in which we live, was far richer than anything I had read before except in the novels of some of the great writers. None of the pragmatists, except James, could write very well, and Dewey was the worst of the lot; his sentences were so clumsy as to be at times almost impenetrable. But with some effort they could be parsed and deciphered.

The pragmatists drew upon sociology, psychology, history, culture, and not least aspects of the mind to construct their pragmatist perspective. I came to understand in later study that their views were relentlessly Calvinist. They had a meliorist orientation to action that never paused for a moment. Although their appraisal of the present was critical, there was optimism in their outlook, a belief in a better, achievable future I had not encountered in many European authors with the outstanding recent exception of Marx. Yet there were also affinities with European philosophy—especially with the conceptions of the active elements of the mind, of the openness of history, and of the existential embeddedness of all human action.

Because Dewey was the most prolific and influential of the pragmatists, his views were the most frequent target of attacks from both right and left. Conservatives saw his liberalism as a challenge to the status quo; Marxists saw pragmatism as contaminated with nonmaterial elements and merely reformist. The European commentary I read was dismissive on other grounds. American pragmatism, some of the European critics said, is not so much a philosophy as an utterance typical of a young nation, meaning that "the utterance" was peppy but immature. Although I did not agree with the negativity of the ideological evaluations, I thought both conservative and Marxist critics had a point: pragmatism did challenge the status quo and was reformist. The Europeans had missed altogether what pragmatism is about.

Of course, I compared the pragmatists' views with those of Marx—not with contemporary Marxists. But there was really not much to compare. Marx's political and economic acumen were unequalled, but his theoretical understanding of human experience and action was narrow. None of the disciplines that informed the pragmatists' understanding had been much developed in Marx's day, and some hadn't yet been born. And although Marx espoused revolution, he hardly shied away from improving the lot of people even if this did not require revolution. Perhaps the contemporary Marxist critics of pragmatism had forgotten that when Marx and his daughter endeavored to shorten the workday they were acting as reformers. In any case, revolution was not quite the shibboleth for Marx as it had become for many of his followers. And the pragmatists were certainly not revolutionaries.

Whitman was a very good teacher. Perhaps because she wasn't too much older—twelve or fifteen years—she allowed me to pursue a variety of tangents. Most of these were not very successful, but I learned from them nevertheless. In one of my forays, I read in a book edited by Sydney Hook, *John Dewey, Philosopher of Science and Freedom*,[5] that Dewey had gone to Mexico with James T. Farrell in the late 1930s to interview Trotsky. Farrell reported that Dewey and Trotsky spoke for hours. Later, on the train ride back to the United States, Dewey told

Farrell he thought Trotsky was a brilliant man, but that his thinking was caught between narrow categories.

The Dewey/pragmatism seminar stoked my desire to develop a comprehensive understanding of human conduct. I had glimmerings of aspects of human experience that I could not yet adequately formulate. If Whitman were to have given another seminar on a related topic, I would have taken it. Shortly after the seminar concluded, however, she suddenly died. She had choked to death on some bit of food she was eating. A Heimlich maneuver might have saved her. It was a shock and a loss. She was a lovely, intelligent person.

In the spring of 1954, I was well into the second of my Kant seminars (about which more later) when the Army-McCarthy hearings broke upon the television screens and claimed national attention. McCarthy looked and acted much like the character "Wiley Cat" in the Pogo comic strip created by Walt Kelly. He snarled and sneered and hissed and even intimated that Eisenhower was unpatriotic. Although he played a secondary role, Roy Cohn among McCarthy's acolytes was as venomous. But in taking on the army and its counsel, Joseph Welch, McCarthy found an adversary far stronger than any he had encountered before. And of course Joseph Welch was our idol.

The hearings lasted weeks. Most of us—students and faculty alike—sat glued to our television sets either in the afternoon (if there were no classes) or in evening replays watching the sparring and ripostes of either side. Many of us—myself included—began to imitate both McCarthy and Joseph Welch, saying whenever we thought the occasion might warrant, "Point of order, Mr. Chairman, point of order," in McCarthy's teeth-clenched hiss, or "Have you no decency, sir? Have you no decency?" in Joseph Welch's finger-shaking voice. The latter question we continued to ask frequently of anyone or anything for a year or so after the Hearings had concluded—a bit of graduate school vernacular of my generation.

Imitation is common but the psychological reasons are not always obvious. I imitated people I admired because I wanted to be like them—that seems to be an obvious reason to imitate. But I also imitated people I disliked, even despised. In this case, the reasons are not so clear. When I imitated a person I disliked I think I was doing two things: attempting to take him into myself and thus master and conquer him, and show him to be as odious or foolish as I believed him to be. This is a bit like taking fear into oneself in order to dominate it. But there are other examples of imitation that are not so easily put into one or another of these categories. According to philosophers' gossip, Jean Paul Sartre was able to do a passable imitation of Donald Duck. The thought of his endearments to Simone de Beauvoir in the squishy accents of the famous duck cheered an otherwise lugubrious journey through *Being and Nothingness*.[6] But did Sartre want to be like the duck?

Although I did not realize it at the time, the teacher who had the greatest influence on my thinking was Fritz Kaufmann. Kaufmann and Farber had met in the 1920s when both were students in Germany of Edmund Husserl, the founder of phenomenological philosophy. Farber had since eschewed what he regarded as Husserl's idealism and embraced philosophical naturalism, but Kaufmann remained a phenomenologist. When the Nazis began to rampage, Farber extended his hand to his old friend, and Kaufmann came to the University of Buffalo.

Kaufmann's main interests were in esthetics and religion, but he was enormously learned in the natural and social sciences as well as in history, and could speak, read, and write in all the European languages. His German accent, however, was very pronounced, and understanding his English was a challenge. It took me a while to grasp that when he said "Blotto," he was referring to Plato, or that when he pronounced the word "ka-teh-go-ree," pausing between each syllable, he was not using a Greek word. Of course, several of his students and I soon began to imitate him.

I took two seminars with Kaufmann devoted to Kant's *Critiques* and some of Kant's lesser writings. The *Critiques* were difficult, and comprehending their meanings was like trying to understand each step of a long, complex mathematical proof in which all the primitive terms, axioms, numbers, and relational symbols are in words rather than in letters and Greek and algebraic symbols. Fortunately, we were using very good English translations of each of the critiques (in which the word corresponding to ka-teh-go-ree appears many times), and, no less fortunate, Kaufmann was a superb commentator and a patient and clear teacher. Kant's vanquishing of Hume's skepticism—a disturbing skepticism that left me feeling I was on intellectual and moral quicksand ever since I had read Hume as an undergraduate—was an enormous achievement. Marx's aphorism, in his *Theses on Feuerbach*[7] (the only comment of his on the subject that I could find), that mere contemplative skepticism (presumably of Hume and Descartes) evaporates in practical sensuous activity, was not much of a solution, in my view. How was this better than Hume's advice that, for practical purposes, we need to assume things in the actual world will hold together, even though we cannot prove that they will? What then when things fall apart? I suppose the sensuous response would be—whoops!

Kant showed me, however, that concepts are always necessary, always part of any description, fact, or judgment. Our minds make essential contributions to what we know. This is as true in the twenty-first century as it was at the time of the Neanderthals, the ancient Greeks, the Middle Ages. The mind's contributions Kant elicited are the famous a priori categories—space, time, and the heuristic, regulative category of causality. They are the fixed points that stand fast against the arbitraries of merely empirical knowledge to which Hume's philosophy leads.

Kant's philosophy also taught me that any knowledge of the world is always an active relation between the knowing subject and the known object. The subject is not and never has been a "camera," merely a passive recording instrument, but a participant in and shaper of what is known. The subject's mind is always at work, always active, in knowing. What things may be in themselves, separate from what we know and experience of them, is blank to us. The Cartesian dualism of subject and object is in Kant's philosophy elaborated and enriched by the concept of knowledge, which is the active synthesis of the subject's perceptions of the object.

Prompted in part by the memory of some of Kaufmann's asides ("Back to Kant!" he had quoted Dilthey as saying), I discovered in later years that Kant's influence had affected most of the great social thinkers of the latter part of the nineteenth century up through the middle of the twentieth: George Herbert Mead, Georg Simmel, Max Weber, Emile Durkheim, and Talcott Parsons, among many others. Noam Chomsky's linguistic theory was also influenced by the Kantian insights. Some part of the seed of my own work was planted in Kaufmann's Kant seminars.

While going through Kant's ethics my memory was stirred by some passages in Thomas Mann's *Buddenbrooks*,[8] and I muttered something to this effect under my breath. Kant's ethics are rigorous and ascetic, an ethics of duty that the will is called upon to realize, an ethical doctrine to which, I thought, Thomas Buddenbrooks subscribed. Kaufmann heard my barely spoken comment and smiled. I did not know at the time that he was working on a book on Thomas Mann, which came out a few years later as *Thomas Mann: The World as Will and Representation*.[9]

My response to Kant and Mann, and to Kaufmann's teaching, formed a sympathetic bond between us. Kaufmann alerted me to some of the work of the contemporary neo-Marxist estheticians of the Frankfurt school, Georg Lukács and Theodore Adorno, that he thought I would find interesting. When I was thinking of the thesis I would write, he suggested I look into Max Scheler's social phenomenology. I began to do so, but almost all of Scheler's work was written in a complex, excited style that was very difficult to translate. Several years later I took up Scheler again and brought out a small book on his work. I found that Scheler, unlike any of the other philosophers I had been studying, explicitly understood the systematic relationships between feeling, knowing, and valuing—relationships of which I had a strong intuition, but did not find much explored even in the work of the pragmatists.

During the 1950s, a steady, mounting din of Cold War hysteria accompanied my studies and at times intruded on them. Nevertheless, although this was a time of confusion for me, it was also a time of growth. My emotional equilibrium was too often tenuous, but the study of philosophy deepened my understanding of many things, and in a way I could not anticipate, gave me greater courage to confront myself.

An important Civil Rights decision by the Supreme Court in 1954 (Brown vs. Board of Education) promised everyone, white or black, equal access to public education. Segregated public transportation was challenged in the Montgomery bus boycott. Eisenhower brought an end to the Korean War, as he had promised he would—and for this many of us, not least I, were grateful. But it was under Eisenhower's watch that Julius and Ethel Rosenberg were sacrificed to the Cold War—grim lessons of the passions in transgression and punishment. And as I learned more of what he was trying to do, my appreciation of Marx's intellectual endeavor grew, and so too did my understanding of its shortcomings.

Notes

1. Penguin Books, New York, 1998.
2. CreateSpace Independent Publishing Platform, 2012.
3. Bristol Classical Press, London, 1995.
4. Routledge and Paul, London, 1972.
5. Greenwood Press, Westport, CT, 1976.
6. Washington Square Press, New York, 1969.
7. Mondial, New York, 2009.
8. Vintage Books, New York, 1994.
9. Cooper Square Publishers, New York, 1957.

6

Other Discoveries

For several reasons, mainly personal but also financial, I took a leave of absence from the university and worked at a variety of jobs. I sought aid for anxieties and doubts that had plagued me for years. Although I never doubted my intellectual ability, my many self-doubts and misconceptions had led to bursts of conduct neither I nor anyone else much liked, and made ordinary day-to-day living far more difficult than need be. One of my professors, a thoughtful, kindly man I liked and respected, saw how miserable I was and urged me to speak with a university counselor. The counselor recommended I see a highly respected psychiatrist who had had positive results in treating university students. Some of my radical friends warned that capitalist psychiatry aims to achieve conformity to the system. But I was too unhappy to worry about that, and doubted this would happen to me. After several months of conferring with this psychiatrist for an hour at a time, three times a week, some of my anxiety and anger had subsided. Saying he thought I could now probably benefit from a greater dose of reality, he urged me to take a leave of absence from the university, get a job, and move out of my parents' house. It was important, he said, that I learn to support and take care of myself. None of this was easy to do. Professor Farber assured me there would be a place in the university for me when I was ready to return. As it turned out, both the work and the continued counseling helped dispel several misconceptions, gave me greater self-confidence and freedom and a better sense of people as well as of myself. Not least, I learned I could talk with most people, and even like many of them, if I was direct and plainspoken—and not angry.

Among the many jobs I had in the years after leaving school, four were particularly effective in softening some of my hardened neurons. One of the first and very short-lived of the jobs was on the line of a Chevrolet assembly plant located in a northern suburb of Buffalo. The work consisted of a series of quick moves: standing next to a slowly moving conveyor belt, I was to snatch the nearest long steel ten-pound tube coming my way and place it on a small platform. The tube was part of the interior of the rear axle. Then, quickly snapping two small metal clips into the slots of a spot-welding apparatus just above the platform, press the buttons that would drop the apparatus and weld the clips onto the tube. After this, I was to toss the tube with welded clips back onto the conveyer belt to continue its journey. Any misstep or hesitation would result in a pileup of tubes, which after a few minutes would stop the entire assembly line.

I am quite strong and well coordinated and at this point in my life was healthy. The tubes were not heavy, but one had to be quick and steady. After an hour I began to flag. And the more I flagged the more anxious I became. I doubted I'd be able to last much longer and feared I'd shut down the whole line. I shouted to the foreman who came over, saw what was happening and took over my spot-welding station. He told me to go to the bathroom for a couple of minutes. This happened twice more that morning. By lunchtime I was a wreck—depressed and exhausted. Two older men who worked farther down the line came over to me. "Come on, kid," they said, and led me across the street to a bar. Each ordered two shots of whisky for himself and advised me to do the same. I did. We chugged the drinks, broke open our sandwiches, ate, smoked a cigarette, and walked back to work. "You'll get used to it after a while, kid," they said. "Then you'll be able to work on the line without thinking." The remainder of the afternoon inched by in a slowly clearing haze. I asked the men the next day at lunch how they dealt with the morning hours. "You take a couple of shots for breakfast, kid," they said. "That's how you do it."

The third day I told the foreman I was quitting at the end of the day. I didn't want to spend a good part of my wages on liquor, be half drunk and have my mind turned off for eight working hours each day. I don't know how the men handled it. They certainly were alert enough to see when I was in trouble. Maybe they also became numb and didn't feel the strain much, as they predicted would happen to me, if I'd stayed on the job longer. They were at least ten to twelve years older and certainly seemed well seasoned. But I feared the cars I would have a hand in assembling would be defective, and I didn't want to contribute to this any longer. The men who had befriended me shook my hand when I told them I was leaving and wished me well. They advised me to go to school, perhaps become a machinist. Anything would be better than being an assembly line laborer.

None of the books and articles I had read purporting to describe auto-assembly-line work came close to capturing the numbing, stupefying quality of the experience. However idiotic rural life might be, I thought, most people who live or have lived such a life have been born into it and know little, if anything, of any other kind. But working on an automobile assembly line is a diminishing experience, however low one's previous attainments might have been.

Yet, despite the robot-like quality of the work, I also saw that the men who had come to my help had not been turned into androids ("robotomized," as a friend put it). The work might be diminishing and numbing, but the men had not become alienated from each other and been dehumanized. They had a network of friends that surely must have helped sustain them. Almost none of the reading I had done on the assembly line had made much, or indeed, anything, of this fact, but stressed the impersonality and degradation of the work experience. The work was treated as something in itself, cut off from its social integuments. Chaplin's *Modern Times* takes this view to its absurd extreme.

This negative appraisal of modern industrial work, which continued well into the 1960s, was radical in intent. But as I saw then and even more clearly in later years, it was often made in tacit comparison to traditional, handicraft modes of labor, and thus harbored—no doubt unwittingly—some reactionary sentiments. It was a kind of left-wing conservatism, which treated modern work solely as enslavement to the machine. Marx himself, in the first volume of Capital,[1] describes in dripping sarcasm the graceful movement of women's hands as they work the textile machines "whilst their babies squall untended at their feet." I doubt anyone could have worked in this sort of environment very long without developing serious mental disturbances.

Working on the assembly line was one of the highest-paying unskilled laboring jobs one could find. I was reluctant to give it up and reproached myself for doing so. Was I not tough enough to take it? But I had choices. The men who had been kind to me had very few. It occurred to me as I walked away that I might have been a momentary diversion for them. I hoped so.

At an opposite extreme from working as a manual laborer, I applied for and was accepted in an executive training program of a huge firm, Sylvania Electronics. This job would be a snap, I thought in my still abundant arrogance, and with my education and ability I would quickly rise and earn the money I needed. The job was to make sure vendors delivered parts in needed quantities and on schedule. If, after several contacts, a part was very late, I would visit the vendor and speak to him directly to determine whether he would be able to meet our schedule.

I visited a company in mid-state that produced castings—metal cases—for all the types of radios and television sets Sylvania was making. Sylvania was a very large customer. This company was much smaller, but sold to many other companies in the United States, Canada and parts of Europe. After discussing Sylvania's needs with the production manager and receiving a satisfactory explanation of their lateness and firm assurances of prompt future deliveries, he took me to meet the CEO of the company.

The CEO was in his late fifties to early sixties. He was cordial, and told the manager he would escort me the remainder of my stay. He asked me a bit about my background. I told him I had been studying philosophy, asked him about his studies. Metallurgy and economics, he said. An unusual combination, but not one that quite prepared me for all of his responses to questions about the company.

The CEO described the many parts that went into the products the company made, the designing of its casts in close consultation with customers, the casting process, and many other features of production. Then he described measures to promote satisfaction in management and the workforce. He emphasized the importance of managers at all levels learning to listen carefully. At times, issues will arise that have no cut-and-dried solutions, but they must be resolved. Good judgment, the CEO observed, is critical for this, and "we" try to select managers who seem to have this ability. By "we" he meant this was not his decision alone, but that of a team of managers. I later discovered a similar general perspective in Chester I. Barnard's *Functions of the Executive*,[2] which the CEO might have read. After this, the CEO described relations with other companies in the United States and Europe; the importance of company representatives communicating well in the various national languages, the need to evaluate market, social, and political conditions of the locale of each company, and other related topics.

The CEO spoke to me at least an hour and a half, possibly longer, and I have given here a bare outline of the topics he covered. It was fascinating and impressive. This was the kind of talk I would have expected from a senior professor, a talk from someone at the top of his or her profession with a command of details and a sure ability to weave them together into a coherent overview. This CEO was a revelation. I had never thought a businessman could think or talk this way. Even though I knew that one of the finest American poets of midcentury, Wallace Stevens, was also a vice president of a large insurance company, I had blocked this knowledge from conscious memory. I had absorbed from many of the radical critiques I had read as an adolescent and some of the work I had done with Gouldner a view of businessmen as being concerned only with "the bottom line," of being intellectually and morally narrow. Why else in the face of the harmful inequities for which their business actions were responsible, I had thought, would they continue to be businessmen? Either they didn't realize the social and moral consequences of what they were doing and were dense, or they didn't care and were vile. This negative view of businessmen and bankers was not held only by radicals. Many poets, writers, and artists considered the bourgeoisie to be philistines, crass in their tastes and rapacious in their lust for wealth. Robert Graves, whose writings I admired, expressed this view forcefully in *Goodbye to All That*.[3] But the examples of Wallace Stevens and now this CEO were contradictions too jarring to fit into the precast mold of my thought, so to speak, and they could not be ignored. This CEO understood very well what his company was doing, and he was endeavoring to be even-handed and fair with his employees.

I kicked myself for having been intellectually dishonest, and of course wondered what other areas of my thinking might be similarly affected. This was not a question that could be answered in the abstract, however, and I vowed to try my best to pay attention to any other contradictions to my thinking that I encountered.

From that day forward, I have been careful not to prejudge businessmen again, but evaluate them as I did priests and pastors and rabbis (and professors), on an individual basis, businessman by businessman. I did wonder, however, why the CEO bothered to speak to me at such length. I doubt he was trying to cool me out; I wasn't important. But was he trying to recruit me to his company? I doubted that too; he never asked me whether I would be interested. More likely, I thought, he was rehearsing a talk he was going to give at a stockholders' meeting. I learned when I got back to Buffalo that he was held in high esteem in the industrial community.

The combination of work and counseling served not only to uncover some of the roots of my anger, but also to lessen much of it. The counseling in particular deepened my appreciation of Freud and the neo-Freudians, and I studied their work as avidly as I had studied Marx. I soon saw that the issue of motivation—of what moved people to act or not to act—so critical yet poorly understood a part of Marxist thought, was being developed by the Freudians with great insight.

I took another job as a caseworker for the county welfare department. And here too a misconception formed in childhood and adolescence was shattered.

The average number of cases—individuals, families—each caseworker had was about 150. The job consisted of visiting each of the cases at least once a month to determine whether their situation continued to warrant welfare assistance. Assistance consisted almost entirely in money, based on a standard of living for families of X number of persons, of individuals without or with other sources of income, and so on. If, for example, a woman with children under sixteen years of age receiving welfare assistance were discovered living with someone earning money, her welfare allotment would either be reduced or stopped. A good part of the work was thus essentially snooping, and I found that distasteful. But given the size of our caseload, the need to visit seven or eight cases in different parts of the city each day meant that the "snooping" (when it occurred) was often perfunctory at best.

My parents had a dread of welfare. Receiving welfare assistance was for them a disgrace mitigated only, and then just barely, by desperate circumstances. The mid- to late 1950s, when I worked for the welfare, was a time of economic boom. I assumed that anyone on welfare had either to be ill, in a sudden bad way financially, or a slacker of some kind. And indeed I met "slackers," but they were not the kind I expected them to be. These were deeply damaged people, too stunted in mind and body and spirit to engage in any kind of sustained work. Most of them were the third generation to be receiving public assistance. They lived with their famines in crowded and filthy warrens—frame houses with cracked windowpanes, peeling paint, and pieces of plank siding missing, some without electricity or adequate plumbing. Set closely together on small, weed-grown lots strewn with rubbish, these buildings, originally designed for two families, now housed six or seven families, sometimes more.

The poor in my caseload were what Marx called the "lumpen proletariat"—the "foolish proletariat," foolish because they were not wage earners. The older caseworkers called them the hard-core poor and many were certain their lot could never be improved. Some of the senior caseworkers believed sterilization was the only effective way of ridding the state and county of their care.

Other Discoveries

I was initially uncomfortable in dealing with these people. I had adopted my parent's attitude and was also influenced by the senior social workers. The hard-core poor were considered the lowest of the low, a filthy, degraded lot, willing to live without self-respect. After a few visits, however, I became interested in them—their singularity made them oddly exotic—and began, in the limited visits I made, trying to understand how they viewed themselves and the world about them. I never asked questions outright, because I was certain this would have alarmed them and caused them to view me with even greater suspicion than a caseworker would normally merit. I listened and watched and learned a few things.

Some of the younger women among the hard-core poor bagged an occasional dollar through casual prostitution, the older men and women in begging and petty thievery. If I happened to show up when they were returning with their proceeds, they would furtively hide or pocket then, but begin to pull them out again and remark upon them as I was leaving. Proceeds were thus shared within the family, much the way a clan would operate. But with the exception of a television set, whether proceeds were also shared with other families—the larger "tribe"—I was not able to discover.

Many of the younger school-age children seemed to have escaped going to school—they were always about whatever time of day I visited. They too might have been enlisted in begging or thievery, but I never saw them engaged this way. The children were on the welfare rolls, but there was apparently no crosschecking between the welfare bureaucracy and the school bureaucracy, and so the children remained out of reach of school authorities. Charles Dickens would have had a field day with this situation.

So far as I could tell, they were not part of any religious group or denomination or involved in any sort of formal religious rituals. Christmas was "observed" in watching television Christmas shows and in small gift giving. But there were no Christmas trees, bushes, or ornaments of any kind that I could see. If records were still available, and I were to dig back a few generations and through mountains of files, I might have discovered the religious origins of these people.

Part of what was striking about the hard-core poor in my caseload was the similarity of their physical makeup. They were generally small, most not well developed, had sallow skin, mouse-colored hair, oval faces, small, yellow eyes, and bad teeth. I wondered then, but of course had no way of determining, whether there was incest among them or simply a great deal of inbreeding. Or perhaps more likely, their bodies were the result of the ravages of poverty.

The existence of such "lower depths" was likely unknown to the people in the cars and buses who drove past a few blocks away. Yet the inhabitants of these depths knew full well of the oblivious passers by. A few had managed to get television sets, and these were kept blaring before family members and friends who remained narcotized by them all day long. The beggars, petty thieves, and occasional prostitutes entered the larger city (where I occasionally spotted them), and there they saw the kinds of people depicted on their television screens, people who were well dressed and groomed, tall and healthy, who did not beg or sell their bodies, but engaged with one another openly, confidently, with a sense of legitimacy and well-being. Comparisons were made with themselves, as I learned from comments I overheard over several months, and they were likely demoralizing. The hard-core poor never tried to leave for long the crannies into which they had secreted themselves. However blighted their lives, they attempted to insulate themselves from the negative judgments of people in the larger society, judgments in which they concurred. This meant that, in sharing the views and general attitudes held in the larger society, they must at some level have disliked themselves, but were, or at least seemed to be, reconciled to their lot in life. They had found a relatively undisturbed niche to which their limited resources could adapt.

Such people are in every city in the country with a population of over a few hundred thousand. Their numbers have since been augmented twenty fold by another segment of the lumpen proletariat, the street people and beggars that have filled our cities over the last thirty-five years. There are no easy ways to reclaim such people to themselves and to us. Sterilization is an abhorrent and frightening measure. Educating the very young and those who would be receptive to education among the older ones, providing medical attention and rehabilitation programs for everyone and jobs for those able to work might be effective in the long run. But the run would undoubtedly be very long, expensive, and uncertain. For such reclamation to occur these people needed political advocates. But the dilemma is, they are virtually unknown, and when known are shunned.

I discussed these cases with my supervisor, a thoughtful, experienced woman who had studied history and psychology in college. In her view, people of this sort have lived in the interstices of every society, and would be found, perhaps in fewer numbers, even in a socialist society, were one to exist. Victor Lidz, a friend with whom I discussed this matter recently, suggested that the number of such people might also be smaller in Scandinavia, the Netherlands, and other societies that provide more care for the poor and stigmatize them less. It is a grim issue not only for the people who live in such misery and degradation but also for the societies that, however unwittingly and unintentionally, foster their condition.

I had other kinds of cases—women with young children who had no other means of support, old people without resources other than Social Security payments, people who could not find work after their unemployment benefit payments ended, and a few cases of people with severe disabilities who were unable to work. Again, some of the senior social workers called many of these people, especially the unwed mothers, the flotsam and jetsam of the society. But this moral condemnation, cruel that it was, also expressed, I believe, a sense of hopelessness among the veteran social workers who had spent years of providing aid to little effect. I understood some of the reasons for this attitude, but would have none of it.

One case of a severely disabled person is worth mentioning because had funds been available, better medical attention and rehabilitation would have helped him. This was of an African American man in his mid-twenties who had been diagnosed since childhood as having gran mal epilepsy. He had little formal education. On our second meeting, he showed me some poems he had written. They were not in any particular form but expressed thoughts and feelings fairly well and in the rhythm and imagery of some lines and phrases quite vividly. He was also interested in magic—an apt complement to poetry—and showed me a few of his tricks. He was cheerful and friendly and, despite his lack of schooling, quite articulate. I liked him and attempted to find ways of getting him good medical attention, but there was no funding in the welfare system for anything beyond the minimum. People of this sort will also exist in every society, whether capitalist or socialist, and the question of allocating adequate resources to help them is not a simple one.

Some years later I realized that I learned many things about social life while working in public assistance. Not least among them is that social life in all its varieties was one of my great interests.

The last nonacademic job I had was as a part-time investigator for an insurance agency. About a third of the investigators were firemen and policemen. They too worked part time, but while on their full-time rounds some of the cops were able to check out a building to see whether it was up to code. After they finished their policing and fire-duty shifts, they came into the office to type up their reports. We got paid per report, and the cops and firemen generally picked up quite a bit of money (about a third of their gross income some told me) by doing this part-time work.

The manager of the agency, however, was an ill-tempered, foul-mouthed martinet. He harbored a six-foot fantasy in his five-foot-two-inch frame. All the cops and firemen and just about everyone else who worked there were taller and more fit. The manager spot-checked all the reports. The most picayune error—a comma missing or out of place, a word slightly misspelled—would jerk him to his feet, body stretched to the tallest, and with rasping, outraged voice and report held high in small shaking fist he would shout to the illegitimately conceived writer to correct the report immediately. Too many of these mistakes, he would warn in an even louder voice, would result in firing. Since everyone made minor typing errors, everyone eventually got yelled at. The cops and firemen merely smiled and shrugged it off. Trying to cut us down to his size and even smaller, some of them said. They saw him and his absurd antics for what they were. I admired their composure and strived to emulate them. It was only with great effort, however, that I was for the most part able to rein in my anger. I detested the manager, and wouldn't mourn his sudden death. There may have been reasons for his conduct, but there was no excuse for it. I did the second best thing within the law, and after a few months removed myself from the office.

I took with me, however, a different view of the police than the one that I had grown up with and been reinforced by my radical outlook. As a grade-school child, I knew only one policeman, Walter, the traffic guard. He was a genial, kindly man, and all the children liked him. For several years, fall, winter, and spring, we greeted Walter, he greeted us and with a smile shooed us off to school. Except perhaps in small towns, I don't think police serve in this capacity any longer.

I liked Walter but hardly thought of this large, friendly man as a policeman. He wore a uniform and policeman's badge and cap, but I don't remember him wearing a gun or carrying a club. (He would hardly need either to monitor schoolchildren and traffic!) But although my parents' attitude toward the police was overtly neutral, they seemed wary. My mother, in particular, was a shade negative, and I discovered the reasons for her attitude when I was in my early twenties.

My mother had had a run-in with the police when she was a young woman. Shortly after coming to the United States in 1922 (she would then have been about twenty years old) she went to New York City to live with an aunt. While there she found work in the needle trades and joined the International Ladies' Garment Workers Union. Within months a strike was called, and she and her fellow workers formed a picket line. The police were called. Soon fights between strikers and police broke out. As I heard the story from my mother's cousin, my mother, furious over the strong-arm methods the police were using, hurled herself against one of the club wielders and began pummeling him. She was certainly an intense and ardent person, but she was slight, the policeman was big and burly, and she was brushed off as though a fly. Thereafter, my mother shrank slightly whenever she saw a policeman with a club or a gun, and although this occurred infrequently, her attitude was communicated to me.

But there was more to it than that. During the 1930s, '40s and early '50s, the majority of the policemen in Buffalo were Polish and Irish. There were probably a few Italian and German policemen too, but there were no African Americans at the time and certainly no Jews. Certainly, because in that period to be a policeman was not considered by the Jews I knew in Buffalo—and this was likely true for most Jews in the United States—a proper occupation for a Jewish man. Policemen carried guns, and guns were viewed with dislike. Times have changed, of course, and there are now Jewish as well as African American policemen in virtually every large American city. Yet, even today, of all the sports in which Jews have become notable, hunting is not one of them. All this meant the police were entirely Christian in makeup (in Buffalo, mainly Roman Catholic) and thus for Jews the police were "other," alien beings from whom one kept a physical and emotional distance.

Added to their "otherness" for me was the politically radical view that the police were lackeys of the bourgeois state whose major function was to preserve private property at all costs. Human life, human welfare came second to the protection of banks, buildings, machines, streets, lawns—anything owned and thus deemed valuable. Given this function, it was inferred that only the most callous, brutal type of person would be suited to being a policeman. And indeed, the tactics of the police in breaking up strikes in the early decades of the twentieth century and the violence with which they and their dogs attacked Civil Rights marchers and political protesters in the 1960s provided ample evidence for this view.

But as I got to know the policemen in the insurance investigating office, I discovered other sides to their make-up. They were all working very hard—twelve to fourteen hours a day—to make a decent living for themselves and their families. All were married; all had children—some three or four. None had a college education. All had been in the armed services during the Second World War. All had seen many horrors and much misery and knew of terrible things that happen to people in the city. Yet all were civil and friendly, and believed their job was to curb as many as possible of the things that were destructive to persons as well as to property. Much of their job, they told me, consisted simply in being a presence that would inhibit unlawful conduct. They broke up domestic quarrels and street fights, chased and sometimes caught thieves, rushed sick people to hospitals or took them to shelters, and depending on their assignment, directed traffic or pursued traffic-law violators. All knew there was an element of personal danger in being a policeman, but they were willing to take the risk because they liked the job; the work was steady and the pension was good.

In his "Continental Op" novels, Dashiell Hammett called a cop a "shamus," and he may have been the first to do so. It is uncertain where Hammett got the name, whether it was derived from the Irish name "Seamus" or the Jewish name for the sergeant at arms of a synagogue. Many policemen at the time Hammett wrote were Irish, and surely some were named Seamus, but there were also Jewish gangsters some of whose Yiddishisms such as "shames" and "finif" (five) had entered the language. In any case, although far more varied and consequential, the work of the police nevertheless serves the community in a capacity similar to that of the shamus of a synagogue. Both police and shamus are custodians. Both are guardians not only of their respective physical quarters, but also of the conduct appropriate to those quarters. Both facilitate orderly relations, one among citizens and the other among congregants. The analogy is an apt one.

But the police are hardly perfect, of course (nor are the shamuses of synagogues). Notwithstanding their training, the police too will respond to threats—sometimes all too readily—with fear and force. They too will succumb to temptations. They must be subject to the same vigilance and constraints as the rest of us. As I began to rethink my views of the police, I recognized again that the dream of human perfectibility, which I had held onto and that was implicitly projected in radical texts, was a dream.

Almost each of my work experiences led me to reflect on characteristics of modern society and whether any of these characteristics, appropriately modified, might also be found in a socialist society. I was—and remain—certain that in every complex society, whether capitalist or socialist, there will be elements of disorder, infractions of the law of one kind or another. We are all quite individualized. There are many ambiguities in rules of conduct. And there is ample reason to understand why deviance of one kind or another will occur. Socialism will not be a cure-all for this, will not produce perfect, uniform citizens. Socialism aims at best—and perhaps this is more important—to provide a more humane and just treatment of human beings. Orderly relations among members will have to be maintained in a socialist society as well as in a capitalist, and the police or functionaries very much like them will always be needed.

About twenty-five years after my experience in working with policemen, I came across a fine, balanced ethnographic account of police work that considerably amplified my revised view: *City Police*[4] by Jonathan Rubinstein.

Notes

1. C. H. Kerr & Company, Chicago, 1925.
2. Cambridge, MA, Harvard University Press, 1968.
3. Cassell, London, 1961.
4. Farrar, Straus & Giroux, New York, 1973.

7

Mannheim, Morality, and Neo-Marxism

After a few years of work and gaining a better understanding of myself and the ways of the world, I returned, considerably sobered, to the university. I had misunderstood large parts of the world. My thinking had been based on simplistic abstractions. Kant had shown me that we cannot think without categories; but we need the right ones in order to see and understand the complex things in the world. Molecules are not morality; different categories are needed to think sensibly of each. And although one or a few features may and often do predominate in a person, he or she is rarely one thing but many things. This is no less true of societies. In my zeal to understand the world, I had been too hasty, and despite being intellectually critical had accepted many ideas and taken on many attitudes on faith. Concepts without percepts are empty, said Kant. I had gained some percepts.

Most important, I had become emotionally more stable. I was economically self-sufficient, had my own apartment, and took care of myself. I no longer avoided contact with my parents' neighbors, as I once had, and even felt comfortable when greeting them. Moreover, my angry flares had become less intense and frequent; only considerable provocation would now elicit them. Whatever it was that I considered foolish or mistaken in other people's views had become for the most part their affair rather than mine and thus did not require correction or chastisement from me. I also learned some things about work that were revelations. Work, even the most physically demanding and menial, was not always dehumanizing. Marx once said that we feel most like animals when we engage in our human activities—that is, when we work—and most like humans when we engage in our animal activates. But although Marx worked long and hard at his research, he never had the experience of doing heavy physical labor. He spoke to and wrote the *Manifesto* for workingmen's clubs. He studied the blue books in the British Museum that recorded the financial structure of much of English industry over many decades—materiel, costs, profits, and wages. He understood the exploitation of labor very well. And because there was so much exploitation, all work, for him, became poisoned with exploitation's injustice and pain. Yet the men I met in the automobile assembly plant who wished they had better paid and more highly regarded jobs had hardly lost their humanity while they were working. They were aware of each other, cared for each other, and helped each other when they could. If they had lost their humanity they would have had no empathy and would not have tried to help me. Moreover, despite having to swallow two shots of whisky to numb the drudgery of their work, work helped give them definition; they were providers, heads of families, attributes in which they could take some pride. The police and firemen I worked with held the same attitude. This aspect of work becomes clear when you see and talk to men who are out of work; they are depressed and anxious, and, if out of work for long, many consider themselves failures—not the industry, not the economy, but *themselves*. False consciousness one could say, if one ignored psychological and cultural aspects of life. The hard-core poor that were part of my caseload are examples of this condemnatory self-judgment. Of course, work has particularly compulsive significance in America. But there are kindred qualities to work in other Western countries, and indeed the world over. Isaac Deutscher, an English Marxist (Trotskyist), understood this well and spoke often of the dignity of work, of the pride in being a worker. Is this attitude less common in France, Germany, Italy, the Scandinavian countries than in England and America? In addition to understanding and appreciating work a little better, I saw yet another limitation to Marx's thought that increased my dissatisfaction with his theory.

    I finished the few courses remaining for a doctorate and got married to a young woman, Suzanne Kottek, who was just finishing her undergraduate studies in history. Before completing the courses and taking my doctoral exams, I was required to write a master's thesis, which I did. The subject was on Karl Mannheim's theory of knowledge and its implications for knowledge of the social world. There were several reasons for my choice.

    Mannheim's *Ideology and Utopia*,[1] subtitled *An Introduction to the Sociology of Knowledge*, was published in Europe and the United States in the late 1920s. The book laid out a challenging thesis and continued to make a scholarly stir for about forty years, well into the 1950s. Although inspired by Marx and Georg Lukács (about whom more shortly), two of Mannheim's teachers, Georg Simmel and Alfred Weber, as well as the great sociologist Max Weber, also influenced his views. I was particularly curious to see how Mannheim would deal with an anomaly in Marx's conception of ideology that Marx himself recognized but did not satisfactorily resolve. The anomaly is this:

In *A Contribution to The Critique of Political Economy*,[2] written just prior to and in preparation for *Capital*, Marx declared that the Greek esthetic achievement, by which he meant the poetry and plays of Homer, Sophocles, Euripides, Aeschylus, and others, remained an *incomparable ideal to this day* (my emphasis). But since ideologies include esthetic standards and are supposed to vary from one age to the next, how could this be? Marx was highly cultivated and enjoyed reading Greek literature in the original. In a whimsical moment he even once compared himself to Prometheus who had "stolen fire from the gods." He explained what he recognized as anomalous to his theory of ideology by saying that ancient Greece was, after all, the childhood of civilization, and the writings of its poets are enjoyed today in much the way we enjoy the works of precocious children. This tortured explanation—the *Iliad* or the Oedipus cycle written by precocious children?—at least has the merit of showing Marx's intellectual integrity in acknowledging, if not resolving, a fact that contradicted his theory. There was not yet enough understanding in Marx's time of what civilization entailed, of the meaning and force of tradition and its transmission over time and among peoples. This would come later with the scholarship of Jacob Burkhart, Wilhelm Dilthey, and Max Weber. How would Mannheim deal with this?

All ideas, Mannheim postulated, their scope and truth as well as their substance, are rooted in the social milieu in which they are authored. There are no ideas that transcend the historical flux. But ideas—ideologies—argued Mannheim, are not only political in intent, as Marx had emphasized, nor do they only express class interests. Each kind of social grouping—whether of generations, professional associations, intellectuals, artists, nations as well as social classes, among many others—has a perspective on the world and generates an ideology that expresses that perspective. Some ideologies express interests the group aims to preserve; others, which Mannheim called "utopias," a future condition the group strives to achieve. Unlike the Marxists who reviled nationalist ideologies and sentiments as false consciousness (a "socialism of the stupid," one Marxist derisively called them), Mannheim in various works analyzed nationalist ideologies as projections of identity whose roots are historical and cultural as well as political.

Mannheim's appreciation of a variety of social and ideological domains that are genuine and not mere "epiphenomena" was more in accord with my own growing understanding of society. Not least, Mannheim's social conception was a welcome relief from the constricted Marxian view of society as consisting primarily of adversarial social classes. I believed his approach could easily deal with the anomaly in Marx's theory by referring to civilizational perspectives. Mannheim's richer conception of society was one of the reasons for my attraction to his work, and likely also its appeal to a broad spectrum of liberal thinkers.

Many critics, however, were quick to point out that Mannheim's thesis was self-contradictory. By his own admission, his voice was not and could not be a disembodied one, standing above and beyond his own milieu. If the universal claim of his thesis were true and applied to itself, then his thesis would be false. (This is a modern version of the paradox of "'All Cretans are Liars,' said the Cretan.") The contradiction was real, but of less concern to me (and I think to Mannheim) than the substantive insights of Mannheim's work. I had also begun reading Husserl's logical investigations at the time (translated by Marvin Farber as *The Foundations of Phenomenology*[3]), and thought Mannheim had overstated his claim. Mannheim's sociologistic thesis to the contrary notwithstanding, Husserl had shown that given the number system base ten, and our definitions of plus, minus, and equals, then $2 + 2 = 4$ is valid with "apodictic certainty," as he put it, for all times and places, in Timbuktu as well as in Berlin, on the moon as on the earth, from the beginning of the universe to its end. This was a universal statement whose origins came from somewhere (whether from a psychological or sociological source is irrelevant, said Husserl) but was true everywhere. The genesis of an idea is one thing; its scope and validity are other things. But I wasn't so much interested in apodictic certainty as in the issues of meaning and understanding in Mannheim's work.

Mannheim had shown how differently groups interpret the world, and how, as a consequence, people talk past each other. He believed "free floating intellectuals" like him, unattached to any particular group, were in a position to understand and relate disparate ideas to their time and place. Intellectuals could thus serve as a kind of "go between," mediating among groups by translating or at least "explaining" each one's ideas in terms understandable to the others.

Mannheim was of the generation that had lived through the unprecedented destruction, bloodshed, and even more important, the social and political transformations of the First World War. I believed (and still believe) his ultimate intention was a healing one, an attempt to help people understand and talk to each other. This would not necessarily promote agreement or sympathy, but without such understanding agreement and sympathy could not occur. I didn't think it possible, however, for anyone to be a free-floating intellectual. One could be impartial in assaying things, but one always selects the things assayed based on one's interests. And interests tie you to something, to a group, to a passion, a profession, a place, a person, a doctrine. However freely he might think he floats, the intellectual is not exempt from such ties. I, who had lived unscathed in the United States through the immense destruction of the Second World War, was now in the shadow of a greater danger to humankind than had existed before—the atomic bomb. I also had healing intentions in mind. This too was an affinity I had with Mannheim. But I had no doubt that my first interests were with my country, my family, my friends, my groups, my perspective. I doubted whether Mannheim's methodological agenda could yield a translation of these particular interests good enough to be truly widely understood.

In his writings, Mannheim gave us a glimpse at a few of the ideological perspectives of interest to him. There are many more. And indeed, if one also considers the profusion and kinds of perspectives in history as well as those yet to come, one must boggle at the thought of translating and communicating even a handful of these among their holders.

The first problem I saw in Mannheim's work was the vagueness in what he was referring to as knowledge. He didn't seem to mean by this term the statements of mathematics, or the sort of analysis Husserl was making about logic and mathematics. Nor was he speaking of the physical sciences. The sweep of what he called knowledge seemed somewhat closer to the anthropological concept of culture. To be sure, scientific ideas also originate in a time and place and are cultural and social products. Their scope and truth claims, however, are based on empirical vindication and logical coherence, and these are subject in principle to constant reevaluation. They are distinct from other ideologies that base their claims to truth on faith or tradition or loyalty or history.

My plan was to distinguish several cultural domains and claims to the truth of their ideologies—religious and nationalist ideologies, political doctrines, civilizational perspectives, mathematics, physical and social science, among others—and clarify the ones among them to which Mannheim's full thesis was applicable. Mannheim's partial thesis, I believed, pertaining to the social conditions in which ideas are formed was likely universal in scope. The a priori categories Kant had analyzed are—let us say for the sake of the argument—always co-present in human thought, but they were not elucidated until the end of the eighteenth century. The equivalent can be said of the propositions of mathematics, such as 2 + 2 = 4. It is an odd puzzle that a universal statement true for all times and places has not been universally recognized as such but had to await being formulated until a specific time and place. But this is, perhaps, also a puzzle with metaphysical implications pertaining to existence and time that Hegel and, in a quite different vein, Heidegger had explored. As a metaphysical puzzle it was not relevant to my proposal. But as a fact it supported my proposal.

The kinds of investigation Mannheim had undertaken, I suggested, were not epistemological in the conventional analytical sense. They were, or could be, social scientific, and as such empirically investigated and subject to the same canons of proof as any other empirical science. But like epistemology, these kinds of study should enrich the meaning of many ideas and provide greater self-understanding among their holders. A sociology of sociology or of psychology or of economics, and so on, would be natural outcomes of Mannheim's thesis. A sociology of Marxism and of the many Marxisms that had been and were emerging in different parts of the world, was also an implication of Mannheim's thesis. But not least, my proposal would obviate the risks and dubiety of free-floating intellectuals serving as interpreters and translators of ideologies.

In the eighty years since Mannheim wrote, many of his ideas have become commonplaces of general intellectual understanding. But when I spoke with Professor Farber of my plan in the late 1950s, he thought I could make a constructive contribution. This would require clarification of what I meant by the different domains of culture. Also implied was the need for the combined resources of many branches of humanistic study, including hermeneutics, philology, and linguistics as well as sociology, history, psychology, and no doubt several others. The study I had in mind would take several hundred pages of analysis, at least. But, he added, given my perfectionist tendencies, it might never be completed! Kindly yet firmly he said he would not accept a thesis over seventy-five pages. This is only a master's thesis! Lay out the most salient of Mannheim's intellectual antecedents. Describe the problems he's dealing with and the methods of analysis he uses. Provide a succinct critique and conclude with a *brief* appraisal of the implications of his work for social knowledge and a few suggestions for further research. I was a bit miffed by this response, but had to admit he was probably right and trying to be helpful. Dutifully, I went to my other advisers.

Professor Kaufmann thought I would find Max Scheler's sociology of knowledge more congenial. But none of Scheler's work on this subject was in English, and his very difficult, idiosyncratic German would have taken me at least as much time to translate as to write my projected several-hundred-page thesis, perhaps even longer. I discovered many years later when I did translate some of Scheler's work (it took less time than I had feared it would) that Kaufmann had been right.

Professors Parry and Moser agreed with Farber. They recommended a few commentaries on Mannheim they thought might be useful. Back to the eighteenth and nineteenth centuries, then, to Kant, Hegel, and Marx.

In the mid-1950s, the Marxian-inspired writings published in America were being considerably augmented by the work of several refugee scholars, in particular Herbert Marcuse, Theodore Adorno, Franz Neumann, and Leo Lowenthal. Even though very little of his work had been translated, the most illustrious of the neo-Marxists was Georgy Lukács, still In Europe the titular father of the Frankfurt School. The many quasi-reverential references to him—Mannheim, for example, even though critical, had written a fascinating and admiring essay discussing Lukács' theory of ideology—endowed Lukács and his books with an intellectual aura none of the other neo-Marxists possessed. A fellow student born in Germany and fluent in the language and I wrote a letter to Lukács asking his permission to translate his book published in 1923, *Geschichte und Klassenbewusstsein* (*History and Class Consciousness*[4]), famous in rarefied Marxist and literary circles as being the most philosophically sophisticated effort since Marx in analyzing ideological issues. Thomas Mann, Jean Paul Sartre, and many of the younger German neo-Marxists had been influenced by it. We never got an answer. Lukács was reported to be under house arrest in his apartment in Budapest for having supported the Imre Nagy uprising of 1956.

My friend and I were quite ignorant of the fuller history of Lukács' early book. A reigning Soviet commissar at the time of its publication in Europe, Grigory Zinoviev, condemned the book as having "regressive

Hegelian tendencies," and all copies that could be found were seized and destroyed by the Soviet censors. (Zinoviev himself was seized and destroyed a dozen years later in the sweeping Soviet purges.). The library did not have a copy of the book, and it was unobtainable except from a private source. All this made the book more desirable. I finally did get to translate part of it in the early 1960s with one of my professors at the University of Wisconsin, Hans H. Gerth, who had a copy of the original 1923 edition. An English translation of the entire book by Rodney Livingstone was published in 1971.

Lukács' analysis of ideology aimed to lay bare the fundamental categories underlying all the thought-ways of the modern bourgeois era. Beginning with the Cartesian philosophy of consciousness and fully articulated in Kant's conception of things unknowable in themselves, an irreconcilable split was believed to exist between all human subjects and all objects—human, cultural, and material. Lukács' concept of Ideology was not limited to analysis of the dominating interests hidden in a particular doctrine or creed, as were the notions of ideology held by Marxists and others. His was an idea of an omnipresent mentality affecting and ordering all human perception and activity, akin to Hegel's Geist and to a civilizational view of culture. Everyone in the bourgeois age, in this view, suffers an alienation from all persons and things. Only in a future communist society, won by the revolutionary proletariat, will the alienation between subjects and objects be overcome. Then and only then, Lukács argued in a more explicitly Hegelian vein than Marx, will man and man, human subjects and the objects of their making become the identical subject-object of history. This mystical, nonmaterialist view alarmed the Soviet censors but charmed the bourgeois writers. The book remains a remarkable effort in the Marxist canon because of the fluency and creativity of its philosophical discussions, rivaled perhaps only by one other, that of Lukács' contemporary Karl Korsch, in *Marxism and Philosophy*,[5] also published in 1923.

Although I was becoming something of a Marxicologist and continued to read many of the Marxist books and journals that came out of Europe, Africa, and South America over the next twenty-five to thirty years, this was more in the nature of following up an earlier interest rather than developing a specialty. The intelligence and creativity of the neo-Marxists were a welcome relief from the plodding apologetics that had weighted the Marxist shelves. The efforts to integrate Freud's theory into Marx's, to develop a deeper understanding of culture and literary and musical art, to clarify political and social processes, to formulate an adequate understanding of history were exactly among the areas in which Marxist theory was weakest or lacking and needed to be developed in order to have as broad a reach as its creator had hoped to achieve.

Yet, brilliant though they were, I began to see more clearly over the next few years that a slender and shaky reed supported the neo-Marxists' theoretical innovations: they were all utopians. Some of them quoted Lenin, but their concerns were not with political action or with the working class. Their critiques, often insightful and illuminating, were predicated on fantasies of human and societal perfectibility. Alongside the illusion of being able to enter deeply into bourgeois society from which the proletariat suffered, according to Marx, were the illusions of perfect communion, perfect freedom, perfect fulfillment in a future, socialist society from which Marxist intellectuals suffered. These imparted an air of unreality to the critiques, which left little room for social improvements other than the most extreme kinds, and thereby weakened their force. Marxism, as Raymond Aron once said, is the opiate of the intellectuals.

Utopias of all kinds—religious, social, political—are an ancient literary genre. Their stories and imaginary settings sometimes give rise to yearnings, perhaps to a sense of hope. At times, their stories are elaborate ironies intended as critiques of things as they are. The trouble with utopias, however, occurs when their imaginary, often quite fantastic scenarios are not left on the page but taken as blueprints to be realized. A few such attempts—Twin Oaks, for example, based on B. F. Skinner's *Walden Two*[6]—seem to have succeeded by readjusting their visions to more realistic dealings with the less-than-utopian external markets and business communities. But over the last century we have also witnessed utopian attempts involving enormous cultural, social, political, and economic reconstructions that have led to unspeakable horrors. At bottom, most modern utopians, whether of the right or the left, are as one; they are self-proclaimed saviors who, on the basis of history, or science, or economics, or sociology presume to tell us what we must do and how we must live in order to be saved. Save us from the saviors! *Perhaps* Adorno among the neo-Marxists, in his not readily comprehensible *Negative Dialectics*,[7] awoke briefly from the dogmatic slumber of an edenic end to the historical process that Marx had inherited from Hegel and passed on to future generations of his followers. History will end only when human consciousness and remembrance end.

After I completed my master's thesis, which was well received, two of my professors, Marvin Farber and Fritz Kaufmann, urged me to consider becoming proficient in German, a language in which my facility was a little better than Sid Caesar's but (still is) spotty. German universities, they thought, would be much more receptive than American to my interests. In the United States, I would likely get a job in a small college and have a career teaching a variety of standard courses in the history of philosophy—not uninteresting when one considers Wilhelm Windelband's or Ernst Cassirer's wonderful treatments of parts of this history. But this was not central to my interests, nor did I want to leave the United States, perhaps forever. Least of all, I was not eager to undertake the considerable effort required of becoming as skilled in German as my European professors were in English. What then? My professors suggested I might consider getting a doctorate in sociology. I had some background already and the field was broadly enough defined to accommodate my interests.

Notes

1. Harcourt Brace Jovanovich, San Diego, 1985.
2. Beekman Publishers, Woodstock, NY, 1972.
3. Harvard University Press, Cambridge, MA, 1943.
4. MIT Press, Cambridge, MA, 1971.
5. Monthly Review Press, New York, 2009.
6. Macmillan Company, New York, 1948.
7. Routledge & Kegan Paul, London, 1973.

8

The New Left

My wife and I arrived in Madison, Wisconsin, in late summer 1959. The small, clean, tidy, and very white city (110,000 inhabitants), which is also the state capital, and the large, sprawling university (36,000 students) were the opposites of what I had known in Buffalo.

The primary reason I had applied to the University of Wisconsin was to study with Hans H. Gerth. He and C. Wright Mills had published a readable translation of several of Weber's remarkable essays, *From Max Weber: Essays in Sociology*[1] (1946), which for many years was the chief source of Weber's writings available to American students. I also knew Gerth had studied with Mannheim, and from hints dropped in a few of his other writings, inferred Gerth knew several of the neo-Marxist writers as well. From my reading in sociology as well as searching through university catalogues, Gerth seemed to be one of the sociologists in the country with whom I thought I might have some intellectual affinity.

The reception for new students given by the Department of Sociology was also on a scale several times larger than anything I had experienced before. In addition to the sociology department in the College of Letters and Science, to which I had applied, there was also at the University of Wisconsin a separate Department of Rural Sociology some of whose members and students were present at the reception. The two departments were distinct, but occasional crossovers between them occurred. All told, there were about twenty faculty members at the reception and perhaps forty or more new and second-year students.

Gerth knew who I was and why I had come to Wisconsin, because I had not only identified myself quite clearly in my application letter to the department but was also pointedly ushered over to him by the chair of the department and introduced. I was clearly going to be his student. I will relate just one story of the many I could tell that may indicate something of the flavor of the man I discovered at that first meeting. As we were chatting about the work I had done in philosophy and was hoping to find some relation to in sociology, I asked Gerth quite innocently what he thought of the department, leaving unsaid the remainder of the question—"for the pursuit of my interests." He hesitated for a moment as though thinking it through and then, answering only the stated part of the question, said in his heavy German accent (which I will not attempt to reproduce): "The more I think of it, the less I think of it." I was startled by this response and must have shown it, but then laughed. "Ja," he said, and then in an attempt to leaven the harshness of his comment, added with a shrug of self-deprecation, "I am a phrase monger."

Phrase monger though Gerth was, and also erratic and disorganized as I was soon to discover, I learned a great deal from him. He came of intellectual age during the years of the Weimar Republic, studied with Karl Mannheim, Theodore Adorno, and Karl Jaspers, was a Social Democrat, wrote many fierce articles in opposition to the Nazis, and with his late first wife, the daughter of a minor noble family, fled in the late 1930s to England and then to the United States. Dorothy Thompson, the newspaper columnist and former wife of Sinclair Lewis, was his sponsor—a fact he thought important enough to mention several times. But unlike many other intellectual émigrés from Germany, as he stated often and in different contexts, he made it clear that "I am not one of the Chosen People."

Gerth's best-known students were C. Wright Mills and Don Martindale, with neither of whom, by the time I got to Wisconsin, was he on good terms. Until I came along, he had not had a student for several years, but need and interest now joined us. Most of what I learned from Gerth was not through classes but through the many informal occasions when we went swimming or had lunch or played duets on the piano or chess, and not least, when we were translating the Lukács book. His knowledge of Weimar Germany—of the writers, musicians, painters, actors, movies, sociologists, social makeup, and politics—was encyclopedic but was conveyed, like much else he spoke of, through free associations. While we were listening to *The Threepenny Opera*, for instance, he stopped the recording just after the words "make a plan, and make another plan" were being sung and went off an a tangent describing the failure of the Dawes Plan to which Brecht was referring. I learned from a little research in the library the following day that the Dawes Plan was an American effort to rescue the German economy after the First World War with billions of dollars in loans tied to the international stock market. The collapse of the market in the late 1920s effectively wiped out the German economy and soon thereafter the Weimar government.

Except for their clothes and large personal library of about ten thousand books, two-thirds of which were in German, and many files and notes, Gerth and his wife had taken little else with them from Germany. Gerth's brother-in-law, Baron von Reventlow, had given him and his wife six small, valuable paintings when they left Germany. About four of them remained stored in Dorothy Thompson's house, in New York State. Gerth referred to one of them as having been painted by a Breugel, although which one of the many Breugel painters it was he didn't say, and I never asked. The baron remained behind, where, throughout the war years, he rode out each week on horseback to place in several dozen mailboxes an anti-Nazi broadside he himself had written and printed. The Nazis considered the aristocracy ineffectual, and the baron remained untouched.

Once, in the midst of our translating, Gerth went to a bookcase, pulled out a book Mannheim had written after he had immigrated to England and inscribed to him. He opened it to show me the inscription. It read: "For Hans, Don't let them get you down, K. Mannheim." This was a hushed and grieving moment that called up the many "thems" from the Nazis to his foreign hosts in all their vagaries. Gerth described the esteem bordering on celebrity adulation in which both Mannheim and Lukács were held in intellectual circles in the 1920s. A novel by Anna Seghers featured the intellectual and political contest between the two passionate men—Lukács, once liberal, who turned to revolution, and Mannheim, who held fast to his liberal views. The book, which was favorable to Lukács, ended in a poignant image, said Gerth, with Mannheim portrayed as standing in a darkened room, alone, staring pensively out a window. The novel made quite a stir in Germany, where Mannheim was considered among intellectual women as something of a heartthrob. This is the only novel ever written and likely ever to be written explicitly about two sociologists, and so has a certain parochial interest. My searches over the years never turned up a copy of it. Gerth's many asides sent me to the library for years even after I graduated.

Although Anna Seghers was explicit in casting Lukács and Mannheim as her two protagonists, these two men appeared in fictional cloak in yet another novel. Thomas Mann's *Magic Mountain*[2] contains long sections of intellectual and political arguments between two men who, I think, are thinly disguised versions of Lukács and Mannheim.

The one, Felix Naptha, born a Jew but now a Jesuit master of casuistic argumentation turned voluptuary, is well known to have been modeled after Lukács. The other, Herr Settembrini, a Mason, a liberal and gentle apostle of reason and life, is, I'm fairly sure, modeled after Mannheim. The kinds of arguments Mann invents for each fictional character resemble in their oppositions and style those of their actual, real-life counterparts. In the novel, Naptha, for no apparent reason, commits suicide. Lukács did not commit literal suicide, but in turning in a kind of sudden act of atonement from his earlier deeply insightful esthetics of modernity to espouse the esthetics of Soviet realism—because of a wager, he said, he was making with history—he committed a kind of intellectual suicide. The sunnier Settembrini, not as brilliant as his adversary, but with a stronger hold on life, lived on. Mann had a sure grasp of the characters of these two men. This is the last instance I know of sociologists figuring in a novel in anything other than a minor, comic role. From the 1930s on, the lives of sociologists have apparently been of insufficient interest to be reimagined in a work of fiction.

Gerth referred often and familiarly to the drawings and paintings of the avant gardists, of Georg Grosz, for example, the movies of Fritz Lang, the architecture of Mies van der Rohe, and I wondered whether he might have known them. Given his detailed knowledge of the period and its players, one might think he would have written something about Weimar. But to my knowledge he never did. He had shown me essays he had written when in Germany, but now, in the United States, he seemed incapable of writing more than a couple of sequential sentences in German or in English. And, in fact, all of his writings in English were done in collaboration with or fully edited by others. It was only later, in reading Peter Gay's *Weimar Culture*[3] (1968) that I was able to put many of Gerth's references and stories, which sometimes fleshed out Gay's treatment, into some kind of framework.

During the year we spent translating the Lukács book (about a third of which we completed), Gerth's comments introduced me to other notable writers, particularly Ernst Bloch, another of the intellectual fathers of the Frankfurt School, and Walter Benjamin. A search in the library turned up Bloch's three-volume *Das Prinzip Hoffnung* (The Principle of Hope)[4] but nothing by Benjamin. It would take another twenty years before works of these writers were translated into English. However, I did find a large book in English translation by one of the members of the Frankfurt School Gerth had mentioned, *Oriental Despotism*,[5] by Karl Wittvogel.

According to Wittvogel, Chinese dynastic rule over huge populations was accomplished through bureaucratic functionaries—tax collectors, traveling magistrates, surveyors—who used the large system of irrigation waterways for extensive and relatively frequent oversight. All this may be true. But although Wittvogel was presumably integrating Weberian elements with Marxian, there is no analysis and little evocation of the complex elements of Chinese patrimonial rule and its normative culture; no mention, for example, of the selection and training of functionaries, the many layers of authority and status among functionaries, the basis of legitimacy of control of the waterways, the nature of sanctions for functionaries and populace when legitimate expectations were violated, or of the degree to which corruption within the Chinese legal and cultural framework might have been considered tolerable, among others. Most important, Wittvogel enormously exaggerated the need of bureaucratic control of irrigation work. A smaller workforce, working steadily and over long periods, was likely all that was needed for such work. This puffed-up, un-Weberian, and rather dreary ecological analysis Gerth dismissed as "hydraulic Marxism," an appraisal with which I agreed.

My teachers in philosophy at the University of Buffalo were right. Even though the sociology department at the University of Wisconsin was a powerhouse of survey researchers who favored empirical-statistical methods, there was room for other approaches. Gerth was schooled in the interpretive methods of the German "cultural sciences" (Geisteswissenschaften), and Howard Becker, the chief theorist of the department, was an advocate of historical and social periodization, for example, the oft-quoted (but I think essentially faulty) distinction between earlier sacred and later secular societies. All societies have both sacred and secular elements. Two junior professors of the department pursued quite different paths, one in phenomenology, the other in behaviorism. I had to take the obligatory courses, but could otherwise go my own way.

I minored in philosophy and in the first two years took three small seminars on Heidegger, Hegel, and existentialism from an assistant professor specializing in modern European philosophy. These stimulating seminars, which concentrated on exploring aspects of the complex ideas of time and representation, partially fed my hunger for a comprehensive understanding of the world and also aided my understanding of Lukács (and later of Adorno and Horkheimer). The professor who taught these seminars, however, left soon thereafter and took a tenured post at a small liberal arts college in the South. I hoped he would have the opportunity to continue teaching and working in his specialty, but was not sanguine of his prospects. My professors at the University of Buffalo were turning out to be right on this score too.

Howard Becker died during my first year at the university and was soon replaced by a young assistant professor, Joseph Elder, who had studied with Talcott Parsons at Harvard. Elder specialized in Indian society but was very well educated in sociology and could easily teach the theory courses. During the second-year theory course, the reading assignments included portions from *The Structure of Social Action*[6] by Parsons. I had begun reading this book as a sophomore and made little headway in it. The discussion of the nature of fact was persuasive, but many of the philosophical, sociological, economic, and historical references and ideas discussed were beyond me, and I put the book aside reluctantly, thinking it was important and I would go back to it again someday. This turned out to be the day, and it was a fateful one for me.

The Structure of Social Action was still a difficult book, and there were many areas discussed of which I was as yet ignorant, but the general thrust of the argument became much clearer. Parsons' synthesizing scheme was the most comprehensive, systematic, and daring I had encountered to date. In bringing together and analyzing the underlying categories of the German, French, Italian, and Anglo-American schools of sociological and economic thought, he had arrived at a small but powerfully generative set of categories implicitly shared by them all. He thus not only broke through the constrictive idiosyncrasies of nationally framed scholarship, but also established a common framework he believed would be a firm basis on which to understand and analyze social phenomena wherever they occurred. Some years later, I discovered Noam Chomsky had achieved an equivalent scheme in the field of linguistics with his ideas of deep structure and generative grammar.

The only other synthesizing scheme I knew of in the social sciences with a reach similar to that of Parsons' was Marx's. If one compares the range of critical scholarship in the volumes of Marx's *Das Capital*[7] and *Grundrisse* (Foundations of the Critique of Political Economy)[8] with the range of critical scholarship in Parsons' *The Structure of Social Action*, the analogous efforts between the two scholars become patent. They each worked through comparable materials with analytical rigor and the same intellectual aim: a rational, empirically grounded theory of modern (and in Parsons' case, perhaps more than modern) social and economic life. Indeed, in the boldness and sweep of his thought, Parsons can be seen as an intellectual—though by no means ideological—successor to Marx. Marx's scheme suffered from the limitations of mid-nineteenth-century economics, sociology, and history, whereas Parsons' thinking benefited from the great advances in knowledge made in each of these disciplines in the seventy-five years since Marx wrote.

A major difference in basic orientation between the two, however—and it is a major one indeed—is that Marx was steeped in the philosophy of Hegel, Parsons in that of Kant and Whitehead. An essay I had read two or three years earlier in English by Emil Fackenheim, "On Kant's Concept of History" *(Kantstudien,* Band 48, Heft 3, 1956/57), had clearly delineated the differences between Kant's and Hegel's views of history. To put it in a nutshell: For Kant, history is the archive of human freedom and creativity. The horizon of history, its trajectory, thus remains open and undetermined. For Hegel, on the other hand, history is charted in the inexorable and ever-growing syntheses of contrary thoughts. The final culminating synthesis of these contrarieties will thus be the end of history, and past, present, and future will become one. These sharply divergent views helped me see some of the differences in philosophical points from which Marx and Parsons had departed and the paths each had subsequently taken.

Some years later, Victor Lidz, a close friend and colleague at the University of Pennsylvania, and I discussed the analogy between Marx and Parsons at some length. Very few scholars have seen this because the ideological blinders at the time these thinkers were both in the center of academic attention (1966–75) were too opaque to permit much more than Invectives to get through. There is often more conflict within than between classes.

I read two other books by Parsons in so many weeks and wrote two critical but constructive essays on certain philosophical issues in his work—preliminary sketches, as it turned out, for what would become my doctoral thesis.

Gerth had met Parsons in Germany when they were both students in Karl Jasper's seminar, but found Parsons' presentation on Herbert Spencer's utilitarian philosophy, even though sharply critical, not to his interest. Gerth did not much care for Spencer. He had glanced at *The Structure of Social Action*, he said, but like many others who merely glanced at the book, took it to be a history of modern social thought.

I showed Gerth my essays, which Elder liked and encouraged me to expand. Gerth, however, was not interested. I made the strongest rational case of which I was able but could not persuade him of what I believed I had seen in Parsons' work.

Parsons' *Structure* and several of his other writings had become by 1960 the chief analytical commentaries on Weber's work in English. Moreover, Parsons had, like Gerth, also translated several of Weber's works. I had heard Gerth make derogatory comments about other émigré scholars who translated German works, saying they treated these works as "real estate investments"—a grubbing, petty bourgeois enterprise without genuine intellectual interest on their part. I knew he considered himself exempt from this charge because he was not merely a translator but also a commentator. Moreover, he and Mills had written an original synthesizing book in its own right, *Character and Social Structure*,[9] which had been positively received. But Parsons could hardly be dismissed on the ground of being an émigré translator. More salient, perhaps, was that Parsons' place in the pantheon of Weber scholars and commentators had risen above Gerth's. I wondered whether Gerth was envious of Parsons' achievements and perhaps loath to express this openly in order not to appear petty and also not to offend me. He was not beyond envy, suspicion, and an occasional flare-up of mean-spiritedness. And no doubt the uprooting he had experienced in his flight from Germany, his discomfort in America (in the late 1960s he returned to Germany, where he lived for several years until his death), and his first wife's recent death fed his often-expressed bitterness. But as is true of all of us, Gerth was many things. He was also caring and generous. In any event, he never said another word to me about Parsons.

By late spring of 1960, it was clear that John F. Kennedy would be the Democratic presidential candidate, Richard M. Nixon the Republican. Anti-Catholic sentiment had been running high even, or perhaps especially, among those who had fallen away from the church, among whom were two of the faculty in the sociology department. But sentiment against "Tricky Dick" Nixon had also been running high, and the outcome was too close to call. The election in the fall of that year was very close, and some of the faculty in the political science department and two of the political sociologists in the sociology department were collaborating on a survey of postelection voter sentiment. I signed on to do some of the interviewing. One of the most striking things I found was how much Eisenhower was disliked by the military, at least the members of the military I interviewed. He had indeed brought the Korean War to an end, but that was not the reason for the dislike. The members I spoke to at Truax Air National Guard Base were angry and resentful over his farewell speech to the nation in which he warned of the global dangers of the "military-industrial complex." The young air force personnel I spoke with took his warning as an attack against the military and therefore against them. Although they had voted for Nixon, they now supported Kennedy, they said, not so much because they were for Kennedy as they were against anyone Eisenhower had endorsed. This degree of political and social myopia was astonishing to me. But one small consequence was that my views of Eisenhower changed. He was a conservative, which was regrettable, but he was much more thoughtful than I had realized; he cared for the nation and the world, and he was a decent and good man.

Many of the friends I made in Madison were graduate students in history. They also had radical backgrounds, were about my age, married, and had children. Through these friends I met a handful of other, younger graduate students in history and English who were editing or deeply involved with *Studies on the Left*. A few of them were in love with Weimar, and since I was happily absorbing torrents of Weimariana from Gerth, we had a further and unexpected sharing of interests. They were democratic socialists, bright, brash, and adamantly opposed to the "Old Left," the socialists of their parents' generation who, twenty-five and thirty years earlier, had held up a mythic, idealized Soviet Union as the model to emulate. By vigorous critique, these New Left students sought to challenge any institution, any circumstance that impeded democratic practices. Their motto could well have been the one Marx had affixed to the masthead of *Rhenische Zeitung* when he became its editor: "For The Critique of Everything."

The faculty members particularly important to the radical students when I was at Madison were William Appleman Williams, professor of American history, George L. Mosse, professor of European history, and Hans H. Gerth. Other than Mosse, I did not meet or take courses with any of the other history faculty.

The undergraduate courses I had taken in history consisted in large part of catalogues of names and dates, dreary chronologies with little analysis. It was a bit like studying biology might have been before Darwin: memorizing the Linnaean classification system. And although I heard many amusing and interesting things about the history professors at Wisconsin, I was reluctant to repeat the kind of experience I had had as an undergraduate. Some years later, I realized this had been a mistake. The historians at Wisconsin were among the finest in the country. They were indeed quite analytical and culturally sensitive, and I would have learned a great deal from them. Not least, almost all of them had been or were still socialists of one kind or another.

In the spring of 1960, the headlines on the front pages of newspapers fluctuated between reports on the Cuban revolution and civil rights actions aimed at striking down voting barriers. Atomic bomb testing in the Southwest deserts was also making headlines because strontium 90, a radioactive byproduct, was being released into the atmosphere, wafting across the country, and contaminating the nation's milk supply. John Kennedy was making presidential aspiration noises to the rumbling accompaniment of anti-Catholic fears. Not least, the military in the form of the R.O.T.C. and the draft was a constant presence and concern for students. And in Madison, the shattering of the atmosphere caused by the fighter planes sent up from the Truax air base at the edge of the city served as frequent daily reminders of the military for everyone.

The reach of the Cold War was steadily lengthening, with clamoring demands for, as well as opposition to, loyalty oaths and increased surveillance measures. Agents of the F.B.I. were investigating professors at the University of Wisconsin and elsewhere. Such agents were apparently following William Appleman Williams daily. According to campus rumor, Williams, who had been a World War II naval officer and staunch critic of the American role in the Cold War, would spot his hatted and suited followers early in the morning, hand each a sheet of paper outlining his itinerary for the day, and with a wave of his hand go off to classes.

Near the end of my first year in Madison, I met George Mosse at a small gathering in the apartment of one of his students. The student was a member of the editorial board of *Studies on the Left*. About five or six other history graduate students and their wives were there, none of whom were formally associated with the magazine. I was the only sociology student among these left-leaning students, a rarity that would cease within a few years. Conversation flitted among the issues of the day, while Mosse fiddled with his pipe and made wry and amusing, but telling asides.

I liked Mosse, liked his comments and manner, and decided I would risk taking his historiography seminar. It turned out to be not only enjoyable but also introduced me to difficult issues in vindicating historical interpretations—a much-needed complement to the more abstract discussions of the subject with which I was more familiar. He was a private man and never spoke of his years in Germany or of his family's social position and loss. His initial publications on political power in early modern England gave no hint of his background. Soon after coming to Madison, his interest turned to nineteenth- and early twentieth-century German culture and institutions, to German-Jewish relations, and particularly to the nature and rise of fascism. These writings, sometimes written as though by an insider, and the discoveries by one or two of his students of the Mosse holdings in Berlin, identified him as one of the "Chosen People," an identification I never heard him mention. Much later, in his honest and moving memoir, *Confronting History*,[10] published in 1999, the year of his death, much of his biography is related.

Mosse was sympathetic to many of the radical students, liked them personally, liked their idealism, their anti-authoritarian zeal, and their courage. But as he said, they were "radicals of the heart, not the head." There are many ways of taking this statement, but I certainly agreed that in 1960 the radical students I met, their claims to the contrary notwithstanding, knew surprisingly less of the theoretical work of Marx or the neo-Marxists than I would have expected. This body of theory is certainly among the parts of the radical "head," but maybe Mosse saw something that I too thought I recognized. There is a romantic appeal in pitting oneself as a radical David against political and industrial Goliaths—an appeal that can override the sort of bookish, European studies of radical thought in which I had been engaged. C. Wright Mills' writings, especially *The Power Elite*,[11] published in 1956, which seemed to be a disciplined, social-scientific unmasking of the powerful enemies of democracy, fanned the radical flames. This was perhaps considered bookish enough.

I wrote a critical review of *Sociology and the Military Establishment*[12] by Morris Janowitz for *Studies on the Left*. A year or two later, however, I regretted having said certain things. I was disturbed by the growing military presence and Cold War furor and swayed by Mills' rhetoric in arguing that business, government, and military leaders were often acting to promote their own interests with little concern for the good of the country. Far worse, these three forces had become a "power elite," argued Mills, that exerts growing hegemonic control over the country. But the more I learned and read, the more I began to see this argument was neither well substantiated nor well analyzed.

There is often as much, if not more, conflict in aims and competition for resources within and among the major elite groups—business, military, and government—than consolidation. This is even true in a totalitarian regime, as Hannah Arendt had methodically documented in her 1951 book, *The Origins of Totalitarianism*.[13] The somewhat paranoid clichés I had used weakened the essay. There was more heart than head in it. I had lapsed into being a victim imperiled by monstrous powers. But in fact Janowitz's study of the military was deeply insightful and prescient. The nature of the American military has changed and its place within the American polity has grown enormously since the Second World War—phenomena that few, if any other, sociologists in 1960 were able or willing to see. In any event, the essay I wrote for *Studies on the Left* made my name familiar to several left-leaning students in other universities. When our paths crossed over the next few years, I was greeted by some of them, total strangers to me, with a friendliness and familiarity that was puzzling until they explained the *Studies on the Left* connection. By this time, the mid-1960s, the radical student movement was well under way and growing rapidly.

During the break between fall and spring semesters in 1960–61, a few of the New Left students went to Cuba. They returned after a week excited and with much news to tell. They had met with Castro, who had taken them on a tour of the island. Cuba, Castro said, pointing to one place after another, is a beautiful island in its setting, its topography, its resources, and its people. But there is also much poverty and much ignorance. Yet, Castro continued, we now have an opportunity for Cuba to become a paradise. But for a paradise to be built here we need to educate almost everyone on the island—the peasants, the fishermen, the tradesmen and service workers and shopkeepers—the millions in the farms and towns and cities—everyone. He called on American and European graduate students and professors in all fields to come to Cuba and teach. Cuba could become a model society. Would we join him and the Cuban people in this great effort?

I discovered in my reaction to Castro's invitation that my utopian thirsts had not been entirely quenched. I was hesitant, but the prospect was tempting. To help create a model society, a socialist society! I mentioned this to my wife, who was dubious. I talked to Gerth, who said, quite directly, no! I should not go. America, he said, needs intellectuals to sustain rational standards, which are always the weakest and the first to be attacked in times of national anxiety. It is your duty to stay here, he urged me. Besides, Castro is speaking now in the afterglow of his triumph. It all sounds very rosy. Wait a bit, we'll see.

During the spring of 1961 Sartre visited Cuba and wrote a glowing report of the Cuban effort. At the end of the spring semester one of the students went again to Cuba, joining C. Wright Mills, who had flown in separately from New York City. The student returned to Madison after a few weeks with glum news. A cult of personality about Castro was being fostered in children and the young side by side with a spirit of militarism. He related two incidents. In a grade school kindergarten during the midmorning snack, the children were asked to close their eyes and pray for ice cream. "Now children, open your eyes," the teacher instructed. There was of course no ice cream. "Now children," the teacher again instructed, "close your eyes and pray to Fidel for ice cream." Skippy cups were quickly distributed among the desks. "Now children, open your eyes." In the schoolyard, slightly older children were parading about with toy rifles, being instructed by their teachers how to aim at targets—presumably American—that might breach the Cuban defenses.

These incidents did not bode well for a democratic Cuban paradise. Sartre, who visited Cuba a few more times, saw none of this and returned to France to sing rhapsodic praises of Castro, Cuba, and especially Che Guevara, whom he called the new man, the man of the future. But then, as one commentator later said, Che Guevara could have told Sartre the Cubans were going to bring down the moon and eat the cheese and Sartre would have clapped his hands in glee. The step Sartre took from *Nausea* to the *Just So Stories* was smaller than I would have imagined.

Most of the radical students I knew in Madison were Jewish and had grown up in New York City, Chicago, Denver, and Los Angles. However rebellious they were, there was for many a generational continuity with their parents. Their parents' aspirations for knowledge, justice, and social inclusion were values for them, and they sought to extend these values for everyone. Their socialism, like mine, had a messianic tinge rooted in their Jewish background—a background not fully extinguished, however assimilated many of their parents and they had become. As with all people, they were angered when their values were violated, but their anger was not as diffuse and bitter as the anger of the veteran radicals I had known as an undergraduate. In some part, I think, this was because the Wisconsin radicals I knew were not members of the Communist Party, which would have set them at odds with the country as a whole. The radicals at Wisconsin were Americans—Jewish Americans, to be sure, but Americans—shaped by American traditions of civil liberties, civil rights, independence, and individual worth. American communities of voluntary associations rather than Soviet collectives of solidary social classes were envisioned in their socialism—as in mine. But no small part of the difference is that none of the Wisconsin radicals had participated in the Second World War and its immediate aftermath. They had not sacrificed their bodies and youth only to return to an America in which there were many of the same inequities they had fought so hard against in Europe. The Wisconsin radicals I knew from 1959 to 1962 were not less impassioned than the older veterans, but they seemed more personally secure, more hopeful, less bitter.

Was there a particular type of Madison radical? For several years after I left Madison some people who had read my piece in *Studies on the Left* said I looked and talked like a Madison radical. But of course, their image was formed even before they had met me by the fact that the magazine was a Madison publication. Besides, no one else said this. Nevertheless, I believe a selection factor that drew certain kinds of students to Madison was at work.

Despite Senator Joseph McCarthy, Wisconsin itself has a long, progressive history. Milwaukee, the largest city in the state, has had socialist mayors from mid-nineteenth century well into the twentieth—over a century. And Madison itself is the most liberal city in the state. All this is fairly well known or certainly becomes known to students in the humanities who are investigating schools and their locations for graduate study.

But more important for students are the professors with whom they wish to study. The attraction of Madison for me was largely the Lukács-Mannheim-Gerth connection. The history department at Wisconsin was filled with nationally eminent scholars, some well known to have socialist views, and they had trained younger scholars who were fast becoming prominent in the profession. All of this was surely attractive to young radically minded students who wished to do graduate work in history—and later in sociology. Paul Buhle has edited a collection of memoirs that provides a fuller account: *History and the New Left—Madison Wisconsin, 1950–1970*.[14]

None of these considerations, however, tells us whether there is a distinct type of *Madison* radical as opposed, say, to a Berkeley radical or a Chicago radical. Jokes, of course, abound. The Berkeley "grundge" was not limited to Berkeley. The only thing we learn is that Madison has had an attraction for students from all parts of the country, some of whom were and perhaps still are radical.

In August 1962, my wife and I and two-and-a-half-month-old son left Madison for Philadelphia. We had been in Madison for three years. I had completed all the courses for the doctorate in sociology and passed the doctoral exams. The dissertation remained to be written, but I had a job as an instructor in sociology at the University of Pennsylvania.

Shortly before I left Madison, Gerth advised me not to become too visible. "Why so, Hans?" Because, he said, in times of trouble the Jews will be sacrificed. And times of trouble, he predicted, will be coming. Better to remain in the background, unnoticed. To which of course I rejoined that this was America, not Germany. Wait, you'll see, he said. Caring advice from one who is not one of the Chosen People to one who is. But Gerth was certainly right in one way. Times of trouble happened, as he predicted, and they continue to happen. But so far, his grim warning has not been borne out.

I have been in dwindling contact for many years with some of the radical friends I made in Madison, and am still in touch with a couple of them. Very few, if any, I believe, were in the core of the more militant radicals that emerged later in the decade. The militant radicals were younger, another generation. By the time the more militant radicals emerged, at least a third of the New Left students I knew had become professors, and a few may still be active as such today. Some went into Southern states and participated in voting drives. Others turned to social work, and a few became journalists. One or two, influenced by Saul Aulinksy's *Reveille for Radicals*,[15] became community organizers. At least one became a stockbroker, and two others settled into being independent scholars supported by inheritances. A few are deceased. I very much doubt any would have participated in the destructive actions that took place at the University of Wisconsin in the latter part of the sixties.

Notes

1. Oxford University Press, New York, 1958.
2. Vintage International, New York, 1996.
3. Harper & Row, New York, 1968.
4. MIT Press, Cambridge, MA, 1986.
5. Yale University Press, New Haven, CT, 1957.
6. Free Press, Glencoe, IL, 1949.

7. C.H. Kerr & Co., Chicago, 1925.
8. Penguin Classics reprint, London, 1993.
9. Harcourt, Brace, New York, 1953.
10. University of Wisconsin Press, Madison, 2013.
11. Oxford University Press, New York, 1956.
12. Russell Sage Foundation, New York, 1959.
13. Harcourt, Brace & World, New York, 1966.
14. Temple University Press, Philadelphia, 1990.
15. University of Chicago Press, Chicago, 1946.

9

Penn Sociology in the Age of Aquarius: 1960–1965

During the years of the college boom, 1950 to 1980, a doctoral student in just about any field who had done reasonably well in graduate school and had good recommendations could get a junior appointment in any one of several colleges or universities. I chose the University of Pennsylvania—Penn—over other opportunities for a few reasons, some rational, some not rational. First, my wife had given birth on June I, 1962, to a beautiful baby boy, and I needed a job. After the euphoria and wonder of the birth and the sense of being connected to all of humankind had subsided, I began searching. I was offered an instructorship in sociology at Wisconsin, but at the last moment, in July, a chance for a job at Penn beginning in September came up. It was time to leave. Penn was supposed to be an excellent school, which meant that students and faculty would generally be intellectually stimulating. Second, there was a promise from the chair of the sociology department at Penn that, assuming enrollments continued to increase, I would be teaching sociological theory as soon as I had completed writing my dissertation. Third, a new department had formed at Penn called "history and sociology of science." I would not be in this department, but it had faculty and programs that might be receptive to my interests in the sociology of knowledge, a related field. Fourth, Penn's sociology department was undergoing a major overhaul. Philip Rieff had gone there a year or two earlier, and other new, interesting people would likely be brought in. Although Gerth, who had spent a year with Rieff at Brandies, did not think well of him as a person and had severe doubts as to the authenticity of his scholarship, I chalked Gerth's judgment up to one of his quixotic moods and paid little attention to it. Part of Rieff's *Freud, The Mind of the Moralist*,[1] was of a high order of insight and scholarship, and he might be a congenial colleague. And fifth, Philadelphia was a big, major city, the kind in which I very much wanted to be.

My wife, two-and-a-half-month-old son, and I packed ourselves into a 1950 Plymouth and drove the eight hundred miles from Madison to Philadelphia in a slow three days. We bought the car for one hundred dollars from a friend. Although twelve years old and without a front grill, the Plymouth was reliable. With its open mouth and faded pale paint it looked like a circus car from which clouds of black smoke should be billowing before it skidded to a stop to let a dozen clowns leap out. But it didn't spew smoke, and the only clown was its Okie-looking driver. The car couldn't go faster than forty-five miles per hour on a moderately steep grade, and after I, dressed in T-shirt and with a three-day growth of beard, explained that to the officers who stopped us on the Pennsylvania turnpike, they looked inside, saw the peaceable kingdom of my wife and swaddled baby boy, and advised us to be careful.

While my wife and son stayed with her aunt who lived near Kutztown, I searched Philadelphia for a neighborhood that would be pleasant and safe and, no less important, in which we could afford to rent a small house or flat. I found one, finally, a row house about an hour and a quarter by bus and subway from the university. I tested the route; it might be possible to read, perhaps even prepare lectures, while traveling. This prospect soon proved to be illusory. The neighborhood also was not as congenial as I had hoped it would be. I stayed at home writing and reading on the days I didn't teach. Soon, neighbors thought I was unemployed. When my wife explained I was a teacher—she didn't say where or what I taught—one of the neighbors asked whether I would tutor her son in algebra. There was an implication I would receive some sort of compensation—very kind, of course, and meant to offer a bit of financial assistance to a needy neighbor. But after we quickly supplied the explanations of where I was employed and what exactly I did, neighbors saw us, and we saw them, as essentially belonging in different social worlds. So much for class-consciousness. Within a year we rented a coach house from a professor who lived much closer to the university, and within five years bought our own house. By then, as some friends observed, my bourgeoisification was well under way. The initial week I spent in Philadelphia searching for a place to rent, and the occasional forays in the city we made later in the year, gave me some sense of the city that added to what I had learned from a bit of earlier research.

In 1962, Philadelphia's population was over two million—about seven times that of Buffalo's, twenty times of Madison's. Like all American cities, Philadelphia is divided into distinct ethnic and class neighborhoods. But a newcomer could grasp little of this diversity, because the city seemed to stretch endlessly in all directions. Except for the central grid of the city, many streets stopped at one intersection only to start up again several blocks beyond—clearly a place in which one could (and often did) easily get lost. Philadelphia has all the features of a big American city—four major-league sports teams, several colleges and universities, famous music and art schools, a large, excellent public library with many branches, a great symphony orchestra, outstanding museums, several daily newspapers, radio and television stations, an immense park system, and a major zoo. Philadelphia also has features that are unique to it—historical buildings such as Independence and Carpenter Halls, the Old Swede Church, the houses of George Washington and Benjamin Franklin as well as other well-known colonists, the Liberty Bell, the preserved colonial streets, such as Elfreth's Alley, and the graveyards of early settlers dating to the 1600s.

Yet, in 1962 Philadelphia did not quite have the feel of a big city. I had been in New York City and Chicago many times. But In Philadelphia—the fifth-largest city in the country at the time—there were no skyscrapers, few office buildings and apartment houses. Philadelphia had many poor people. At ten in the evening, the city shut down—the movie houses emptied, the handful of restaurants closed. The streets became darkened and bare. Most people lived in houses, which gave the city a domestic, family-centered look. The city was a place where people lived and worked, but other than that there seemed to be little energy. The streets were dirty. There was crime—there is always crime—but the city was quiet.

All of this was puzzling and a bit dismaying at first. Buffalo was livelier; Madison was cleaner. But as a young instructor and father, my energies were absorbed in work and family; there was little opportunity—or money—to avail myself of the pleasures of a big city.

Much in Philadelphia has since changed. The city has lost population, mainly people of the middle class, and the suburbs have sprawled over what were once miles of adjacent farmland. Many industries have left—either shut down or moved elsewhere—but several new, technological industries have sprung up and drawn some younger people into the city. With new leadership the old city has been developed into many blocks of chic townhouses. There are now many skyscrapers, many tall apartment and office buildings, many restaurants and theaters and much music of all kinds. The waterfront has been partially developed, and there are plans for further development. And the city, at least the central part of the city, now stays open many more hours than in 1962. There remain of course the streets that stop and start erratically. And there is still and always will be crime.

In some ways, the University of Pennsylvania has mirrored the city. In 1962 Penn was beginning to shake off decades of faculty inbreeding coupled to the practice of drawing a large proportion of students from the local community. With the exception of the professional schools (medicine, law, engineering, the Wharton School of Business) and the university museum, many of the professors in liberal arts had been trained entirely at Penn. The result was a stodgy provincialism that left Penn in the great college expansion following World War II at a competitive disadvantage.

New university leadership in the late 1950s was beginning to shake the university out of its lethargy. Drives to increase university endowment were initiated that have continued to the present. Scholar-administrators widely known in their fields were brought in from other universities to serve as chairs of several departments and charged with transforming their professional staffs. The inbreeding that had clotted Penn's faculties for decades was halted, and students from all parts of the country were actively sought. Three new faculty members in sociology were hired a year or two before I came, and three more, of which I was one, were hired in 1962.

We were told much of this at the dean's reception for new faculty— an occasion that only remotely resembled the down-home, noisy, alcohol-free, and shirtsleeved reception for new graduate students at Wisconsin. The dean, as it turned out, headed the Wharton School of Business and Finance, and this is where the sociology department was housed—an unexpected and surprising fact, about which more soon. I wore the suit I had bought for interviews (my only one), and parked my grill-less and embarrassing car two blocks away. The building in which the reception took place was nondescript, made of cinder blocks, but the gathering was in a (faux?) oak-paneled room a bit larger than a classroom, with an Oriental–style rug on the floor, a bar and black bartender in white coat at one end, a table with name tags on it nearby, and a number of upholstered chairs and walnut tables scattered about. A young woman gave me a name tag, offered a glass of wine, and took me over and introduced me to the dean. The meeting was perfunctory but not unpleasant; the smoothly dressed dean smiled, shook my hand, and welcomed me to the university. ("Glitchik vie gluhz,"—smooth as glass—my grandmother would have said.) He was adroit in pronouncing my name correctly. After this, I wandered about introducing myself to the eighteen or nineteen other new as well as older faculty members. I soon encountered David Lavin, another new professor in sociology, whom I had met a few days earlier. It was a relief to find someone I knew at least slightly, and we remained together for the length of the reception—and indeed, have been friends ever since.

Unlike the Universities of Buffalo and Wisconsin, which are in the middle of the country geographically, culturally, and socially, Penn is East Coast and projects in the look of its faculty and buildings an older and much higher social status. Whether faux or real, the oak paneling and Oriental rug, the wine in glasses rather than in plastic cups, the polished wooden rather than Formica tables, the well-tailored faculty—all spoke of an economic well-being and higher social place than the more slap-dash appearance of persons and places at the other universities I had known. A friend to whom I described all this sought to allay my initial unease by assuring me that "nothing is too good for the proletariat." I have since learned that Penn in 1962 was closer to the bottom of the private university status ladder, with Harvard, Yale, Princeton, Chicago, Stanford, Brown, and Columbia at the top. The practice begun in the late 1950s of augmenting the faculty and replacing retired professors by bringing in new people from other universities has with few exceptions continued. By 1990, Penn—the entire university, not only its professional schools—had become one of the premiere research universities in the country with a distinguished faculty and a select body of undergraduate and graduate students. Partly as a result of the market-like recruitment of faculty from all parts of the country, coupled with the growth of the research function, Penn has, like every other large public or private research university, taken on many of the trappings of a corporation in which the entrepreneurial spirit predominates.

Although its history is quite different from that of other liberal arts departments, the sociology department also benefited from the new hiring practices. Sociology evolved from the Department of Political Economy, which was formed at the beginning of the twentieth century. Under this older rubric, the department was housed in the Wharton School of Business and Finance. It was as an instructor in the Department of Political Economy that, over a hundred years ago, W. E. B. Dubois did his famous study, *The Philadelphia Negro*.[2] But although the Department of Political Economy was renamed after a time as the Department of Sociology, sociology remained for many years in the Wharton School, and as such was overseen by the dean of the school.

Since the Wharton School was quasi-independent of the larger university and well endowed, one of the presumed benefits to this arrangement was that the faculty in Wharton would be receiving slightly higher salaries than the faculty in arts and sciences, which, if true, would have been an unanticipated and welcome boon to a beginning instructor with college debts, a grill-less car, and a young family to support. Although presumed, and likely correct, the benefit was difficult to prove since the university is a private institution and salaries are not made public. (I learned soon enough that the concern over salaries is one of the rites of spring for a majority of the faculty, lowly instructors and senior professors alike.) Another benefit, this one actual, was in the quality of students. The Wharton School was famous not only for its excellence but also because it was the only business school in the country with full-fledged undergraduate as well as graduate programs. The school attracted students from all parts of the country as well as Europe, Asia, and South America. The final selection from these applicants yielded a bright group of students. The downside, I feared, was that a business school ethos might affect the humanistic branches of sociology that I favored.

The Department of Sociology did move to the School of Arts and Sciences in the mid-1970s, which, even though arts and sciences was much poorer, did not have any discernable effect on salaries that I could see. Several members of the department, however, believed salaries were negatively affected over the years. But if so, most members, and not least I too, were willing to pay a price to feel more intellectually comfortable ensconced in a liberal arts environment. Bottom lines are not always the same.

Another curious feature of the sociology department, at least curious to me, was that most of the newly hired faculty members were Jewish, whereas there was not even one Jew among the older professors. Much the same ethnic difference obtained between older and younger faculty at the University of Wisconsin, a fact I noticed but made little of. An analogous difference had not yet developed among students at Penn. Most freshmen students at Penn in 1962 were not Jewish, as was true for senior students as well. One index of this was that Hillel, the Jewish student organization, was quite small both in membership and physical quarters. The influx of Jewish students began to occur about a decade later, and with this Hillel also grew. By the 1980s Penn was widely reputed to be a "Jewish school," and Hillel had moved into its third and much larger building.

Many Jewish students may have been prompted to go to Penn because in 1971 Penn had elected as their new president Martin Meyerson, the first Jew to lead a major private university—a radical departure from the anti-Semitic attitudes that had dominated Penn's Board of Trustees before the Second World War. (A doctoral student researching the history of higher education found in the Penn archives a document put before the Board of Trustees in the 1930s proposing the university be relocated from west Philadelphia to Valley Forge, a suburb thirty miles north. The reason given: Penn would thus be insulated from the rising number of Jews moving into west Philadelphia.) However, the anti-Jewish sentiment lingered well into the 1960s and beyond. In the mid-1970s, while approaching the auditorium for a university-wide discussion on issues of university financing, I overheard a few senior professors arguing in a side hallway. They were discussing whether president Meyerson would be successful in increasing state subsidies to the university. Milton Shapp, a Jew, was then governor of Pennsylvania. One of these gray eminences stated loudly and flatly, "You need a Jew to deal with a Jew." This seemed to clinch the argument. (My parents might have wished the argument clinched by all their bones being broken.) Their attitudes were contemptible and commonly found in many universities, but I think—hope—their kind has since diminished.

But as for the professors in 1962, the main noticeable difference between the two groups in the sociology department that I could detect was a generational one. The older faculty had completed their studies in the 1930s and early 1940s, the younger faculty in the late 1950s and 1960s. There were differences in topics the two groups studied and some differences in jargon as well as in methods of research. There were also differences in style. There was no one among the older faculty like Gerth, but of course there couldn't be; Gerth was one of a kind. The professor who taught theory, for example, was polite and always well dressed and manicured. He had done consulting for the State Department on matters relating to Spain and Portugal. There were some fine Spanish philosophers that I knew of—Miguel de Unamuno was my favorite—but I didn't know of any Spanish sociologists. Since this professor was retiring personally and just about retired professionally, I never did find out much about Spanish sociology. In political matters the older professors were, with one or two exceptions, either fairly listless or moderate to right leaning. The exceptions were not merely leaning but practically recumbent with the right.

The younger faculty members were a bit less formal in manner than the older ones, and more interested in restaurants, movies, and popular culture. Perhaps most important, the older faculty had more or less ended their scholarly work and were looking forward to retiring; the younger faculty were just beginning. And not least, the younger instructors were more attuned to the political and social ferment that was arising, whereas to many of the older faculty such developments were a repetition in new dress of what had happened before. Nevertheless, although scholarly and social relations were limited, the two groups made efforts to be friendly and, given their differences in status and outlook, by and large got along well. The same pattern of generational and ethnic differences was repeated in most of the departments in the university and likely in universities and colleges throughout the country—a consequence of the barriers broken after the Second World War.

The change in status from student to teacher was a large one, somewhat analogous to going from being a child to a parent, but taking much less time, fortunately, and far less difficult. I had a brief preparation of sorts, since I had recently become a father and enjoyed being such. I soon made friends with other young instructors. But the uncertainty and anxiety of being junior faculty in a new and strange setting in which senior faculty, however cordial, were evaluating much of what you did was an experience harkening to our recently outgrown adolescence. This served to bind junior faculty in mutual support, which sometimes overrode our competitiveness. In my first years, the wives and children of three of the junior faculty in particular, David Lavin, Seymour Leventman, and a year or two later Ralph Ginsberg, got along well with my family, and we all became good friends. Norman Kaplan, a new associate professor of the department, also became a good friend. Kaplan's research compared national differences in scientific laboratories—between, say, the social organization of chemistry laboratories in Russia versus those in Germany—and he also had considerable knowledge of the literature in the sociology of knowledge. He was older, a veteran of World War II, about the age of my youngest uncle. And although he took a slightly avuncular attitude toward me, we enjoyed each other and talked a great deal. He was the only member of the department at that time who had some comprehension of what I was doing. I was fond of him.

The senior person with whom I soon became close friends and remained such until the end of his life was E. Digby Baltzell. He was the youngest of the senior professors, had gone to Penn as an undergraduate, and after serving in the navy during the Second World War did his doctoral studies at Columbia University with Robert K. Merton. Baltzell was the only member of the department who went out of his way to meet new people, learn of their interests, and show them the university and city. He took me to lunch soon after I arrived, asked me about my research, where I went to school, and who my teachers were. We talked for two or three hours that day and never stopped talking together until his death. His research (about which more later) clarified central features of the American class system and also of democratic processes. He was the only member of the department whose work had been stimulated by the study of Marx. I learned a great deal from it.

Philip Rieff, with whom I had hoped to develop good collegial and intellectual relations, was a disappointment. We made friendly overtures to each other and shared certain interests, but soon discovered unbridgeable antipathies. Gerth's judgments of him and his work were not as quixotic as I had hoped them to be. Our relationship settled into a distant civility. Although his ultra-political conservatism may have played a part, I don't think this was central in the differences that developed between us. He was clearly a man of considerable ability, but also one with a supercilious manner that I and many others found disagreeable. His work fell off sharply over the years. The negative preachments in his Freud book became dominant and increasingly strident in his later work, which never again approached the quality of his book on Freud.

As an instructor, I was no longer a recipient of knowledge and dependent on professors; now I was the provider and had to take the lead. But I was not without some experience. I had given lectures in some of my classes even as an undergraduate and served as a teaching assistant in graduate school. Most important, I wanted to be a teacher, wanted to emulate the teachers who had influenced and nurtured me and taught me so much.

I was startled at first, and admit to being a bit put off, to learn that undergraduates owned the Jaguars, BMWs, and Porches parked around the campus. There was nothing remotely like this newly rich display of opulence at the University of Wisconsin where the cars undergraduates owned, if they owned any, were an old Volkswagen beetle, Ford, or grill-less Plymouth. But Penn, I had to remind myself, was an Ivy

League university. The cost of going to Penn in 1962 was twelve to fifteen times greater than going to Wisconsin. There was clearly an economic factor in the selection of students, and I hoped there was an intellectual factor as well.

I don't believe my teaching was affected by the fact that many students came from households whose economic wherewithal was far greater than mine. At least, I hope it wasn't. Given our respective roles of teacher and student, the economic differences made no difference. The disparity in wealth between us was eclipsed by the opposite disparity in knowledge and authority. Of this I was confident. And these latter differences were the important ones. As I got to know the students, moreover, the kinds of persons they were—whether they were honest and decent and tried their best—was the principal consideration in my responses to them.

Most of my students were in liberal arts programs rather than in the Wharton School. The style of teaching I found most comfortable was quasi-Socratic, but of a much more active kind than that of my philosophy professor Marvin Farber. I would lecture for a bit, and then engage the students in a give-and-take discussion of the materials until reasonably sure the students understood the materials. Sometimes we did not quite complete the reading assignment, but it was more important to understand what was read than to read everything but comprehend little.

I did not use a standard text. The thirty or so introductory texts I had reviewed in preparation were patronizing and hackneyed; some were saccharine and cute, as though produced by the Walt Disney Studios; and many were appallingly ignorant. I put together a set of readings from original sources that would introduce students to the basic ideas in the field—essays, research reports, chapters from monographs, and a few short paperback books. I assigned *The Communist Manifesto*, thinking this would provide a brief, overall view of the concept of class and one of the ways of understanding the parts of society as making up an organized, systematic whole. Many of the students, I was startled to learn, had never read the essay, and many had never heard of it. This was in 1962. By 1980, the essay was regularly assigned in many high school history classes. Although students sometimes grumbled at the amount of reading—a mere 100–150 pages per week on average—the courses went well. There is a difference, however, between what is taught and what is learned. I tried to introduce students to a sociological perspective, but am unsure whether or to what degree this was assimilated.

In mid-fall 1962, about six weeks after classes had started, the Cuban Missile Crisis erupted. The nation was put on alert. Troops, ships, and planes were massed and made ready for nuclear war with Cuba and Russia. The crisis lasted about one week. My friend Dave Lavin thought Philadelphia, with its shipyards, might be a target for Cuban-Russian missiles. We discussed plans to leave the city, take both our families in his VW bus, and drive to some central, safer state—Colorado, say— where there were lead mines.

We didn't do this, of course, and the missile crisis was resolved soon enough. But I had misgivings about President Kennedy's actions. I had opposed the anti-Catholic drivel that had been spewed against Kennedy in 1960, but was ambivalent about his presidency. He was charming and witty and young and handsome. The Peace Corps that his administration had established was a fine program that inspired many. But it seemed to me that his was the overt beginning of the American Imperial Presidency. His early action toward Cuba—the fiasco of the attempted invasion at the Bay of Pigs—was taken with only belated consultation with the Organization of American States—an organization to which we as members were responsible. We were lucky, I thought, there was not a widespread anti-USA uprising in South America. The students were also frightened by the missile crisis, but their fears soon receded, and the remainder of the school year passed in relative calm.

I had had no fellow black students in my classes when I was an undergraduate. Now, however, there were two black students in the classes I was teaching. Both were very bright, and both were sophomores. One was on a full scholarship. He was a beautiful writer, expressed ideas plainly and with a metaphorical sparkle. We became friendly. He showed me some stories he had written and told me a bit about himself. The stories were charming—funny and with ironic punch. He had discovered books early and found in the novels and stories he was reading a world of wonders far richer than anything in his environment or in what he was being taught at school. Although he had formally declared an early interest in being a sociology major, it was clear to me he was going to become—was already—a writer. His family was large, his parents poor. He had applied for and won a somewhat obscure scholarship that had one stipulation: full tuition for four years if the student maintained an overall B average each semester. He should have no problem, I thought. He was getting an A in sociology, an A in English, an A- in history. But his grade in physics, he said, was D; in math F. His grade point average for the year so far was about a C, below the required B. I didn't think this would be an insurmountable problem. Given his intellectual ability, a little tutoring in the mathematics he hadn't been taught in high school would set him straight. If the chairman of my department put in a word of support for him, I was sure the scholarship committee would defer judgment for another year. I of course wrote a strong letter, but I was among the most junior of the faculty and unknown. A positive word from the senior and very influential chairman was needed. It was at this moment I discovered bigotry in what I believed would be the least likely place: in my department.

One of the basic teachings of anthropology is that there is no fundamental genetic (or so-called racial) difference in intelligence among blacks, whites, Asians, or any of the populations of the extant human species. The findings of all the social sciences—sociology, anthropology, and psychology—had concurred that most of the differences between peoples were attributable to variations in cultural and social conditions. This was the basis of the Supreme Court's decision in Brown vs. Board of Education in 1954. One hardly needed to be chairman of a sociology department to know this. Indeed, mitigating negative social conditions—for example, high birth rates in poor countries—was what many of the members in my department, including the chairman, were trying to do. Fewer children would, presumably, receive more resources.

I spoke to the chairman; described the gifts of my student, the terms of his scholarship, the situation he was in, and what I thought could be done to help him. After listening with head bowed he sighed and piously reflected on the sad fact that this young man's chances of succeeding in the world under present social circumstances were extremely slight, indeed just about nil. It would be cruel, he said, shaking his head, to mislead this young man, and a waste of scholarship funds to encourage him in a course that will very likely end in failure. He is reaching far beyond what he can expect to achieve. Best this is happening now, before he gets any farther. He should find a job someplace where he can fit in. And with a smile—which I cannot expunge from my memory to this day—he turned to other, doubtless more pressing matters. I suppose I might have thought of burning the chairman in effigy, if I were eighteen years old (I clearly thought of it then), but I had learned my lesson. I tried to reason with him. The civil rights movement was making progress. Each positive step we took would improve chances for blacks. This student was not a big risk; the scholarship investment was small. There was more to gain than to lose by supporting him. The chairman listened but remained firm in his decision.

I had thought the chairman was a decent man. He had been a Quaker and a conscientious objector during the Second World War and was now a Unitarian. But he was also, I saw in his response, worse than uncaring. He seemed oblivious of the gains the Civil Rights Movement was making and the many efforts under way that would make his view of the world less probable. His decision would end this young man's tenure at the university. It was grotesque to claim his decision was in keeping with the nature of the world and therefore for the student's good. The chairman had been trained as a demographer and thought in statistical generalities. He couldn't see the trees for the forest. The world was changing and could only be further changed and improved by acting upon it. But not in this case. The trouble with the chairman was not his demographic mentality. He was a racist. My mother would have called him a roach. My father would have ridiculed and dismissed him with a Yiddishism that said it all: "You're the one peeing on this kid's back, but saying it's raining." From that moment on, my respect for this chairman, and with it my trust in him, evaporated.

But alas, he was not the only one of his kind. I discovered over the years that a few other members of my department were also racists. Their self-proclaimed, but seldom realized, good intentions for the poor of other countries were far outweighed by the actual harm of their racial attitudes at home. I was stunned to discover this attitude was held by sociologists who, I thought, of all people should know better. When hearing of persons doing and getting away with cruel and unjust things, my otherwise gentle and reticent grandmother would murmur "zol zay alle tief in drerd lign!" (May they all lie deep in the ground.) It was a sentiment I too murmured often to myself over the years.

Twenty-five years later, I learned my student had become the writer I thought he was and had worked himself up to becoming editor of a major black newspaper in Philadelphia. The other black student had become a physician practicing in New York City. Both had found places where they could fit in.

In spring of 1963, I was invited to the philosophy department for afternoon tea. Marvin Farber, my philosophy professor at the University of Buffalo, signed the invitation. Unknown to me, he had been brought in a few years earlier, while I was at the University of Wisconsin, as the new chair of philosophy at Penn. I looked forward with pleasure to the prospect of seeing my old professor again, and I think this may have pleased him too; I was one of his students who was making good, so to speak.

One of the first professors of the philosophy department I met at the tea was William Fontaine. He was the only black philosopher I had ever met, and so far as I knew also the only black professor at the university. He was a shy man, soft-spoken, bent and frail, and did not look well. He had an interest in Mannheim's theory of interpretation, and we chatted amiably for a bit, spoke of getting together perhaps early in the fall semester, and we then moved on to speak to other people. I did not see Fontaine again. He was quite ill, as it turned out, and died a few years later. He was a singular man; the few former students of his I met in later years spoke admiringly of the clarity of his thinking and teaching. A biography of Fontaine by Bruce Kuklick, *Black Philosopher, White Academy: The Career of William Fontaine*,[3] was published in 2008 by the Penn Press.

Through Farber's good offices, I met and soon became friends and colleagues with other members of the philosophy department, particularly Abraham—"Abe"—Edel and his wife, Elizabeth—"Betty"—Flower. We remained good friends until their deaths almost three and a half decades later. Edel was a learned and gentle presence, often casting dispelling light on the darker, more contentious sides of philosophical matters. As an undergraduate, I had read one of his books and several of his essays on ethics in science and learned from them. He carried his learning lightly and without pretense. He could as easily sing a Yiddish folk song as discourse on recondite aspects of the verb "to be." His knowledge of social science was broad, and we often discussed issues in the social history of ideas.

Flower was expert in American philosophy and had written several works on ethics. She was a bit younger than her husband, Abe, but like him gentle and open, a very good teacher, unpretentious and easily given to laughter. Martin Luther King, Jr. had been one of her students—a fact she never mentioned, but one that I learned many years later. We shared a few students over the years, which was great fun because the students would tell each of us amusing things about the other. For several years, I participated with her and her husband in inter-faculty seminars, one on philosophy and social science, and another on the social sciences and psychoanalysis. These were among the kinds of experiences I had hoped to find in university life.

Meeting these and other members of the philosophy department brought me over the years into contact with scholars whose views often enriched my own. One of these philosophers, Mihailo Marković, came to Penn each spring semester for several years. He was a prominent "humanistic Marxist" who emerged in the post–World War II years from Yugoslavia. He was a man of courage and high intelligence, and, unlike many people I've known, had no difficulty accepting criticism—indeed, welcomed criticism, if it clarified his thinking. He was a chess grandmaster of international standing and could have beaten me within five seconds had I been foolish enough to play a game with him. Nevertheless, I ventured some non-chess-related criticism. He did not appreciate, for example, the powerful hold of religion and tradition upon the conduct and outlook of people of *all* classes, but saw traditional views merely as ideologies, more or less intentional expressions of "ruling-class" interests. I recommended some of Max Weber's comparative historical studies to him, which analyze the subtle and extensive reach of "traditional" normative ideas—the Confucian ethic in China, for example, compared to the Protestant ethic in America. These ideas not only express ruling-class interests but also channel attitudes and conduct of all classes, ruling and ruled alike. I have no idea whether he ever read these studies. At a conference on social evolution in which we participated, he still held to Marx's simple stage scheme of historical change and contended that Japan, for example, remained basically a "feudal" society. This was just before all television sets, computers, cameras, and most cars were being made in Japan. Amazingly talented serfs, wot? I countered that capitalism can take many forms, that Japan had a fully developed capitalist economy, and recommended that he look at Robert Bellah's *Tokugawa Religion*[4] for an elucidation of this phenomenon that was contrary to Marxist theory. But again, I have no idea whether he ever read the book.

However, I was sympathetic to many of his views on socialist humanism and began to study several of his writings. But he returned too soon to his benighted homeland for me to get to know him well, and to my regret we did not discuss any of the issues of socialist humanism. I have not been able to find out what happened to him after he left the United States. He died in Belgrade in 2010.

The philosopher I met at Penn who had the greatest influence on my thinking was G. E. M. (Elizabeth) Anscombe. Her monograph *Intention*[5]—deceptively simple, yet cutting to the bone—was of inestimable value in clarifying my thinking on how to understand human action. I heard her lecture, was introduced, read her monograph and one or two of her commentaries on Wittgenstein, but did not get to know her.

Farber left Penn within two years to return to Buffalo, New York, where he retired as a university professor emeritus. I did not see him again.

At the end of my first year of teaching, my wife, one-year-old son and I drove to Buffalo to visit parents and relatives. Many hadn't seen the new baby yet, and there was the usual cooing and squeezing and kissing and gargantuan mounds of food. But there was a surprise in the visit I hadn't expected, and it made me reflect again—and I have never stopped reflecting—on questions of assimilation, identity, and class. One of my uncles, Max, turned to me and said, "Nu Hershel, now that you're a professor you won't be able to talk to us anymore." Could he possibly have meant this? To show that I could still talk to him, I described some of my colleagues in the most colloquial Yiddish I could dream up. X is a shtik oldz, I said, und farshtet gurnisht (a piece of wood and understands nothing). Y is a funfer (someone who talks a lot but says nothing). Q is a klieger (a smart one), aber er zitst mit tzikvaitchteh nuz und keekt avek (but he sits with wrinkled nose, and looks away, meaning he's haughty and acts as though everything around him is foul). R is uingeshtupped mit khokhma und a guten mann, takeh a mench (stuffed with knowledge and a good man, truly decent). And then, for the main course after these little appetizers, I told him the story of the chairman and my young black student, winding up with a simple epigram: "Zol er shtinkin frim kup"—literally, he should stink from his head, a not-too-oblique way of saying his head should lie in a pile of dung—to which my uncle roared and strongly agreed. There was no doubt after this that I could, and would always be able to, speak to my relatives. The bitter/sweet irony in this exchange is that out of their love for me my family had encouraged and supported me in becoming educated while at the same time knowing that by so doing a gap would open between us that might be unbridgeable, and we would lose each other. How many millions of times has this happened in American life? Gaps had opened between my family and me, of course. But there were also bridges.

After returning to Philadelphia, I went to Washington in August 1963 to join the great civil rights march organized by Bayard Rustin. The march was astonishing in its immensity, and everyone was clearly excited. Given the seriousness of the occasion, however, the marchers were relatively constrained. Most of the men wore suits and ties, the women dresses, and all walked arm in arm, tens of thousands, old and young, black and white, men and women, singing "We Shall Overcome." There was not a whiff of marijuana in the air. There were no histrionics. And at the end of the day we all heard Martin Luther King, Jr.'s great, hopeful speech.

Two of my Wisconsin friends who had moved to Washington to do research in the Library of Congress and teach at the University of Maryland were also at the march. I had been reading Antonio Gramsci's meditations on Machiavelli and state power in *The Modern Prince and other writings*[6] that had been translated and published a few years earlier (1959) and appreciating many of his critiques—of Marx, some of the later Marxists, Stalin, and the Soviet state. His conception of culture was not as rich as that of the neo-Marxists of the Frankfurt School, but his understanding of the political entanglements and consequences of cultural innovations was more sophisticated. Gramsci was, after all, the founder in 1921 of the Italian Communist Party, and understood far more concretely than the Frankfurt theorists what political action was about. But what kinds of institutions—economic, political, legal, social, and educational—would safeguard the democratic side of democratic centralism—an idea that Gramsci favored?

The idea of democratic centralism was essentially Lenin's, and it became overwhelmingly *centralism* in the Russian-Soviet context. At the march, I was introduced to a young woman, an assistant professor of history at one of the local universities, who had also been studying Gramsci's writings. We agreed it was unclear how socialism organized along the lines of democratic centralism could be developed in America, France, or England. Unlike Marković, she understood quite well that the cultures and political and legal traditions of each nation were considerably different and constrained all their members. But we both realized that Gramsci's views on the matter were essentially programmatic and undeveloped, shaped by his Italian experiences. Much thinking and studying would be required to gain a better understanding of the national contexts in which democratic centralism—or at least some forms thereof—might be viable. Within a month or two of this conversation, the young woman left the university for other parts, and, except for our conversation at the march, I never met or heard of her again.

I remark upon this because it was at the time quite unusual to find anyone, man or woman, but especially a woman, interested in and able to discuss Gramsci. Perhaps Flower and Anscombe could have—no doubt would have—but they were so exceptional as to prove the point. There were only two women graduate students at the University of Wisconsin who had participated in discussions with the much larger contingent of male students. Within a few years, this gender imbalance was corrected.

The interest in Gramsci's writings has since become largely historical. In reading Gramsci, it became even clearer that my sympathies and views were now closer to social democracy, of which the civil rights march in Washington seemed emblematic. And for this Marx was hardly needed. It was not at all surprising that my Wisconsin friends had similar views. We enjoyed and marveled at the march, and wondered whether this massive outpouring of people, following the Birmingham marches earlier in the spring, would finally persuade Kennedy that supporting the civil rights movement would be politically expedient. Although I'm sure some were there, I saw no one I knew, students or faculty, from Penn.

The spell of hopefulness cast by the march was broken within three months by the assassination of President Kennedy. The initial waves of suspicion in the wake of the assassination—was it the work of the CIA? the Soviet Union? Cuba?—that swept over a great many people, including students, collected into paranoid pools that slowly drained and after several years finally evaporated. The rapidly enacted Great Society programs of President Lyndon Baines Johnson provided a needed boost in morale for much of the nation. But the healing programs and the renewal of hope they had created were overshadowed all too soon. The Vietnam clouds that had been gathering for over a decade were darkening.

In 1965, I began to teach the two undergraduate courses in sociological theory, one semester of classical authors, another of contemporary. The theory texts were much fewer but suffered from deficiencies similar to the introductory texts. Once again I decided to use original sources, lecture, and lead discussions.

Each undergraduate student at Penn, regardless of major, was required to take one course in sociology, usually the introductory course. But unlike these courses, the theory courses drew students from a much smaller base, the sociology majors who were required to take them, and the occasional philosophy, political science, or history student interested in the subject matter.

Students seemed to enjoy the introductory classes I taught but said they were much more difficult than they had been led to expect. It was in teaching these courses that I discovered sociology at Penn—and likely at many other schools—was considered a "gut" course, a course one could pass with little effort and garner at least a "B." I, however, graded "on a curve," and accordingly gave many more Cs than As or Bs, and even a few Ds and one or two Fs. D or F in sociology? Unheard of!

I developed a reputation for being "tough," which I rather liked, but I also didn't want to deter students from majoring in sociology because I was considered *too* tough.

At the outset of one of his graduate seminars on Max Weber, Gerth announced that everyone would get at least a "B." He told us he only wanted students in the class who were interested in the subject; the others could stay away. The anxiety over grades since the end of the Second World War, he said, had become so obsessive that interest in grades was pathological and interfering with what students were learning. Whether one had obtained an overall average of 3.2 or 3.3 or 3.4 and so on was tallied up with the same sharp-penciled exactness and zeal as a Puritan calculating costs and profits in a countinghouse!.

Gerth was right. Many professors who fully understand this have nevertheless given in to student anxiety or the prospect of poor teaching evaluations and loosened their standards. Grade inflation and the concomitant devaluation of grades have been the inevitable results. I tried my best to resist this. With the exception of one or two graduate courses in which I followed Gerth's example, and the changing of a few undergraduate students' grades whose work was sufficiently on the edge from a B to a B+ or an A- to an A, I by and large succeeded.

I spent much of the summer of 1965 completing the writing of my dissertation (which I will comment upon in a later chapter), selecting the materials for my courses and deliberating on how to teach them.

I decided to divide each of the theory courses into three segments. One-third of the course in classical theory would be on Marx, another on Weber, and a final third on Durkheim. Each segment would begin with a brief biographical sketch of the theorist, including a discussion of the intellectual and social-cultural setting in which he began his work. The bulk of each segment would be taken up by an exposition of the theory and some of its contemporary developments. Each segment would conclude with a brief critique of the theory in question.

My aim in the Marx segment was not only to lay out the range of Marx's thinking from his youthful writings as a left Hegelian to his mature years as the author of *Capital*. I wanted to show the students that his was a supremely serious *intellectual* endeavor, not only (but of course also) polemical and political. He understood culture and history from Hegel, socialism and the collectivity of social classes from Saint Simon and Proudhon, utilitarian economics and individualism from the English economists and philosophers. The uniqueness of his work is in its creative weaving of these disparate intellectual strands into a single comprehensive theory, not German, not French, not English, but including and intending to surpass them all. Marx did not consider himself a sociologist—the word was hardly used when he wrote—but a political economist. Nevertheless, every social thinker in the generation that followed him, many of whom did call themselves sociologists, responded to his thought. The analytical and substantive shortcomings of his theories (some of which have been mentioned in previous chapters) were soon apparent. His economics, though illuminating in its elucidation of commodity production and the compulsive demands for their markets, was inadequate and faulty—utility theory, for example, had not yet been developed in his lifetime; his philosophy of history, essentially Western centered and based on assumptions of necessary progress, was shown by later scholarship to be misleading; his understanding of normative culture was virtually nonexistent, his view of the social world as consisting primarily of classes was simplistic and inadequate. And although hardheaded and realistic in many ways, he was also a utopian. But his theory also advanced the understanding of modern social life. Marx was the first great analyst of capitalism and of work. The following segments of the course were designed to show how other scholars had advanced his most general central theme, the nature of modernity, and developed this with greater richness and insight. Both Weber and Durkheim assimilated Marx's thought and supplanted it. Yet no one went to the front lines murmuring the names of Weber or Durkheim, whereas many did go to the front lines invoking Marx. This too—the hopes and aspirations Marx had projected—I wanted students to understand.

By a piece of good luck, I was invited to join the Shawnee Leadership Conference, a Quaker-sponsored group, for a week in August of 1965. This was to be held in Vermont. We would get free housing and food; there was swimming nearby, and going there would provide a much-needed and cheap vacation for my family and me. We packed ourselves again into our grill-less car—we'd had it for three years and found it really was reliable!—and drove to Vermont. As it turned out, several of the young people who had participated in the Selma-to-Montgomery civil rights marches in early spring would be arriving at the Shawnee Conference. The televised images of the nonviolent marchers set upon by the dogs and beaten by the club-wielding sheriff and his deputies flashed through my mind again as they had flashed coast to coast several months earlier and as they are still remembered today. I wanted to meet these young people. Some of them would be about the age of the students I would be teaching, and I wondered whether there would be any similarity of outlook between them. A majority of the young civil rights marchers who came to the Shawnee Conference were white. Like almost all other late adolescents I've known, they were playful and openly passionate in their beliefs. Some had been beaten and jailed. But this experience served only to affirm to them the rightness of their cause, and they had not wavered in declaring it. In one of several discussion sessions, an older marcher, perhaps in his early twenties, observed that it was a brave but simple thing to put one's body on the line and march, as they all had done. But the road ahead, he thought, would be much more difficult because it would require political and economic action. And to travel on this road, he concluded, many kinds of skills were needed, not merely brave bodies. I was impressed by this young man's judgment and tried to follow his career, but soon lost touch. After a week of talking with and listening to these young people and other counselors, my family and I returned to Philadelphia heartened and refreshed.

In early fall 1965 a Philadelphia friend, Michael Brodie, took me to hear Bayard Rustin speak at a luncheon of the local Jewish Workmen's Circle, a socialist group. I admired the precise quality of mind in Rustin's writings and was a bit in awe of and curious about the man who had organized the great civil rights march in 1963.

Rustin had light brown skin, was lean, tall, somewhat hawklike in appearance, intense in manner, and spoke in a slightly Anglicized accent. He was advocating a Marshall Plan for American cities and seeking the support of labor unions. It was a well-thought-out proposal, and he had won over the largely elderly audience. In the question period following the talk, someone asked Rustin whether he thought socialism would abolish evil. Rustin's answer was simple: socialism will reduce pain and suffering of many kinds but will not extinguish the capacity of people to do cruel things. Forty-some-odd years after Rustin proposed it, there has been some rebuilding in the large cities—in Philadelphia, Chicago, Minneapolis, Boston, New York—but much more deterioration in the smaller industrial cities and towns, the "rust belt," in which large unemployed populations languish. There is talk again of plans to rebuild American cities. Wars, poverty, disease, ignorance, and cruel acts have continued.

Except for the responses of a handful of exceptional students, most of the theoretical materials I tried to teach during the fall and spring semesters of 1965–1966—whether Marx's, Weber's, Simmel's

Durkheim's, Freud's, Malinowski's, Parsons, Mead's, Schutz's, or even Tocqueville's—fell like so many stones. Students did respond in the contemporary theory course to some of Mead's and Goffman's work and bits of Parsons' essays, but many had difficulty in the classical theory course in seeing society as a *system*—the sociological idea par excellence—rather than as a set of discrete, aggregated parts. The constraints of such noneconomic norms as legal contracts on economic activity that Durkheim analyzed, for example, were too challenging to the rationalist, self-interested bottom-line idea of the profit motive for most students comfortably to grasp, and, even when grasped, too much against the grain of received wisdom to believe. One can always get around contracts, sir!—as one student put it. Despite this preparatory cynicism for the adult world, the students were unfailingly polite, most of them studied (I think), but the materials were abstract, different from anything they had encountered before, and interest was low. In some part, I believe, this was due to the kinds of students who had come to Penn a few years earlier and were now juniors and seniors and finishing up. Had the radical temper beginning to affect students at Wisconsin, Berkeley, Chicago, and Columbia reached the more insular students at Penn, this might have served to enliven them.

Among the group I taught that year, however, were some very able students as well as a few brilliant ones. One of the students in my class wrote a paper that was published while she was still an undergraduate. She went on to get a PhD in sociology and has since made notable scholarly contributions. Two others went on to do graduate work in political science. And one young woman became in later years the president of the University of Pennsylvania. (I really don't remember what grade I gave her.) But the interest of students was uneven, and most did not have the money or the desire to pursue lengthy professional training; they went on to civil-service jobs or became schoolteachers or social workers. Sociology—at least my course—was not the "gut" students had expected. But sociology is not for everyone. In any case, within a decade all this changed, and Penn became a much-sought-after school with a livelier student body.

In reflecting on the theory courses after the year was over, it dawned on me that I was also contributing to the students' difficulties. I was treating the ideas too reverentially. They were being presented as though sacred, and I was acting as their priest, leading the student-congregation in their worship. But in setting the ideas above and beyond me, they must have appeared to the students as being even more distant from them. I needed to bring the ideas down to earth, to help the students make the ideas their own, to translate the abstractions of sociological theory into terms closer to the students' everyday experiences. Sociology isn't worth the paper it's written on if it doesn't help to illuminate your life—as indeed it had mine.

In addition to tapping my own life experiences and expressing my enthusiasm for the ideas, I decided in the second year also to recommend and occasionally assign novels and stories that would exemplify one or another theme of the course—by Dickens, Gogol, D. H. Lawrence, Melville, Thomas Mann, Sinclair Lewis, F. Scott Fitzgerald, Saul Bellow, Isaac Bashevis Singer, John Updike, and in following years several others. The idea of doing this occurred to me when a friend who had studied at M.I.T. with the great economist Paul Samuelson told me Samuelson had assigned Mann's wonderful novel *Buddenbrooks*[7] as the best exposition of mercantilism to be found. I followed this example and also yielded to some of my literary as well as sociological interests by commenting not only on the substance and sociological significance of the stories they were reading but also on differences in the language in which they were written. In this way, I could bring out aspects of the period and place—the culture and social makeup—of their composition. This would provide points of comparison with their own lives. As my old high school teacher said, there is more to a piece of writing than its overt meaning. To some extent, these literary materials served as exercises in self-reflection, and when successful helped students locate themselves. The following year (and thereafter) my teaching went well. The courses, however, were always considered tough.

Notes

1. Doubleday & Company, New York, 1961.
2. University of Pennsylvania Press, Philadelphia, 1996.
3. University of Pennsylvania Press, Philadelphia, 2008.
4. Free Press, New York, 1985.
5. Harvard University Press, Cambridge, MA, 2000.
6. International Publishers, New York, 1959.
7. Vintage Books, New York, 1994.

10

Pot and Protest

In 1965, the Vietnam War was rapidly moving toward the center of public concern. Students were apprehensive and at some universities already protesting. The duration of the draft had continued far beyond the Second World War in which it was last initiated, as my friends had predicted it would.

In fall 1965, several graduate students and professors organized a series of university-wide lectures by experts at Penn and other universities on the history, culture economy, and politics of Vietnam and other countries in the region. As the war grew in scale, so too did attendance at the lectures. Almost all the speakers contested the "domino theory"—the major reason the government had been giving over the past twenty years for the American involvement in the region. Even speakers who thought the domino theory might have some merit had strong reservations about its certainty. After many years of occupation by the Chinese, the Japanese, and the French, and an enforced division of the country, Vietnam was undergoing a massive internal struggle to become unified and regain full independence. If, after decades of struggle, the Viet Cong forces were to win, it was hardly likely they would hand the country back to the Chinese, from whom they had fought so hard to free themselves. Although sharing many things, each of the countries in Southeast Asia had distinct cultures and traditions as well as long, complex histories of political and economic relations with one another and with the West. They were all dependent on each other in some ways, but each also had strong traditions of independence. If one country were to become Communist, the others would certainly look on, but would be unlikely either apishly or fearfully to follow. The more the domino theory was invoked, the clearer it became to many of us that it was Cold War fear rather than actual understanding of the region that was driving the American engagement. None of us had a good idea of how to get a handle on this fear and calm it enough so that the situation in Southeast Asia could be more realistically appraised.

But there was more than fear involved, as we began to realize. Coupled with American fear was ignorance of the attitudes and concerns of the people in the region and the arrogant belief that against mere third-world countries American power and technology were insuperable. We had no means of proving otherwise. Only the future would tell.

In spring of 1966, a group of junior and senior professors from Penn, of which I was one, went to Washington to speak with our congressmen as well as with members of the administration. We were part of a nationwide assemblage of professors. Appointments had been made in advance. Our aim was to urge consultation with experts at the universities—not merely with the domino theorists of National Security and the Departments of Defense and State.

The congressmen listened to us politely; some seemed interested, talked with us, asked questions, and thanked us for coming to speak with them. The person sent by the administration to meet with us was unexpectedly rude and arrogant. He acted as though it were a pointless use of his valuable time to speak to such naïve types. We were sheltered and soft, his clipped manner seemed to imply, and couldn't be expected to understand the hard realities of the situation; he could barely conceal his contempt. The well-known experts on Southeast Asia among us were not acknowledged, not even recognized! This man was foolish and ignorant, and his manner only increased our antagonism toward the administration. But we also recognized that in his attitude the administration was showing its intransigence, and the United States would likely remain in the war until either Vietnam was defeated or another administration called an end to it.

Robert S. McNamara, the secretary of defense under Presidents Kennedy and Johnson, died in July 2009, thirty-four years after the Vietnam War ended. The "architect of the Vietnam War," as he was called, spent the last third of his life publicly acknowledging that "We were wrong," and urging us to re-evaluate our attitudes toward our presumed rational superiority. Fifty-eight thousand American lives were lost in the Vietnam War, and hundreds of thousands of Vietnamese lives as well. This is the burden he bore. It was finally over for him.

By 1967, protest marches were being held weekly in many American cities and broadcast on television screens for all to see and to hear the chanting of "Hey, hey LBJ, how many kids did you kill today!" Mohammed Ali became a national hero, not merely to boxing fans, when he refused to go into the army on religious grounds. After declaring to his draft board in a sentence much quoted thereafter that

"I ain't got no quarrel with them Viet Cong," Ali was stripped of his heavyweight boxing championship title and jailed. Some students began to flee the country, going to Canada, Sweden, and South America. Others—it is impossible to tell how many—quietly slipped into the countryside, where they attempted to live out of reach of authorities. Draft counseling centers sprang up in universities across the country. I joined such a center at Penn. Michael Brodie, a lawyer and one of my Philadelphia friends, became expert in a sub-field of law that was quickly developing aimed at finding legal recourse for resisting the draft.

I believe most professors tried, but it was impossible to keep all of this out of the classrooms. The anxiety and anger generated by the war blazed more fiercely every day. I had only to mention the name Karl Marx for some students—not all—to leap up as though ready to go to the barricades. Marx was unread, more associated with protest than with intellectual effort. Among other students, a mood of disaffection from the government and the general society was taking hold. A withdrawal of interest from politics, conventions of personal relationships, appearance, possessions, classes, studying, was spreading. This was not true of the majority of students, but of a sizeable enough minority to be seen everywhere. The use of marijuana and psychoactive drugs was becoming widespread and open. Whether or not said explicitly, it was as though many students had begun living according to the mantra associated with Timothy Leary: "Turn on, Tune in, Drop out." The few younger professors who got caught up in drugs and open sexual expression and experimentation soon left the university and perhaps academic life forever. The counterculture antedated the protest against the Vietnam War by some years and continued after the war ended. But the two accompanied each other, and for a time the energies in each formed a kind of synergy of protest.

The graduate students were also affected. They were older and ostensibly engaged in professional training. Yet many had developed the view that just about all organizations were corrupt. A provisional exception was granted retrospectively to university practices during the Second World War. Secrecy is anathema to the university's mission to teach and to produce and disseminate knowledge. But given America's powerful and dangerous enemies, the standard of free and open communication was suspended. Universities turned their research efforts into secret endeavors that would aid the American military. After the war ended, several influential atomic scientists, as well as many other scholars, expressed concern over constraints placed upon research sponsored by the military. Many naively assumed—despite the Cold War—that secret military research in the universities would be ended. Moreover, since the large and growing research facilities that had become central to universities were now being funded by a host of independent and national foundations not associated with the military, it was believed that universities hardly needed military funding anymore. Or didn't they?

With the increase of American involvement in Vietnam, many universities, Penn included, neither invoked the Cold War or the funding needs of their laboratories, but steadfastly denied any involvement in secret, military-sponsored research of any kind. After years of such denials, discovering that the universities had been untruthful all along and were still issuing false disclaimers was not exactly trust inducing. With mounting anger at this breach, students began describing the universities as "the soft underbelly of the system." As one of my more sardonic colleagues remarked, however limited students' understanding of the idea, at least they were beginning to have some recognition of society as a system.

The attrition rate among graduate students rose. Like the undergraduates, several graduate students were also dropping out, in part disillusioned by the university they had found to be, after all, as rotten as the rest of the society. Some asked me to bring my family and join them in a commune they were planning to form. They said it was unlikely I would get tenure; the university was just exploiting me and the other junior faculty and would let us go the first chance it had. I was touched by the affection of these bitter students but bade them good-bye and wished them good luck.

Had some of my sympathies reinforced the students' negative attitudes? Perhaps. I was against the war and disgusted with the university administration for having been dishonest. But I was certainly not alone in this. When secret research had been uncovered at Penn, the faculty senate publicly censured the president, which led to his resignation. And although I was not an advocate of the counterculture, nor did I indulge in its practices, I was curious about those practices, the modes of dress and display that were reminiscent of the agrarian life of colonial times, the ritual of passing a "joint" among persons at a small gathering, the simple musicality that had become threaded into the countercultural style. Except for disapproval of drugs and dismay at the anti-intellectualism of most of its adherents, I looked with favor on the efforts of many of the young to be more inclusive, to bring men and women, black and white, older and younger into the same community. Like many of my older colleagues, I was concerned about the consequences of the irresponsible sexuality that was being practiced and often imposed by the young upon each other. But I thought the breaking of some sexual taboos might have positive consequences. I tried, however, sometimes successfully, to adhere to Gerth's injunction to maintain and advocate rational standards. But effective advocacy also requires a sympathetic audience, or at least an audience with some affinity for what is being advocated.

The students were not only morally disillusioned. In some part also, many of the students who left had found the demands of graduate work in sociology (and perhaps in bourgeois life generally) too rigorous, finding they not only lacked but disliked the discipline needed to gain professional skills. They had complained all along of the difficulty of the graduate program and of their distaste for certain courses. I hope they found more congenial work.

Despite an increasing dropout rate, the Age of Aquarius was also becoming the Age of Sociology. Since sociology provided a perspective on society and in some quarters a critique, sociology became in this period of conflict and confusion one of the most popular subjects in the university, and the influx of new students far exceeded those leaving. There were at Penn almost three hundred undergraduate majors in sociology in 1967, and all classrooms were filled to overflowing. In the following year the number of majors in sociology jumped to four hundred; in 1969 to five hundred. The number of students accepted to the graduate program was also increasing. During the peak years, from roughly 1968 to 1973-4, the Department of Sociology at Penn—which numbered at most about twenty-five faculty members—gained forty-five new graduate students each year. In 2005, by contrast, the number of undergraduate majors had fallen to a fifth of what it had been in 1970; the number of graduate students had been reduced similarly. And these small numbers hardly reflect the interest in taking sociology courses during this period, which quickly ballooned into the thousands and by 1974 began as quickly to deflate.

The nine new instructors brought into the sociology department in the second half of the 1960s to teach the burgeoning numbers of students were in their mid-to-late twenties, about eight to ten years younger than I. They were liberal to left leaning, some leaning a bit more than others. All knew something about Marx, some more than others, but none was by any stretch of the imagination a Marxist or a socialist. They were decent, modest, middle-class, and liberal. All were cynical about power, and suspicious and fearful of those they believed were in any way associated with the powerful. Power, as one put it as only an academic would, is an onanistic aphrodisiac, used by those who wielded power to retain power. Their sympathies may have been with the downtrodden and the poor, but neither their words nor their work was much taken up with such people. They were of the middle and looked at and taught about the middle.

But the middle, it became clear, did not hold for long. With hardly a pause between them, in the next year and a half one eruption after another shook all the generations, young and old, and it seemed that, if the country weren't torn to pieces, it would be changed forever.

In late fall of 1967 Eugene McCarthy began his campaign for the presidency. Many students, excited by McCarthy's antiwar and antigovernment platform, began to campaign for him door to door. The McCarthy campaign generated hope among students on campuses across the country and boosted antiwar efforts. But for a great many of the students actively engaged, the combination of pot and protest served to narrow their understanding and their interest. After many years of protest, too much of the world became "political." Culture, history, institutions, morality—all fell for them under the cynical wheels of power.

In February 1968 Walter Cronkite announced to the nation that the war in Vietnam could not be won and urged that we should negotiate a peace settlement.

In early spring of 1968, students at the University of Pennsylvania occupied College Hall, the main administrative building. Despite denials by the university administration, some—ambiguous—information had been found that secret research was still being conducted. Distrusting and angry, students demanded access to research records that would clarify the matter. The university resisted. The students took eight-hour shifts round the clock in manning the building; they were polite, did not interfere with classes or university business, but vowed to remain until all records of research were made public. The chief of the Philadelphia police, Frank Rizzo—a big, tough cop with a reputation for bashing heads, but also with an uncanny ability to get people to call him Frank within thirty seconds—dispatched to the university two riot trucks bristling with helmeted men, tear gas masks, guns, and clubs. They parked on the street nearest to the occupied building, motors running in readiness, while the chief informed the provost they were ready to quell the rioters. The provost thanked the chief (whom I believe he always addressed as "Chief," never as "Frank") and assured him he would be called, if needed. This piece of good judgment by the provost helped keep the campus relatively calm. The trucks eventually drove off. The students finally broke into the files but found no evidence of secret research.

In April 1968 Martin Luther King, Jr. was shot and killed. Riots broke out in many dozens of cities nationwide. Television and newspaper reports showed fires and looting in Los Angeles, Detroit, Chicago, Washington, Cleveland, and New York. Philadelphia rioting was contained and subsided quickly.

Among students, civil rights issues were no longer paramount. King's death was shocking, a horrible example of racial hatred. He was mourned, but students' interests were fastened on the war and the upcoming presidential election. Some students threatened to shut down the Democratic convention in Chicago, if McCarthy or an antiwar candidate were not nominated. McCarthy won the Wisconsin primary in spring of 1968.

Johnson halted the bombing in Vietnam and withdrew from the presidential race.

In late spring 1968 tens of thousands of students and workers rioted in Paris. And thousands more radical students in Bordeaux, Berlin, Frankfurt, London, Rome, Madrid, Barcelona, Mexico City, and Prague were photographed for all the world to see marching and rioting in antigovernment demonstrations and being beaten by the police.

In June 1968, after winning the California primary election, Robert Kennedy was shot and killed.

In August 1968 national television networks at the Democratic convention showed the Chicago police clubbing and tear-gassing thousands of antiwar demonstrators while Mayor Daley looked on.

In the fall of 1968, some liberals declared they would vote for Richard Nixon rather than Hubert Humphrey because Humphrey's stand on ending the war was vacillating. The war was a Democrats' war, they argued. Nixon would end it.

In late fall of 1968, Nixon was elected President of the United States. Bombing in Vietnam was resumed.

In 1969, the Stonewall riots against gays in New York's Greenwich Village evoked another nationwide reaction. Gay students at Penn and other universities began to reveal themselves and drew responses of disapproval and indifference. The administrative secretary of the sociology department was volubly affronted when she saw two young women kissing in the hallway. Declaring that the world was going berserk, she lobbied faculty unsuccessfully for a few months to have public decency rules enacted that would sanction such conduct at the university. In one of my classes, a sallow, scrawny male student appeared one day with reddened lips, skirt, high heels, and parasol. His legs remained unshaved. Students snickered but said nothing; nor did I. He sashayed out of class at the end of the hour apparently unfazed. He didn't look very attractive either way.

The national furor unleashed by the war in the second half of the 1960s seemed like the madness of biblical times when cities fell and lions roamed the streets. A revolution of sorts had been in progress, but it was not the kind envisioned by Marx or Lenin or Trotsky or Shachtman or De Leon or Gramsci. I wondered whether Hannah Arendt's observation on revolutions would apply to this one too, that like the revolution of the planets, the one now in progress would also describe a circle and after a time return to or near its origin.

I was asked in early spring of that insane year of 1968 to take over the administration of the undergraduate program in sociology, beginning in the fall. I accepted. Many of us were finding it difficult to do much intellectual work that year. Accounts were coming in almost by the hour, each one more disturbing than the other, of terrible destruction in Vietnam and turmoil in the country and the world. Herminio Martins, an English friend who had been at Penn a couple of years earlier, wrote and asked what was happening in the country. I could only answer with a couple of words: frenzy and furor.

To do something positive, to immerse myself in practical work that had the promise of building rather than tearing down, was an unexpected and welcome opportunity. I had some thoughts on how the undergraduate program might be improved. I also wanted to foster greater trust among the undergraduates.

Junior faculty taught the majority of undergraduate courses. Before the spring semester was over, I canvassed several of the senior faculty to ask whether any who were not already teaching an undergraduate course would consider doing so. With one immediate exception, that of E. Digby Baltzell, their responses were noncommittal or equivocal—a bit like members of Congress, I thought, who weren't certain what was happening but wanted to keep options open.

Baltzell told me he preferred to teach undergraduates. Whatever they did after finishing college, whether they went to work or into politics or business or law or medicine, very few undergraduates went on to become professors. Graduate courses were intended to train only the small handful of future professors. It was more important, he thought, to give the much larger number of students who will take up a wide range of posts some perspective on society. And the best place to do that was while they were undergraduates. This was an example of what my grandmother would have called "sekhel"—good sense.

The other exception to the senior faculty's equivocations on teaching undergraduates occurred about a year later. This exception, which in a few years proved to be a fateful one for me, was Reneé Fox. The medical school had brought her in as their new medical sociologist. I had read one of her essays on unanticipated consequences in experimentation, "The Case of the Floppy Eared Rabbits," and found it illuminating and, not least, delightful to read. She wrote and thought well, an uncommon combination for a sociologist. Several of us believed she really belonged in the sociology department, and after brief departmental discussion she was voted in as a joint member. As soon as I asked, she said she would expect to teach an undergraduate course, adding that faculty in her view should teach both undergraduate as well as graduate students. I very much liked her intelligence and candor, and most of all her principles—characteristics I would get to know well in later years when she became chair of the department and we worked together.

At the first faculty meeting, early in September, when I was formally introduced as the new undergraduate chair, Dorothy S. Thomas, an internationally famous demographer in the department with perhaps a year or two to go before retirement, surprised me (and I'm sure everyone else) by making a short, very pointed statement on the need for the well-known senior faculty to teach at least one course to the undergraduates. "Students come here to hear you," she said, pointing to Thorsten Sellin, the internationally known Swedish criminologist who had been a member of the department for many years, "and me," she added. "And it's only right that we teach them." Sellin made indecipherable Swedish-sounding noises (he had not taught an undergraduate course in many years) while other senior members of the department who were also not teaching undergraduate courses sat stony-faced with eyes averted, not knowing to whom Thomas' unerring finger would next point.

I hardly knew Dorothy Thomas, had not talked to her much since I came to the department, and did not speak to her about giving an undergraduate course. But I certainly did like her! She was a tough, no-nonsense person, as she had to be in order to get as far as she did. She was the first woman professor in the Wharton School. In the mid-1940s, she published a two-volume study of the economic effects of internment upon Japanese Americans during the Second World War. In 1991, almost fifty years later, the United States Supreme Court relied on her earlier study in order to establish reparation payments. She had begun the Population Studies Center at Penn, had done pathbreaking research, and trained dozens of first-rate demographers. She was small, dark-haired, wiry, and indomitable. She was also a fierce chain-smoker. I didn't think so at the time, but in retrospect, it may well be that with the exception of being American born, Protestant, well educated, a professional, and very forthright—a pretty large set of exceptions!—aspects of Thomas' appearance and manner were a bit reminiscent of my mother (but only when my mother, who was also a fierce smoker, was excited. Normally, my mother was gentle and quiet-spoken.). Thomas had been married to the late W. I. Thomas, one of the founders of the Chicago school of sociology, to whom she referred, when she spoke of him at all, as "W. I." Some of the junior as well as senior faculty were intimidated by her and used to make silly jokes that would in some way be diminishing of her. But in fact, she was shy, hiding behind her bark, and responded openly and attentively to anyone who was straightforward with her. I believe Thomas did give an undergraduate course on demographic methods in spring of 1969, but Sellin, smiling but essentially removed, demurred, relinquishing the task to his loyal protégé, Marvin Wolfgang. Wolfgang continued to teach a popular undergraduate course in criminology for several years, until he took over as chair of the department.

Unlike sociology undergraduates in many other universities, the ones at Penn did not have a "club," an organization in which they could meet with one another, discuss ideas, exchange information about courses and professors in sociology and other departments, explore graduate training, career options, and so on. If the club developed well it might—I hoped it would—bolster student morale and make useful recommendations to the department about teaching formats and new courses.

I set about trying to get such a club started. A few senior and junior students in my courses were eager to be the nucleus, and so the club was launched with biweekly meetings. The membership was never large, but there was a stable core of about twenty to twenty-five students, and they were effective in calling the attention of many other sociology majors and undergraduates in general to happenings in the department. They also organized a pizza party (sans beer) each semester and prevailed upon the chair of the department to fund it. All this was good for students as well as faculty.

One of the senior professors asked me in a tone both quizzical and critical why I was doing "all this"—meaning, I thought at first, why was I wasting my time with undergraduates. We happened to meet while walking across campus, and the tone of his question seemed overtly friendly. But I thought I also detected small notes of anxiety and asperity in what he asked. He was not asking me what my motivations were, which was of no concern to him, but what my purposes were, what I was attempting to achieve by dong "all this." He was a fairly intelligent man, somewhat puffed up—the kind Gerth called a "careerist"—and made much of his ability to get research grants. But the truth is, he was not much more than a glorified technician, and his many research reports, doubtless briefly useful to policymakers, were soon out of date and left to disintegrate in the library archives. Nevertheless, he was a senior professor, and his personal as well as professional appraisal of me could affect my future promotion.

Rather than answer him simply and directly, which would have been the wiser course, I replied flippantly that I believed in socialism in our time, and this was a step in that direction. In responding this way, I was addressing the barely sounded anxious notes underlying his overt question. Socialism, after all, is concerned with the common good. My response, I realized a nanosecond later, was a passive-aggressive needling of him, a rebuke for his having been remiss in allowing the undergraduate program and students to languish. In neglecting to perform an important part of their professorial duties, he and some of his colleagues had been unconcerned for any good other than their own. Would my efforts with the undergraduate program—socialist indeed!—embarrass him into teaching? He laughed, and I hoped he hadn't caught the implied slap of my reply. Before turning off to his destination he made a point of telling me he had just received another research grant. Why was he telling me this? If this man, a senior professor and at least fifteen years older, were so needy of approval from even a lowly instructor, he could be dangerous. I congratulated him and thought to myself, *So? Go stand on your head!* We never became more than nodding colleagues. I found out many years later that he had been an orphan, and by dint of ambition and hard work was able to channel his obviously good native intelligence into becoming a professor at the University of Pennsylvania. Quite an accomplishment! But one needs good parents or good early models to become a good teacher. He soon removed himself to another department, where he managed never to teach an undergraduate course.

The anxiety aroused among junior faculty when there was uncertainty in dealing with senior colleagues was palpable. One of the wags among the junior professors suggested that the first line of *The Communist Manifesto* be brought up to date by including the "class struggles" between senior professors and junior professors. In any event, I was obviously no exception to this, but the knowledge of other job possibilities, should I not be promoted at Penn, kept me on a slightly even keel. Some junior professors are extraordinarily adroit at setting out very early to determine who the influential senior professors are. Once they've mapped the influence terrain, they attempt to cultivate friendships with these professors. One junior professor, a bright and attractive man, was astonishingly successful at this sort of thing and within a short time managed, to the envy and anxiety of his fellow instructors, to establish friendly, first-name relationships with a large raft of senior professors in several departments. But the energy and time he expended in doing this left him with little of either to write or publish a word. To his astonishment, if not to that of his peers, he was not promoted and left the university. Some sort of public-relations work would have been better suited for him.

As I was preparing to leave the University of Wisconsin for Penn, Joe Elder, my thesis adviser, counseled me not only to do my best in teaching, but also to discharge my committee duties faithfully, and, no less important, to maintain a civil and friendly demeanor with all my colleagues. I consider ad hominem arguments nonarguments and except when greatly provoked rarely descend to them. Although I might on occasion have such thoughts, I also never call anyone stupid or an idiot to his or her face. Nevertheless, I was known in Wisconsin for not hesitating to challenge anyone, professor or student, if I thought his or her views were greatly mistaken. If I were to follow the implications of Elder's advice, I would have to curb my propensity to challenge. Very few people, certainly very few professors, are like Marković—open to criticism if it will improve their thinking. I think I can accept criticism, if it's made honestly and without rancor. Whatever challenging I did would have to be done politely, gently, and preferably in private. I think I was succeeding in not irritating most of my colleagues, since several other senior professors liked the changes I was making and were overtly encouraging. But I must admit, my lips parted occasionally when I thought certain intolerable idiocies were being done or spoken.

In mid-semester, my mother died. Two weeks earlier, she had heard the television replay of Vladimir Horowitz's return to Carnegie Hall after many years of absence and seclusion. His playing was wonderful, with no loss of mastery, and we spoke about his recital with pleasure. The grief over her death gripped me for most of the academic year. I went to Buffalo for her funeral and to be with my father, sister, aunts, and uncles, and participated in the Jewish ritual of mourning. I returned to the piano after a hiatus of over twenty years and played the easier of some of her favorite pieces. I put a great deal of energy into the undergraduate program, trying to stave off the melancholy, which finally began to recede. I did not appreciate until then the unfathomable depth of such feeling. After several months I was able to resume reading and concentrating on my work. Her life had been a mangle of work, duty, sacrifice, hopes, and suffering. But there had been some pleasure and love. I knew that.

11

Negation of the Negation

In summer of 1969, I decided to revise my dissertation for publication. The dissertation was an analysis of the sort some philosophers make of theories in the physical sciences in which underlying categories are brought out and their meanings appraised. Arthur Pap's book *The Apriori in Physical Theory*[1] (1946), is an example. This had not often been done for the social sciences, and not yet for the most ambitious theoretical enterprise by an American social scientist in the twentieth century, namely Talcott Parsons' theory of social action.

What struck me as I studied Parsons' work was the prevalence in his formulations of necessary reason. In his first work, *The Structure of Social Action*,[2] he believed he had found a set of categories fundamental to and necessary for an adequate scientific theory of the many components that make up social action. These categories were not in themselves the scientific theory but the framework for such a theory. But then, in his following works, in which he was developing a scientific theory, new, substantive categories were brought out. They too were considered necessary for understanding the makeup and functioning of social life. Although fascinating and insightful, this was, to say the least, an extraordinary tack in a scientific theory that is supposed to yield propositions of sufficient reason—that is to say, propositions that with the appropriate qualifications can be used to make predictions. Of course, one could say—and I am more inclined as I get older to say this—predictions are nice, if you can have them, but coherent understanding and insight into the social world are more important. And, indeed, Parsons' work was producing a great deal of coherent understanding and insight. But this was not the sole contribution Parsons was content to make. He was also explicit in wanting to develop a theory capable of making predictions. Given the form of his reasoning, however, he would be unable to do so. Why then did he pursue this line of reasoning?

None of the many critiques of Parsons' work I had read called attention to the form of his reasoning. But the more I read in Parsons, the more his reasoning appeared to me to be analogous to that of Kant's. Indeed, many of his formulations were linguistically similar to Kant's; rather than saying, for example, "if x, then y"—a statement of sufficient relation—he would say that y was *impossible* without x—a statement of necessary relation. Was Parsons, like Kant, also trying to resolve skeptical dilemmas, trying to construct a foundation for social knowledge that could hold fast against the buffetings of relativist arguments, ideologies, claims, viewpoints, approaches? I thought this was very likely the case and set about in my dissertation, which was titled *The Apriori in Talcott Parsons' Social Theory*, to explore and, if possible, confirm it.

This was hardly all. Although I considered the central analysis of my dissertation sound, I realized in continuing to read Parsons' work that many parts of what I had written were unsatisfactory. Parsons was remarkably consistent in the basic principles of his thinking, but there were many new developments and shifts of emphasis in his work over the years to which I had not been sufficiently attentive. I had taken his earlier formulation of the kind of theory he was trying to develop as final. In fact, he had in his early as well as later work many such formulations that were dissimilar, not well or even at all integrated. Moreover, I had caught glimmerings of a barely stated assumption underlying his work of a much larger whole, a kind of metaphysical orientation, of which his work and the actualities in the social world to which it referred were related. Puzzles therefore remained, at least for me, as to what kind of theory he was trying to construct.

In the years following my dissertation, a critical literature arose on Parsons' theory that was of a vehemence I had encountered only in political diatribes, never before in scholarly critiques. Claims were made that Parsons' theories were ahistorical and could not deal with change. These allegations, which I knew from my study of Parsons' work to be ignorant and false, were but a prelude to personal attacks. Parsons was characterized as a bourgeois ideologue ensconced in Harvard, the apex of academic privilege, where he was contriving theories that served to safeguard the status quo.

Alvin Gouldner, one of my former teachers, took the lead among these critics. In a book-length assault, *The Coming Crisis of Western Sociology*[3] (1970), mainly against Parsons, but also against Erving Goffman, Gouldner mounted an attack of unrelenting fury. I had never read any scholarly work like this before. Gouldner portrayed Parsons' theories as obstacles to human freedom and betterment, and with the exception of a bit here and there, must be struck down and surpassed.

If his words had been translated into physical actions, Gouldner would have been charged with assault and battery.

Gouldner's book was written in a national environment of social and political turmoil. Younger people, certainly younger academics, were the most vociferous in challenging one another and others on "where they stood," or "where they came down" on a variety of issues, political, personal, and among academics, professional. The professional etiquette of respect for colleagues of different opinions was dismissed as an artifice to preserve the status quo. Class and its near twin, power, were the enemies, and they were sought and found among virtually all "establishments" in the country, universities included. Although some older academics had sympathy for the sentiments of their younger colleagues, most held fast to scholarly standards of objectivity, evidence, and consistent reasoning. There were exceptions, however. Scholarly standards once held sacrosanct were swept away by the winds of protest.

My responses to Gouldner's book were several. From my experiences as his student twenty-two years earlier, when he was in his early thirties, I knew him to be very bright but also quick to anger. Stories of his verbal assaults on those with whom he disagreed were common. I was not surprised to learn that his anger had at least once boiled over into physical expression. In June 1968, the *New York Times* published a story that he had physically beaten a graduate student at Washington University in St. Louis.

Yet, despite my wariness, I still felt some gratitude to him. He was the teacher who had introduced me to the great social thinkers Weber, Durkheim, and Parsons. He had insisted my arguments be backed by rock-hard reasoning and evidence, and had worked to help me come as close to this standard as I possibly could. Marx, he had once said, had made a man of him, Merton a scientist. He did not ask his students to be Marxists, but he expected no less than rigorous, scientific work from them.

It was as a skeptical scientist that I examined Gouldner's most recent appraisal of Parsons. His book was a kind of sociology of knowledge, a field of which his teacher, Merton, was an exponent. Marx, Mannheim, Max Scheler, among others, were the forerunners of the effort to clarify the social sources of ideas. Unless monitored by scrupulous standards of comparative and historical evidence, studies in this vein could give way to irresponsible attributions of motive and thus of substance. Yes, Newton was a mystic trying to reach God. Did this make his celestial mechanics scientifically worthless, a mere artifice to hear behind each formula the whisperings of the angels?

There is a critical counterexample to Gouldner's argument that revealed his evidence to be irrelevant and his reasoning unsupported. The counterexample is in Noam Chomsky's work, professional position, and political attitudes. Chomsky is a professor at M.I.T., not exactly the nadir of bourgeois academic privilege. In necessarily abstract terms, his work analyzes the common, deep structure of *all* languages and certain of the rules that permit meaningful utterances to be made. Parsons' work, also in necessarily abstract terms, analyzes the common, deep structure of *all* societies and certain of the mechanisms that permit societies to function. There are many other points of comparison, such as the Platonic and Kantian-like qualities of their constitutive categories, the assumptions they both make of ubiquitous human creativity and voluntarism in speech and action, as well as many others.

There is a striking analogy between Chomsky's and Parsons' theories. There is also an analogy in their professional positions. Given Gouldner's argument, one would expect the allegations made against Parsons also to apply to Chomsky. But of course they do not. How could one explain in Gouldner's terms the fact that, far from "safeguarding the status quo," Chomsky is a political radical who is vigorously critical of the status quo?

Instead of grounding his analysis in comparative evidence, Gouldner had lapsed into seeing under every word of Parsons the mutterings of an imagined persecutor, an abridger of freedom. And although Gouldner invoked a future "freedom," it was a freedom that was undefined and empty, and the society in which this empty freedom could flourish was therefore also undefined and empty, a void for his readers' fantasies to fill. Gouldner's Marxism was hardly the expansive and substantive kind of a Marković. In practice, the Marxism of Gouldner's book was sloganeering and demagogic, intent on exposing and destroying bourgeois ideology, but masquerading as science. The more I thought about this anomaly to Gouldner's argument, the more convinced I became that Gouldner's animus against Parsons was neither rational nor even political, but derived from some other source. The case Gouldner was making against Parsons was too ferocious, too personal, too laden with appeals for an empty "freedom" to be considered rational. But I did not then or to this day have a clear understanding of what the source of Gouldner's animus could be. This was the more puzzling since Parsons was a well-known liberal and outspoken advocate of equal rights for African

Americans, Asians, Jews, Hispanics, women, and radicals. Indeed, he had been placed on McCarthy's "black list" for his outspoken support of alleged Communists at Harvard! Parsons hardly had the attitudes of a conservative thinker. I knew I would have to reckon with Gouldner's analysis in my book. At this point I also knew what the title of my book would be, *Ideology and Social Knowledge*.[4] I would clarify the distinction between the two. Marx, a highly educated product of the nineteenth century, asked that his work not to be considered as ideology but as science, and judged as such. Evidence, logical coherence, and comprehensiveness are the rational, scientific standards to be used. Parsons' work is the product of a highly educated social theorist of the twentieth century. As knowledge, it should also be evaluated by the same standards applied to Marx's or to any scientific theory. And like any other scientific theory, Parsons' theory should be open to rational improvement, and replaced as a better, more comprehensive one is formulated. I was sure of my ground. I was also distressed that Gouldner, whose intelligence I had once admired, had apparently thrown over the standards he had held high and taught me to abide by. I never heard a word from him.

For the book I was planning to write I also decided to study the work of several philosophers and logicians who dealt with matters kindred to those of Parsons—Anscombe, Ernest Nagel, Charles Taylor, G.H. von Wright, among others. I applied for a sabbatical year beginning in fall 1971, during which time I would write what I hoped would be a much-improved book.

Other than Joe Elder, my thesis adviser, I knew only one other person with whom I could discuss the range of issues I wanted to write about, Herminio Martins. I had met and become friendly with Herminio a few years earlier when he had spent a year as a visiting professor at Penn. He was part of an active intellectual community in England and knew many of the people who wrote for the *New Left Review*, including Perry Anderson. Herminio was now a lecturer at St. Antony's College, Oxford, and encouraged us to visit. My wife and I agreed that among foreign countries England would be easier since we could more or less speak the language. In June 1971, borrowing some money from my father-in-law and ordering our first new car to be delivered in London, we set off.

Notes

1. Russell & Russell, London, 1968.
2. Free Press, Glencoe, IL, 1949.
3. Basic Books, New York, 1970.
4. Blackwell Publishers, Oxford, 1973.

12

Emanations

With their vast collections of books, periodicals, manuscripts, and records of all kinds, the great libraries of London, Paris, Rome, Milan, Madrid, Berlin, Leipzig, New York, Washington, Harvard, Yale, Oxford, and Cambridge are to the modern world what the library of Alexandria was to the ancient. Although the increasing digitization of the world's reading matter in the twenty-first century may place access to these intercontinental materials within everyone's easy reach, in 1971 it took many hours of air travel and days of finding and settling into living quarters before I could step into the great, round reading room of the British Museum Library in London.

The curved rows of the library's tables and lamps and the many scholars bent over them reading and scribbling greeted me. This was the room in which Marx had worked for over twenty years, sorting through the data of manufacture in the blue books that formed the empirical basis of his analysis in *Capital*. The attendant told me many first-time visitors asked where Marx had sat. I asked too. "You'll have to try each seat, guv," the attendant answered me, "until you feel the emanations."

About two days a week, I went to the Library of the British Museum or the fine smaller reference library at Swiss Cottage, near where we lived in Highgate, to do my research. All of the writing I did at home. As far back as I can remember, each visit to a library, whether large or small, has engendered an experience in me difficult to describe; I have a sense of safety and well-being mixed with excitement and an urge to enter and explore the wonders that will be revealed in the pages of the books. I have always had this experience in libraries, even foreign-language libraries, wherever they are located. It is akin to the experience the great blind poet and writer Jorge Luis Borges spoke of when he sat among the nine hundred thousand books of the National Library of Argentina in Buenos Aires, of which he was the director. They are, he said, his windows to the world. One does not need to read the books to feel this; one merely needs to be among them. Walter Benjamin describes something like this experience in his essay "Unpacking My Books." But I am a child of The Book, as were many of my teachers, and so too were Marx and Benjamin, and perhaps to this fact may be attributed one of the sources of the experience I am trying to convey.

After we were settled in London, Herminio introduced me to Leslie Sklair, a former student of his teaching sociology at the London School of Economics. Sklair read portions of my manuscript as they were turned out and made useful comments. Henry and Ruth Cooperstock, American sociologists on leave from the University of Toronto with whom we had become friends, lived nearby. Henry had studied with Merton and Seymour M. Lipset. He also read parts of my manuscript and made helpful comments. Friends in Philadelphia, particularly David Lavin, who had lent me his portable Olivetti on which I typed my manuscript, and his wife, Marguerite, wrote encouraging letters. Herminio also introduced me to Roland Robertson, a sociologist who was encouraging of my work and with whom I am still in contact. Except for one event that shook me deeply for several weeks and I feared might scuttle the whole project—the death of my sister in January 1972—the book was completed in eight months of steady, hard work.

In February of 1972 I was visited by a graduate student from Penn. He was a historian working on an aspect of modern German history, and he brought some newspapers from Germany he thought I would find interesting. He had taken a reading course with me on the Frankfurt School, and we had spent many hours discussing Georg Lukács' work. Lukács had died six months earlier. The German newspapers the student brought had long obituary articles on Lukács' influence and work. Again I wondered how Lukács, who had written with such delicacy and insight on esthetic forms in which the psyche is expressed, was able to shift gears so suddenly, consign the great literature he had once prized to a historical attic, and become a spokesman for and analyst of politics in art. This transformation had taken place in the few years after his book *History and Class Consciousness*,[1] was condemned by the Soviet critics. How had he been able to throttle his sensibility and intelligence? He said he was making a "wager with history." In his last years he had been working on his esthetics. I had not read this last two-volume work and don't think I ever will. History had won out.

I finished the writing of my book in April of that year and set about looking for a publisher. Yet again, Herminio came to my aid. He introduced me to an editor at Basil Blackwell publishers, who sent the manuscript out for evaluations. In my mind, the book was a kind of long letter to Parsons. But beyond that, it was intended to be read by the small number of experts in the field and was not the kind to make money. University presses publish this kind of book as an academic service. After almost two months of anxious waiting the evaluations came in; Basil Blackwell agreed to publish the book in England and also arranged for their American associate, Wiley-Halsted Press, to bring the book out in the United States. This was an enormous relief for me. My promotion to associate professor with tenure and my family's well-being depended upon the publication of this book.

I wondered what my radical friends might make of this book. Would they even read it? It was a very far cry from *Studies on the Left*. Parsons had become the black beast of the radicals, but I looked upon his work with favor. Would I be viewed as a turncoat? I had been intellectually critical of Marx's work for years and had not been shy about stating these criticisms, but never for a moment, either as critic of Marx or praiser of Parsons, had I given up my conviction in the value of a socialist society. My guess was that the book would be too specialized to be read by many but that it would cast a pall upon me nonetheless. If this actually happened, so be it. I believed in the book and thought it made a contribution. As for those who would challenge what I wrote on ideological grounds, I would say, as my grandmother might have said, "Ikh hob zay alle in buhd"—literally, "I have them all in the bath," which means they can go jump in the lake.

I found many things in the writing of this book, but short of recapitulating all that I wrote, a few may be mentioned here. First, some part of what I called Parsons' metaphysical orientation, of which I had had an earlier inkling, came into much clearer view. This was close to the philosophy of organism of Alfred North Whitehead, one of the philosophers who had influenced Parsons' understanding of science. One of my professors, Marvin Farber, told us that in lecturing on cosmology Whitehead once struck his forehead with the palm of his hand and said, "By this act I have affected the farthest star in the universe." This little anecdote, so typical of Whitehead's ability to find the simple example that expresses the essence of a complex idea, reflects Whitehead's belief in the interconnectedness and dynamism of all things. The gases, elements, galaxies, stars, and planets are not simply there, stacked up and inert as though in some kind of interstellar warehouse. They continually act on each other and on us, sometimes with great, sometimes with small effect. But reasonable though we might consider this belief to be for the objects of the natural sciences,

Whitehead intended its scope to include biological, moral, esthetic, social, and psychological things as well—that is to say, *all* things—and this is not, nor perhaps can ever be, fully articulated by the limited reach of scientific understanding, whether of modern science or the science that will develop in the future. It is a belief that for Whitehead was derived partly by speculation, partly by rethinking the traditions of philosophical cosmology and metaphysics, and partly by generalized inference from what was then known—a kind of *impress*, as he might say, the universe made upon him. But many things are not known. New physical, biological, esthetic, and social phenomena continually appear. Furthermore, as Whitehead himself emphasized in his discussion of misplaced concreteness, distinct, nonreductive principles organize the phenomena of each domain, physical, biological, moral, psychological, social, and so on. The metaphysical-cosmological belief in a supra organizing principle that organizes, but does not reduce, all the subsidiary organizing principles, which is what the philosophy of organism aims for, remains unrealized, not more than a belief. And in this sense, it is a kind of higher physics, a few-times-removed cousin, perhaps, to the cosmology of Spinoza. But as with all beliefs, this one orients the holder to think about and look at things in a certain way.

The social sciences in Parsons' time were even more fragmented than they are in ours. In the 1930s they were largely atheoretical and empirical. Each had gathered much information, but their findings were often unconnected and thus yielded only a partial understanding of human actions. Human activity was increasingly portrayed either in psychological, economic, social, cultural, or political terms. Yet, although not well understood or recognized, at some point the subject matter of any one of the human sciences always touches the subject matters of all of the others.

Given his organicist assumptions, Parsons set himself to develop a theory that would relate the findings of the social sciences, if not the social sciences themselves. Human action always consists of psychological, economic, political, social, and cultural elements related in complex ways. The understanding of the nature and relations of these elements in social life has been the overarching aim of his theory of social action.

Parsons, however, was not only a theorist. He set about translating his theory into practice by founding the Department of Social Relations at Harvard, which introduced students to the full range of the social sciences. This department flourished for about twenty years and trained a generation of creative and eminent scholars.

Much of Parsons' epistemology is Kantian, as I tried to demonstrate, but not his metaphysics. He believed in an actual world of interrelated objects that can be analyzed. He studied and was respectful of those who worshipped a Supreme Being and analyzed their beliefs and practices. But although a descendant of Jonathan Edwards and son of a Congregationalist minister who became head of Marietta College in Colorado, he was a "backsliding Protestant," as he characterized himself, implying that he had moved away from observing the ritual practices of his forbearers and those he studied. I shared his organicist and epistemological views; indeed, the implicit organicism in his work was one of the reasons for its appeal to me.

Although it is unclear whether Marx held metaphysical organicist presuppositions, it is not completely out of the question that he might have had them. He had studied the cosmologies of the Greek atomists and written a dissertation on them. One might see a metaphorical extension between the Epicurean view of the conditions of the movement of atoms, which he had analyzed in his dissertation, and his later views of the social environment of individual human actions. Neither atoms nor persons function in a void. But this is not quite yet organicism; there is only an analogy and an implied interconnection in his dissertation between different things. A cosmology of sorts is suggested by Engels' *Dialectics of Nature*,[2] but this seems in its ultimate projection more reductionist than organicist. While not without interest, the question of Marx's cosmological-metaphysical views has not, to my knowledge, been carefully explored.

I much admired Parsons' efforts and accomplishments but was also quite critical and saw several serious shortcomings in them. The many qualities of action had been abstracted by him to yield a four-function framework, but the relations among the functions—how energy and resources from any one is transferred to the others—was unevenly understood. Moreover, the propositions Parsons was using in characterizing the workings of each of the four functions were logically heterogeneous. Some part of the work of the economy, for example, could be explained by laws that yielded predictions. Cultural meanings, on the other hand, could be understood after the fact, so to speak, by interpreting the significance of human actions that had occurred. I sketched four explanatory modes that I thought Parsons was using but that remained poorly related in his work. This left his theory vulnerable to breaking apart into four different emphases, in which concentrating on any one might give scant or even no attention to the other three. The questions of political or social structure might become so predominant, for example, as to ignore cultural or psychological influences, or vice-versa. The explanatory problem was something I thought I might turn my hand to in the future. Four years later, Victor Lidz and I contemplated integrating the explanatory modes in action theory, but, for reasons that will be discussed in a later chapter, we have so far not yet done.

I could find nothing in Parsons' work that merited the radicals' critique other than the fact that he wasn't a Marxist. If one reads through the gamut of his writings, it should be clear that he was a liberal and a meliorist—similar in his political and social views to John Dewey and George Herbert Mead. But in a time of great social agitation—from the mid-1960s to the mid-1970s—liberalism was not enough for those who wanted a drastic revision of society. He was only an intellectual radical. He mainly wanted a drastic revision of our understanding of society. It was not the right kind of revolution.

I did not spend my time in England solely in the library or at my desk. England is the mother country of Canada, where I was born and spent my early childhood. A dialect of the language spawned by England had become my own. Like many Americans, my wife and son and I were exposed to bits of English life through novels, poetry, histories, movies, and three or four of Shakespeare's plays. We had to see the country for ourselves, explore as much of it as we could, and get a feel for its qualities. Of course we knew we could never get very deep into English life. The novelist Mordechai Richler, who was born and raised in Montreal, said that even after living twenty years in London, much still remained and would likely always remain opaque to him. This from someone particularly sensitive to the life and language about him! The culture, religions, and history, the things cherished and taboo, the many markers of social class, the relations among classes, the public etiquette, the (sometimes unfathomable) kinds of sports, the view and ranking of foreigners, the kinds of humor and the things made or not made fun of, the taste in food and drink and clothes, the view of themselves in relation to Americans and Europeans, and more, much more. We could not expect to get very far in all this, but we tried.

Much of what we had learned of the England of the past three or four hundred years was not to be found in 1971–72. The Sherwood Forest in Nottingham, where Robin Hood and his merry men had done their daring deeds, now consisted, to my son's and our dismay, of one large, lone tree. It was the gnarly sort Errol Flynn could have scampered up with ease. It may still be standing in 2013. The rest is housing development. But beautiful, rolling Cornwall and Dorset, the Lake Country, thatched roof cottages, hedgerows, imaginatively named pubs, Tintagel, Oxford, Cambridge, Bath, and Canterbury, and not least, fresh fish and chips were all wonderful and still there.

And of course there is London, grown immense and international, occupying a land mass more than six times that of Philadelphia and having a population easily six times larger. This great, constantly growing city, remarkably though not yet fully repaired by 1972 from the destruction it had suffered during the Second World War, could never be fully known, not even by the Baker Street irregulars.

Social class is something that many Americans who travel to England are interested in, and we were not exceptions. At times a tradesman—an attendant at a petrol station, or the workmen who were installing new metrically measured windows in our house—would address me as "squire." This amused me but signaled they recognized me as an American, and I was thus at least in their eyes middle class. But how indeterminate the term "middle class" is compared to the more precise designation of landowner or lower-order nobleman, which is what squire used to, and to some extent still does, refer to. We Americans speak of lower, middle and upper middle as well as upper classes, and mean differences in wealth and lifestyle. The British make similar distinctions—we are now both bourgeois nations. But the British have a different history and make additional distinctions as well.

There are members of the aristocracy who are impecunious but still accorded certain deference. This became quite clear when we visited several English castles and great houses open to paying tourists. Most of our fellow tourists were English. The fees charged for admission to these palaces went into the much-depleted and in some cases empty coffers of their owners, the descendants of titled aristocratic families unseen by the tourists but still visible from time to time in public life. Several of these families lived in sequestered apartments in their palaces. The tourists ooh-ed and ah-ed at the rugs, furniture, heraldic arms, and paintings, were given a brief history by the tour guide of the family and the times and circumstances of acquisition of their various possessions, and moved on with the understanding that the family still exists, their once great wealth much diminished or gone, but their place within English history recognized and their descendants still due a degree of respect. This remnant of what was once held high becomes a shade more emotionally distant with each passing decade. But it is a remnant that helps define England and will probably continue to do so as long as England exists.

Americans also have preserved the houses of their founders and great leaders—Washington's in Mt. Vernon, Jefferson's in Monticello, Lincoln's in Springfield, Roosevelt's in Hyde Park. But these houses are, at best, bourgeois palaces, publically owned and no longer occupied by their founder's descendants, who have been for the most part folded into the anonymity of American life.

Americans not only take note of the class of persons they meet, but more often than in England also of their ethnicity. And sometimes in America ethnic identity is more important than class. In addition to the few, somewhat tucked away houses of the nation's founders, Americans continue to build museums and centers in the nation's major cities devoted to displaying contributions to the nation made by a great many different ethnic populations—African, Irish, Spanish, Indian, Native American, Jews, Chinese, Swedes, Japanese, Italian, German. There is nothing like this in England. I could not help but wonder what Marx would have made of this profusion of ethnic identities and their importance had he lived in America rather than England. "The history of all hitherto existing societies (except for America) is . . ." and then what?

We discovered that English understatement, part of the cliché of the educated upper-class English gentleman and the butt of American jokes, actually exists. We were returning from France across the English Channel. The seas were very choppy, the ship was rising and falling steeply, and about half the passengers were sick, moaning and throwing up. My son's and my equilibrium still held fast, fortunately, but my wife was having a difficult time of it. The gale winds were blowing more fiercely with each passing minute, the rain was pounding ever harder, and I began to fear the increased lurching of the ship might loosen the moorings of the cars stacked below decks, which would cause them to crash into each other and possibly damage the ship. I exclaimed with some anxiety to the casually dressed man sitting next to me, about my age, with legs crossed—and what I saw as I turned toward him was an imperturbable face—that this is an awful, ghastly trip and asked whether they were all like this. In a calm Oxonian accent he murmured that, hmm, yes, the waters were a bit ruffled. I thought this response was very funny and laughed, and he, I'm sure, was again confirmed in his view that Americans are a boisterous lot.

But I wondered, in reflecting on this incident, whether the intention in this gentleman's response was to create a distance from me and others, particularly those not of his class; but whether or not this was the intention, this certainly was the result. Something of this sort, probably not as extreme except among Englishmen manqués, occurs in the United States too.

We also learned a few idiomatic expressions that seem to have become common among all classes in England. My ten-year-old son traveled on all the Tube (subway) routes in London, then quite safe, and saved his cancelled tickets to prove it. As he told us, even though he sometimes overshot a stop he never got his knickers in a twist. This expression (which we have used ever since) probably originated in some music hall ditty.

When the cottage we rented was built, about ninety to a hundred years earlier, it must have been situated near the edge of the rapidly growing metropolis. At that time, the Highgate cemetery, not far from where we lived, was new. Jews were permitted to be buried there, and this is where Marx's body lay.

Cemeteries are like the rings of a tree. They are usually built at the edge of a city, and their locations tell you how many times and how much the city has grown. The old Highgate cemetery, where poets once went to have night thoughts, lay a few miles closer to the center of the city. It had clearly been untended for many years, was overgrown with weeds and vines, and many of the worn gothic stones were cracked and toppled. It had become a Charles Adams creation. The new Highgate cemetery was clean, trimmed, grassy, large, and much visited.

Marx's grave loomed in a well-cropped clearing that could, and often did, hold a few dozen people. It consisted of a huge, leonine bust of Marx atop a pedestal, the whole standing perhaps twelve to fifteen feet high. When we visited, several Chinese tourists were also there, many standing with heads bowed in front of the bust, some continuing to bow for many minutes. A few were placing little bouquets of flowers all around the pedestal. On the front of the pedestal was printed Marx's concluding exclamation from his *Theses on Feuerbach*,[3] "The philosophers have interpreted the world in various ways; the point, however, is to change it."

We had caught glimpses of Marx's bust from the movie *Morgan*, in which the mad protagonist carries his (Trotskyist?) mother piggyback to see Marx's grave. But what we saw in the film did not give us a clear idea of how massive the gravestone is. Across the way, on the other side of a ten-foot-wide path that lay between them, was another grave, that of Herbert Spencer. Spencer's gravestone was much smaller, quite modest, and, except for us that day, his grave was without visitors. There is a well-known department store in England called "Marks and Sparks," short for Marks and Spencer. Separated though they had been in life and death, commerce seems to have united the prophet of revolution with the prophet of evolution.

Manchester, the titular site of the industrial revolution (which we didn't visit), still existed, but none of the nineteenth-century textile mills, of the kind that had provided Engels and his family with their fortune, were any longer functioning. The remains of many of these mills still dotted the country as museums. I saw one of them when I went to the University of Leeds to give a guest lecture. The innards looked like a fiendishly clever torture device designed to immobilize several hundred people. But the more I looked, the more it seemed to me the design that went into the making of this machine was probably similar in its logic to the IBM Hollerth card sorter. Both machines could perform tasks that combine things—threads for the one, punch cards for the other. The working of the great mass of the mill's apparatus, however, the metal and chains and wood, was much noisier and, I'm sure, much dirtier than the smaller, modern sorter.

Knowing that our finances would be limited, we had bought a VW camper bus, and with this for two summers we toured England and much of continental Europe. The great museums of many countries, the landscapes, dwellings, people, languages, cuisines, and, far from least, campsites that we explored from Norway to southern Italy are subjects for another book. But two experiences we had are pertinent for this book. One concerns churches, the other a relationship between a Communist, a cathedral, and a pope.

It is a commonplace for American or European travelers to note that America, unlike Europe, is a country of many religions and many churches. There is hardly a town, even the smallest, that doesn't have at least a Catholic and one or two Protestant churches, and in slightly larger towns there is often a synagogue as well. But these generalities, although true, need a bit more information to give them substance. If one looks up "churches" in the yellow pages of a Philadelphia telephone directory, one reads in small print the names and addresses of well over a thousand Protestant churches of a great variety of kinds and denominations, many dozens of synagogues and Catholic churches, both Orthodox and Roman, several Bahai churches, mosques, meeting houses, Unitarian churches, as well as several other places of worship that do not define themselves either as Christian, Jewish, Islamic, Hindu, Buddhist, or any combination thereof. It is a bit astonishing even for an adopted native like me to recognize the actual profusion of religions and churches in the United States.

What was particularly noticeable in France and Italy, and to a lesser extent in England, was the place the church has in every small town we visited or passed through. The church, and in France and Italy this means the Roman Catholic Church, stands in the center of the town, holding the town's inhabitants, as it were, in protective embrace. Those who are in the town but not of it, or who live just on the outskirts—and in France and Italy, these must be very few people indeed, perhaps gypsies or immigrant laborers—are in effect unsheltered. They live outside the penumbra cast by the church, outside and unprotected.

As I reflected on these towns, it occurred to me that this sense of being outside and unprotected is what Jews must have felt who passed through or, if they were permitted, lived on the outskirts or in the segregated quarters of these towns in earlier centuries. It is what my grandparents might have felt and my parents when they were children. The sense of vulnerability evoked by these reflections made me shiver but also made me grasp how America, despite its strangeness, disappointments, profane attractions, cruelties, and seeming disarray became such a haven for Jews. Religious life in America is very strong indeed, but the churches are not the main source of protection and safety.

When I returned to Philadelphia I mentioned these reflections to a colleague, Otto Pollak. Although they were new to me, I assumed these features of European Jewish life were quite well known. Pollak, however, became quite excited. He was a Jew from Austria, a refugee from Vienna, who came to the United States in the late 1930s. Vienna is a great, imperial city with all the trappings of such, royal houses, gardens, parks, museums, theater, concert and opera halls, and it too is overseen by soaring Roman Catholic churches. Pollak urged me to consider studying the comparative effects of churches on the Jewish experience of safety and belonging in Europe and America while there were still enough Jews remaining of the older generation in America to interview. He thought the outsider experience was more sharply felt among European Jews, but he wasn't certain. But I had more pressing concerns and thought a graduate student might be interested in taking this topic on for a dissertation. Alas, no student was interested in this, and I should have undertaken the research myself. Nevertheless, Pollak's response seemed a partial affirmation of the value of my insight.

While travelling in Rome we visited the Vatican museum. We saw the beautiful *Door of Death* on St. Peter's Basilica—the door through which funeral processions used to pass, hence the name. The plain, unadorned representations carved on the door of the deaths of Jesus, Mary, Abel, Joseph, and several others, including earlier popes and martyrs, were striking in their human, nondeified quality. In this sense the door was in keeping with Michelangelo's *Pieta*—a divine sorrow, but also a human one. In their style the figures on the door resembled some of the relief carvings that we saw several years later on the plaques and columns of the Franklin D. Roosevelt Memorial in Washington, DC. The carvings were of no one in particular but simply of people, which is the point.

We learned that the sculptor of the *Door of Death* was named Giacomo Manzù, and that he was still active in Italy in 1972. We also learned that Manzù was an avowed atheist and, if not a "card-carrying" member, very close to the Communist Party. Pope John XXIII, who had called the Second Vatican Council, and was the author of the famous encyclical "Pacem in Terris," had strong ecumenical views. He had selected Manzù's proposal, we learned, over the others submitted in full knowledge of Manzù's political and atheistic convictions.

Although I have no idea whether it is true, as some stories allege, that Pope John and Manzù became friendly and liked each other, I have no doubt there was some affinity they had for each other based on their common humane concerns. Manzù did busts of the pope, and they likely had several conversations that, one might reasonably assume, did not consist simply of idle chatter. The stories of the relationship between the two men reminded me of Silone's *Bread and Wine*.[4] John and Manzù, however, were not a fiction, and I wondered whether this kind of relationship between a priest and an atheist radical could happen in any country other than Italy—in America, for instance, or England or France or Germany or Spain. As I soon learned when we returned to the United States, something of the sort was actually happening in South America. Espousing "liberationist theology," Catholic priests in Brazil, Uruguay, and Peru were joining in common cause with radicals to aid the peasants and the poor. Nether radicals or the church are of one piece.

We learned a great deal while living and travelling in England and the Continent. Perhaps I in particular learned something many travelers speak of, but I never thought would happen to me: I learned how American I am.

I have spent a large part of my conscious life reading European novels, playing and listening to European music, studying European philosophy, sociology, and psychology, and learning from European-born and -trained teachers. I have assimilated many American versions of these subjects too, but my mind, or so I thought, has been in Europe. By the end of September 1971, however, a few months after we had settled in England, I began to feel a kind of lack. The feeling induced a touch of irritation caused by a sense I had misplaced something and was missing it but unable to identify what it was. I simply shrugged this off until a letter came from a friend in Philadelphia. The letter asked which team I would bet on in the upcoming World Series between the Pittsburgh Pirates and the Baltimore Orioles.

I am not much of a sports fan. Some baseball, some basketball, a bit of tennis, occasionally a boxing match—that about sums up my interests in sports, which occupies about a total of fifteen to twenty hours of my time *per year*. But the World Series! That was it! I missed hearing the radio announcers and the crowds' roaring behind them, missed seeing the newspaper headlines and photos, missed the sometimes heated or joyful analysis of the day's game by my friends, missed the replay on TV of particular moments of the game. This was as much a part of my experience of fall as—every cliché one can think of—seeing the leaves turning color, noticing the days getting shorter, feeling the air getting sharper. There is a germ of truth in clichés. The World Series is the part of fall that I had been missing in the fall of 1971. This bit of self-recognition made me wonder what other parts of my Americanicity I had been oblivious to.

Of all the things we enjoyed and the important things we learned while in England, discovering how American I am turned out to be the most personally important and unexpected of them all. This recognition of who I am led me to imagine anew what my grandparents and parents and some of my teachers must have felt, and by extension what every immigrant to America must have felt. But unlike me, their homelands were lost to most of them forever. But however much they may have grieved, and for some the loss was surely felt very deeply, I reminded myself that most also adapted, and if need be, I'm sure I would adapt too. I wondered how the students I knew who had become expatriates in response to the Vietnam War and the draft were managing in their host countries. "Workers of the world unite!" urged Marx. Only by giving up their national identities would this be possible. "You cannot be a Roossian, or French or Turk or Proossian," as Gilbert and Sullivan might say, "You are a Proletarian, a Pro-o-o-o-o-o letarian." Not likely to happen in the foreseeable future.

Notes

1. MIT Press, Cambridge, MA, 1971.
2. International Publishers, New York, 1940.
3. Mondial, New York, 2009.
4. Signet Classic, New York, 1986.

13

Der Alter Goy

I returned to the University of Pennsylvania in fall 1972 as an associate professor. Reneé Fox had been appointed chair of the sociology department. For many years, the chair of the department had alternated between a criminologist and a demographer drawn from the two largest and strongest sectors of the department. But over the past ten years new sociologists were brought in who specialized in other areas, and their numbers exceeded those of the criminologists and demographers combined. The year before I went to England, I joined several junior and a few senior faculty in expressing the view that the next chair be someone who represented the newer, more cosmopolitan make-up of the department. We agreed that Reneé Fox was the obvious choice for this position. With the leadership of E. Digby Baltzell, this view was presented to the dean, who saw its merits and approved Fox as the next chair. This was not only a palace coup confined to the sociology department. Fox was the first woman to take the chair of any department in the Wharton School and, I believe, of the university as a whole. Small revolutions are sometimes a prelude to larger ones. Other than the small-scale uprising in the sociology department, which had been quiet and peaceful (but with lingering resentment from the powers that once had been), the university was calmer than it had been a year earlier.

The publication of the *Pentagon Papers* was clearly having its effect. The war, it was widely believed, could not last much longer, and war protest was consequently not as intense as it had been. Students spoke and passed out flyers in support of George McGovern in the upcoming presidential election, but without the same degree of passion as there had been for Eugene McCarthy in 1968. The daily revelations of the Watergate follies—Democratic Headquarters being broken into, desks overturned and files strewn, meetings in phone booths, paper shopping bags filled with cash—seemed as though scripted by Terry Southern and played out as a national joke brought to us courtesy of President Nixon and staff. The joke or, better put, the jokers, absorbed national attention, and the whole sorry mess was seen by many to be moving toward a deep pit of disgrace into which President Nixon and his realpolitik administration would finally fall and be removed from national sight.

Although ubiquitous, drug use seemed not to be quite as flagrant as it had been. Who needed *much* dope (although *some* was obviously still felt to be needed), a few students said to me, when one could watch television news, which was almost as much of a turn-on as anything one could inhale and was free?

Reneé and I hit it off well from our first meeting. I liked her intelligence, view of the field, the high quality of her research, and her attitudes about people and teaching. She asked me to continue administering the undergraduate program for one more year while she got her bearings, which I was glad to do. She also surprised me by saying she had read my book in manuscript, which I had sent to the preceding chair, and thought highly of it.

I had not known up to that point that Reneé knew anything about Talcott Parsons' work. She then told me she had studied at Harvard and that Parsons had been her major professor and adviser on her doctoral dissertation, a study of the relations between doctors and patients in an experimental ward, published as *Experiment Perilous*[1] in 1959. Her specialty was medical sociology, not sociological theory.

The sociological study of doctors and patients is something Parsons had explored and written about in his 1950 book *The Social System*,[2] which was perhaps the beginning of the sociology of medicine. In any event, none of Parsons' students could get away without considerable exposure to and training in sociological theory. "A fact," said Parsons, "is a statement about one or more phenomena in terms of a conceptual scheme." The "fact" can be about medicine, migration, delinquency, drug addiction, employment practices, and so on. Only by clarifying the conceptual schemes that have permitted "facts" to be described can facts be understood and their meanings and relationships analyzed. And Reneé had from her earliest work on analyzed many medical and social "facts" and made vital contributions to understanding their significance for medicine and the larger society.

Reneé then jolted me with another surprise. Talcott, she said, would be retiring from Harvard in June 1973; there was a chance of his coming to Penn as a visiting professor in spring or fall 1974. If I were an Englishman of the sort I had met on my voyage across the English Channel, I might have murmured something like, um yes, pleased to hear that, I'm sure. To put it mildly and calmly, however, I was immensely excited! Immensely!! I very much wanted to meet Parsons and talk with him. The former chair had sent him a copy of my book, and he had sent back a glowing letter in support of it. It is a letter I treasure. But I had never seen him, had no idea what he looked like. I was fairly sure my book would be out by the time he came to Penn and was eager to discuss many ideas with him.

The fall semester set off at a fast pace. The singularity of a woman as chair of the department, an occurrence that soon became nationally known, attracted more women applicants for graduate study in sociology at Penn. Some of the older male members of the department grumbled there was a danger the field would become "feminized." But this was a "danger" the younger and even a few of the older faculty welcomed.

The mood of the department lightened and became more intellectually animated. The younger faculty in particular seemed to be more cheerful, and this, students told me, was also expressed in their teaching. The new graduate students who had been admitted before Reneé became chair were not less political in their outlook but seemed more interested in studying sociology.

In fall 1972 the faculty recruitment committee invited Victor Lidz to talk to us. He was teaching at the University of Chicago and being considered for an appointment at Penn. I was particularly interested in Lidz because his vitae stated he had studied with Parsons and was working on a dissertation on Emile Durkheim's theory of solidarity. I liked Lidz's talk and manner, corresponded with him after he returned to Chicago, and strongly supported his appointment to the department. This was one of the better decisions I have made. Soon after Lidz came to Penn, we discovered many affinities between us and became close friends and colleagues. We have remained such ever since.

I stepped down from administering the undergraduate program at the end of the spring semester of 1973. The number of majors had grown, the curriculum had been augmented with new courses and cleared of several old ones for which there had been no enrollments in years, and the undergraduate club was functioning well. The undergraduate program had not yet become quite socialist, as some of the older faculty might have feared that it would, but it seemed to be better meeting the needs of its members.

The graduate program was also changing. Victor and I offered several new seminars in theoretical sociology that we taught together—one on the German tradition, another on the French, a third on the Anglo-American, and a fourth in contemporary theory, largely American. This was not only an exercise in teaching bodies of knowledge that we considered important for all sociologists to have some familiarity with. This was also, as it turned out, an opportunity to have extended intellectual exchanges with each other and with the students. Neither of us had team-taught before. But we went at it without holding back, took turns lecturing, questioned each other and the students, argued, agreed, disagreed, left things open, and managed it all with high spirits and a sense of adventure. Victor was especially good on the French materials and I on the German. One result was that when we got to examining Marx's theory, students had a fuller understanding of the place of these traditions in Marx's work.

What I believe students got from our collaborative teaching, in addition to learning some substantive theory, was the pleasure that could be had in learning and examining and furthering ideas. They also learned something that was sorely needed, given the times: professors could disagree and also respect and like each other. What Victor and I got, in addition to the pleasure of the experience, was a deepening of *our* understanding of these bodies of knowledge and of the many things required in constructing a good, viable theory.

The "draft" was finally abolished in 1973, and it was clear the Vietnam War would soon be over. Student protest wound down very quickly. The turmoil of the preceding decade, however, had implanted a suspicious, cynical attitude among many graduate students that could blossom full blown at what was considered the slightest deviation from moral standards.

Spiro Agnew, whose sneering recitation of William Safire's alliterations ("nattering nabobs of negativism") made him look and sound ridiculous, was found out to be the crook many had long suspected him of being. He resigned from the vice-presidency of the United States in disgrace. Gerald Ford, a decent man, replaced him, and although not disgraced was soon discovered to be lacking in grace when negotiating the Colorado ski slopes. It seemed oddly appropriate that the insanity of the war years under the leadership of a near psychotic president should end in a postlude of cartoon-like absurdity.

When Victor Lidz came to Penn in fall 1973 he was quite fortuitously given an office next to mine. As our friendship and collaborative ventures grew, we thought it would facilitate communication if we could have a window installed between our offices. This would have required breaking through a wall, and of course it did not happen. We began to dash from one office to the other whenever we wanted to talk to each other. The frequency of these dashings doubtless contributed to our cardiovascular health.

My book did come out; there were a few glitches I hadn't caught, but it was readable. It was also remarkably small! All that work, that thinking and churning, all those doubts, and finally the finding of my voice produced . . . this? But I was elated. I gave copies to relatives and friends and colleagues. Norman Kaplan wrote to me from Boston saying he thought the book was "pretty good"—high praise from Norman, who thought some of Parsons' work was only "fair." And in general I got very good responses. But I awaited Parsons. I wanted to give him my book in person.

Between the mid-1960s and the early 1970s, six members of the senior faculty retired. Only two had been replaced. A slightly larger number of junior faculty members had also left the department, five because they didn't get tenure, two for sociology departments in other universities they found more attractive, and one who died. New faculty members were, therefore, fairly constantly being needed, and this was a need not limited to Penn alone but experienced for the same reasons by universities nation-wide. The inevitable result was development of a "shopping mentality" by candidates for universities that would offer them the best possible deals. As one wag put it, with a nod to T. S. Eliot, "Through colleges professors come and go/ comparing the salaries high or low."

The 'shopping mentality' was not limited to academics, of course. Since the end of the Second World War, American business and professional institutions of every kind have also been affected. The expectation that had existed for decades of a career-long tenure in a university or college, a company, hospital, firm, or ball club had become for a great many professionals a thing of the past. Loyalty to and affection for a school still existed, but these were sentiments undergraduate students largely developed. Professionals of every kind—doctors, lawyers, professors, scientists, corporate executives, and athletes—were on the move, selling their reputations and skills at the best possible price. Loyalty, under these circumstances, was hardly possible to develop, and if developed was often characterized as foolhardy. The inexorable growth of the market and with this a concomitant growth of a "buying and selling" ethos, a full-fledged market culture in virtually all sectors of the labor force has gone farther than even Marx, who had analyzed these things a century earlier, might have foreseen. By 1950, the United States of America had become the foremost capitalist, market-driven nation on earth.

As the chair of the recruitment committee of the sociology department, I played a role in augmenting the labor force of this niche of the academic enterprise. Had I become a lackey of the powers that be, analogous to the sergeants Marx described as doing the bidding of their industrial masters? (This is the closest Marx came that I could find to considering bureaucratic elements in capitalist organizations, an issue that his successor, Max Weber, developed with great insight and detail.) However this question might have been answered, I would not have been disturbed in the slightest. In fact, I was eager to find the very best people available to bring into the department. And indeed, I think my fellow committee members and I found excellent candidates. With the exception of two of these candidates, Willy De Craemer and Elijah Anderson, all were quickly approved by the department.

De Craemer was Belgian and a Jesuit priest. He had received his doctorate in sociology from Harvard and had founded the Bureau of Sociological Research in the Belgian Congo a decade and a half earlier. His most recent ethnographic study of a Catholic-Bantu charismatic religious movement in Zaire was accepted for publication in the distinguished series of African anthropological studies put out by Oxford University Press. It was published in 1977 as *The Jamaa and the Church*. He was being considered for a five-year appointment as associate professor. Reneé and he were good friends—indeed, had done research together in the Congo.

For the past few years De Craemer had been teaching at York University in Toronto, Ontario. His English was virtually unaccented and fluent, his credentials impeccable, but several department members were reluctant to having a Jesuit priest in their midst. It was the usual bugaboo about the dangers of a priest teaching in a secular classroom. Even though he didn't wear a collar, would he subtly (he was a Jesuit, after all) indoctrinate his students, insert "Catholic attitudes" into his lectures? Would he be objective in his teaching? Given the fact that his record addressed these issues forthrightly and was available for all to read, the questions about him were unreasonably anxious. All the letters about him, from the faculty at York and Harvard where he had taught, and from officials of the Congolese government where he had lived and done research for several years, stressed the fidelity with which he separated his role as teacher and researcher from that of priest. Partly as a courtesy to Reneé, he was finally voted in.

Anderson's candidacy proved to be more troublesome. He is African American. Several attempts over the past years to bring African American sociologists into the department had for one reason or another failed. *This* one really belonged in a school of education; *that* one belonged in a psychology department, and so on. (*This* one accepted an offer from Harvard, *that* one from Princeton. Were we not good enough? Or were we, perhaps, stricter than our Ivy League brethren in selection criteria?) Anderson, however, was through and through a sociologist. He had been trained by and worked with Gerald Suttles at the University of Chicago and Howard Becker at Northwestern University, received his doctorate from Northwestern University, and was teaching sociology at Swarthmore College. His credentials were excellent. He should have been a shoo-in.

It was unclear to me at first whether there was something about Anderson in addition to the mere fact he is a black man that touched off the intense negativity of some of the presumably left-leaning younger members of the department. That they were vocal supporters of civil rights and affirmative action made their responses more puzzling. Was he not radical enough? (If a Bobby Seale had shown up, half the faculty would have run for cover.) He spoke well but did not wear a dashiki. Then perhaps he was not black enough? But in addition to his brown skin coloring he had also slight black Southern inflections in his speech. Or perhaps he was too black? In fact, he was a soft-spoken, courteous, conventionally dressed middle-class man.

Anderson's work brought out how important "middle-class values" were even to the members of a seemingly marginal black community—namely, the inhabitants of the Chicago bar and liquor store he had studied for his doctoral dissertation. This was published a few years later as *A Place on the Corner*[3] and received wide critical acclaim. Sobriety, thrift, responsibility, courtesy were elevated by all the members, hoodlums, and wine-heads alike, above all other virtues, and those who embodied them, the regulars, the ones who could be counted on, who paid their bills and were decent and respectful of others, were given special status and honor. As Alexis de Tocqueville and many other historians and sociologists have shown, these "middle-class values" are American values par excellence.

Some of the more politically radical members of the department found Anderson's study surprising, perhaps even disconcerting. They assumed that poor, black men would be ready to revolt at the first opportunity. They challenged his study, believed that it must be defective and slanted in favor of his bourgeois biases. Although there was plenty of covert racism in this response, there was not only racism. To impugn his study was not only to challenge the objectivity of his methods but equally to impugn the eminent senior "establishment" sociologists who had monitored and approved the research. It was thus implied that his advisers were also bourgeois ideologues and willfully distorting the "true interests" of the men he had studied. But he had actually observed and studied the men in his portrayal for several years, something that is virtually impossible for a white sociologist to have done. They were not the objects of a wish or a fantasy. They became angry at the indignities they suffered from each other and from whites. But their anger had little political significance. Their notion of dignity was, in fact, an American one. They wanted to be treated as the Americans they were. His study opened a window on a part of American life that is opaque to most white and also many black people. We learned that very poor, not-well-educated black Americans are, as the noun designates, Americans. They have lived in and partaken of this country and its culture for generations. Why should they be anything other than Americans?

Anderson had a doctoral degree and was being considered as an assistant professor. This meant that he had had not only four years of college but at least four to six more years of graduate training in sociology. All of his schooling had been at first-rate universities with first-rate sociology departments. The professors who had written recommendations for him were among the leading sociologists in the field. But now, in 1973, after much professional training, research experience, and several years of teaching at a premiere college, he, with all those years of schooling and credentials, was being considered for a position at Penn.

One of the faculty members deciding on Anderson's candidacy at Penn was a recently tenured associate professor of sociology with a well-advertised reputation for supporting liberal causes. Before making a decision, he said, he wanted to see Anderson's high school record. (A Yiddish expression leapt to my mind: this man was a scoundrel even in his mother's belly—"a paskudnyak in di mama's bukh.") In the almost twelve years I had up to that time been at the University of Pennsylvania, I had never heard this request being made of a candidate for a professional position, not even of a student applying to the graduate program. I might not have been hired myself, if such a request were to have been made of me (which some of my colleagues likely might have wished that it had). The request was silly, voted down, and never again made of another faculty candidate. Anderson was hired over this and other irrational objections, but the acrimony of the discussions on his candidacy left a residue of distrust and resentment. This was not the first time, but it was still dismaying to discover racist attitudes simmering in places one would least expect to find them. These attitudes flared again several times over the years and served further to weaken the tenuous collegiality of the department.

Despite mainly covert opposition, Anderson developed friendships and good collegial relations with several members of the department and the university faculty. He turned out to be a boon for the department and the university. The superior quality of his work has won him over the years a national and international reputation.

During the years when I first became politically involved I had rarely encountered black radicals. I was eighteen years old at the time, and this was a puzzle to me. I assumed the economic straits most black people were in would have made them receptive to socialist ideas. Of course, my activities were confined almost entirely to the university, and few black students or faculty were then, and for many years thereafter, in universalities. There were black radicals—W. E. B. Du Bois, Richard Wright, Paul Robeson—but they were intellectuals and artists, not a large group in any population. A later generation of black radicals, some of whom, like Angela Davis, were Communists, appealed to a small portion of new, middle-class black students in colleges and universities and perhaps even more to the New Left students, who were mostly white. These students, black and white, were vocal, but not in great numbers. I assumed the Black Muslims, who were already noticeable in Buffalo, New York, in 1950, were drawing off black people who might otherwise have become involved in radical politics. I came to realize as I learned more that this was not even partly true.

It took me some years to appreciate the enormous importance of the African American churches for black Americans. It is the black churches, invented by black Americans themselves, that gave some hope of salvation in a cruel and many times seemingly hopeless world. It is the black churches that provided a community for people who had been torn from their communities. It is in the black churches that a people could express its suffering and its joy in prayer and song.

Although I felt self-conscious the first time I went to a black church, the impassioned sermon and responses of minister and congregants and the joyful communal singing quickly captured my attention.

I had encountered something like this before, not identical but similar. The small Hasidic synagogue to which my grandparents went fairly often in the 1930s, to which I sometimes accompanied them, was also marked by outbursts of singing and joy. The cantor would dance his way to the lectern, singing and clapping his hands as he went, and lead the congregants in song. The black minister gave a sermon, the rabbi a d'var Torah, pretty much the same things. Church and synagogue both were noisy, festive, attentive, sorrowful, joyful, filled with prayer and music. And both styles of worship emerged in analogous circumstances. The Hasidic movement appeared in the eighteenth century in Eastern Europe, where Jews were living under dreadfully oppressed circumstances. The black churches were formed in the United States in the eighteenth century as a small haven against the ravages of slavery. Both were expressions of enhanced spirituality and self-worth. Jews, however, considered themselves to be a people with a salvationary mission; blacks did not. This was among the important differences between them and probably one of the reasons more Jews than blacks were drawn to socialism or Communism.

It was with reflections such as these, evoked by the contentiousness over Elijah Anderson's candidacy, that I went to a small gathering in the history department. Friends would be there and one or two new appointments; not least, there would be much-needed intelligence and civility. And there, as though in response to my reflections and questions, I met Nell Painter, a young assistant professor, thoughtful and a pleasure to talk with. She said she was engaged in a study of a black Communist, Hosea Hudson. There were not many such, she agreed, perhaps partly because, in addition to the hold of the black churches, Communism in the United States had roots in the Soviet Union, and is not only antichurch and antireligion but truly foreign to the black American experience. But more immediate and ongoing, both of us thought, were the hostile attitudes of white workers and the obstructions white unions had thrown up against black workers joining them.

Despite grinding poverty and frequent indignities, the racial and religious identities of black Americans, not less than their American identity, insulated them from the alien appeals of Communism. Most black Americans wanted to enter fully into American life, but were being continually thwarted from doing so. The fire next time, as James Baldwin told us, would not be ignited by Communist tinder.

Painter told me a little about Hosea Hudson at that meeting. Her book, which came out a few years later, told me much more. Its title is *The Narrative of Hosea Hudson: His Life as a Negro Communist in the South*.[4]

Hudson was born in 1898, spent his early years in the South as a sharecropper, then moved to Birmingham in the 1930s to work in the steel mills. There he met a Communist union organizer who befriended him. He soon also became a union advocate and joined the Communist Party. With the encouragement and aid of the Communist Party he went to New York City and in a Communist school learned to read and write. He continued to work for unions, and despite widespread national and local opposition remained undeterred in his loyalty to Communism.

Hudson wrote an autobiography, *Black Worker in the Deep South: A Personal Record*.[5] Although enlightening of many aspects of his life, this book has been carefully monitored by ideological hands and is less revealing of his personal experiences and attitudes than the book he did with Painter. He has written a few other books. By all accounts, he was an extraordinary man, intelligent, courageous, and steadfast in the convictions that sustained him in painful and difficult times. Some have held him up as exemplary of the radical black man. But there are few other black men or women who have been radical along the same lines as he was.

Nell Painter soon left Penn. She has since written many books and become one of our eminent American historians. It has been Penn's loss.

In fall 1973, Reneé gave Victor and me a sheet of paper sent to her by Talcott, as she always called Parsons. It was interesting but puzzling, had a diagram on it and some headings. Since after staring at the sheet for a bit I couldn't decipher what it was about, I paid little further attention to it. In fall 1974 she gave us and now Willy too a second sheet of paper. She thought we would find this sheet interesting, and we indeed did.

I read and somewhat less than more understood what was on that new sheet as well as the sheet of paper we had received earlier. As on the earlier sheet, the heading on this one read, rather portentously, "Paradigm of the Human Condition." The subtitle read "Telic." "Telic," as I guessed, and soon found out from consulting the OED, is an adjective that means purposive. The word is derived from the noun telos, which means ultimate object or aim. I knew that Parsons was fastidious in the distinctions he made and thought it important to note the difference between the noun and the adjective. The noun designates something specific; the adjective is a modifier, it designates a degree of things, of more or less, and can be applied to a great many different nouns. Under the titles, a matrix of four boxes had been drawn. Within each box a label was placed generalizing in shorthand Max Weber's analyses of the primary attitudes and orientations of the world's major religions. In Parsons' labeling, these were the combinations of mystical and ascetic with inner- and otherworldliness. Over each box Parsons had put one of the letters, A, G, I, and L, representing the constituents of the four-function scheme he had developed (adaptation, goal attainment, integration, and latency, or the value orientation of the system). I wasn't sure at my first reading what all this meant, but it seemed to me Parsons was on the verge of developing another large extension of his theory.

Later in the fall, I spent several days, on and off, pondering the new sheet of paper Reneé had given us. Victor, Willy, and I talked about this. In the theory of action the religious-cultural quadrant of the action system is understood to guide, in the cybernetic sense of having more or more general information, each of the other quadrants, namely, social system, personality, and mind. The relationships among the parts of the system in the theory of action Parsons was continuing to develop are held to be analogous to that of a thermostat and a furnace: elements with more information but less energy govern elements with less information but more energy. Parsons had now fashioned a more general and economical way of characterizing the orientations of the world's major religions. Was he then thinking of re-analyzing more pointedly how each of the sub-systems is affected? Each of the subsystems also has four functional parts. To trace the guiding effects of the newly understood religious orientations upon these parts and their reciprocal effects on each other would be a complicated, indeed a gargantuan task. So much was unknown! So much more analysis had yet to be done! I wasn't sure whether this could be accomplished in my lifetime. And Parsons was almost thirty years older. But was this really his intention? I was, as were Victor and Willy, far from certain.

Another venture for which we knew Parsons was preparing was an attempt to analyze the entire action system in relation to its nonaction environments. Since he had begun to analyze some of the constituents of the telic, the governing or guiding quadrant of the action system, and since the action system had organic properties, it was a natural scientific question to ask to what the system as a whole was adapting. Shades of Darwin. And of Whitehead! But also, and perhaps primarily, shades of Max Weber. The sociology of religion, in Weber's treatment, was an attempt to understand religion as a response to such experiences of human existence as birth, pain, suffering, love, and death. The religious systems that had been developed around the world could thus be seen in sociological terms as kinds of adaptations to, and ways of understanding, these experiences.

I had been reading a recent translation of Max Scheler's *Man's Place in Nature*[6] (more accurately translated as *Man's Place in the Cosmos*). Was Parsons going to try something similar? If he was indeed preparing to undertake this sort of thing, I was fairly sure one of the main differences from Scheler would be that he would be rigorously naturalistic, whereas Scheler was always reaching for the transcendental. Could this be done without a large degree of speculation? So very much was not known. A large degree of speculation might be productive, but speculation alone would serve to weaken the theory. Victor and I were quite uncertain of *our* speculations on this, and we continued to wonder what the diagrams on this sheet of paper actually portended.

There are some scholars who may find aspects of themselves represented in Saul Bellow's *Herzog*.[7] I am one of them. Herzog has a running dialogue, actually a series of imaginary letters that he writes, with thinkers long dead who have meant a great deal to him. Herzog is Jewish, but is what he does particularly Jewish? It *feels* Jewish. Tevye, the character created by Scholem Aleichem, does the same thing with the First Author, God. And Moses is the one who started it all. (Herzog's first name is Moses.) I too still ask questions of thinkers, dead and alive, who mean a great deal to me. I wonder what Kant, Hegel, Marx, Weber, Durkheim, Simmel, Mannheim, Freud, and over the past several years particularly Parsons would think of this point or that, why they didn't take X into consideration, or how they would respond to Y, and so on. My understanding of the world and of myself is sometimes deepened by questioning these thinkers and trying to imagine their responses. It is as though they and I were contributing to an ongoing, ever more encompassing Talmud, providing commentaries on the meaning of our lives and the world. I do not sit in my bedroom as my grandfather did studying Rashi's commentaries on the Torah or the Babylonian Talmud propped up on a small table in front of him. I sit at my desk in a carpeted, book-lined study reading a pdf file on my computer monitor. Rashi, the medieval French Jewish sage, and Parsons, the twentieth-century American Protestant scholar, are vastly unlike. So too are my grandfather and I. Still, both Rashi and Parsons spent a lifetime interpreting and clarifying seemingly divergent texts. The differences between my grandfather and I are, perhaps, not so great after all.

At least for a year, and possibly longer, if we were lucky, Penn would soon gain an illustrious figure in social science, Talcott Parsons. With a few interludes as a guest professor in other institutions, he had spent his entire academic career at Harvard. He was due to arrive at the beginning of the fall semester, 1974.

I stopped in at the main sociology office to learn whether Parsons had shown up yet. There was the usual beginning of semester milling, students and various people coming and going, phones ringing, syllabuses being dropped off and picked up, and the secretaries looking somewhat harried but keeping the flow of traffic moving. No, they hadn't seen Professor Parsons. Victor stopped in. I asked him whether Parsons was here yet. He laughed and said, yes, he's right over there behind you, pointing to a man standing next to a table and looking at one of the course outlines. The man was quite a bit older, bald, rotund, short, perhaps five feet one or two inches tall. He wore glasses and had a gray mustache. His multi-tweed jacket was wrinkled, and his tie was nondescript and crooked. There were cigarette ashes on the front of his jacket. He looked, one of the secretaries told me later, like "Papa Frohman," the character created by the Tasty Cake Company to represent their home-style baked goods.

This was Talcott Parsons? I expected a man perhaps six feet tall, lean, slightly bent in a scholar's mien, with lined face and long gray hair, a noble forehead, a reflective gaze, someone on the order, say, of Ernst Cassirer or Bertrand Russell—a man, that is, who was a kind of objective correlative of his work. Of course, Immanuel Kant, who is considered by many to be in the company of Plato and Aristotle and the greatest philosopher of the modern age, was not exactly a model of masculine beauty either.

I went over, introduced myself, and welcomed him to the university and the department. He was, I discovered, quite shy. He knew who I was. Victor, thank goodness, helped smooth the awkwardness of the situation, and we went looking for Reneé. (Victor has since reminded me many times of my first reactions to Parsons, but assured me that they didn't show. I hope he's right, but I'm not sure I trust him.)

At the request of the editor of *Sociological Inquiry*, Parsons wrote a review of my book. Although praising it, he was also critical, and emphasized the fact I hadn't considered the economic interests that were a large part of his early work. This, I thought, missed the point of my book, which was not concerned with the substance of categories but with their form and relations. Victor and the editor of the journal agreed with me and urged me to respond. I did in the clearest, most constructive way I could. Parsons read my response and decided to include it, as well as his review of my book, as a chapter in his next publication, *Social Systems and the Evolution of Action Theory*.[8] He gave me a copy of this book inscribed "to my esteemed co-author," which I treasure. He was not afraid of honest, nonpersonal criticism.

Parsons taught three graduate courses and one undergraduate course at Penn: one on social evolution, one on the media of interchange among the parts of the social system, one on the rudiments of action theory, and one on American society. These were distributed throughout the academic year, two courses each semester. But since he was on campus only one week of each month, Reneé, Willy, Victor, and I each took one of the courses and filled in during the weeks he was away. Victor and I also sat in on each other's courses. We each taught our own roster of regular courses as well. Parsons' courses were fully enrolled, and the students were attentive. He came in with a fresh set of notes each day. Victor, who had taken similarly titled courses with him when he was his student, told me the notes were new and the ideas rethought and also presented in a fresh manner.

Parsons spoke plainly and with precision. One student asked him, for example, whether he thought Senator Joseph McCarthy was a fascist. After a moment's thought he answered by saying he thought McCarthy was more fascistoid than fascist, and then went on to explain the difference. This exactness impressed the students and impressed me. His ability to draw sharply etched analogies that clarified an idea was also fully at work. Some students told me they thought he was like a Zen master. Other students, the undergraduates mainly, said they thought he was like Yoda, the grandmaster of the *Star Wars* trilogy who trained Luke Skywalker in the ways of the Jedi This latter simile was more exaggerated than anything he might have come up with but clearly evoked by his physical stature and mastery of a great range of materials and ideas. He might have been amused but embarrassed by being compared to a Zen master but would have been dumbfounded by the comparison to Yoda. He rarely went to movies. (Although they never said anything to us, I suppose students likened Victor and me to Obi Wan Kenobe.) The students were impressionable and sweet tempered, a combination that made them receptive to him and to his lectures. Several went on to become professional sociologists.

Teaching with Parsons was like getting another graduate education for me. His learning in all the social sciences and in history and biology was impressive. But unlike Gerth, who was also learned, he was disciplined and coherent. He was also intellectually daring, as we all knew and discovered again when Reneé arranged a meeting with him and several of us—herself, Willy, Victor, and me—a week after the semester started.

Copies of the sheet of paper with the title "Paradigm of the Human Condition" Reneé had given us earlier were distributed. Parsons spoke. The issue he was considering was the responses of the entire action system to its environments. The action system did not exist suspended, so to speak, in thin air. Its parts were constantly reacting not only to its internal environments, namely, its other parts; the system as a whole was also reacting to external environments of many kinds. The human organism is not the action system. But the birth, gender differences, characteristics, life cycle, and ultimate fate of the human organism are among the things to which our minds, personalities, social systems, and cultures including our religions respond. His aim, he said, was to clarify aspects of these environments and modes of our reactions to them. This was a staggering project, but also a very exciting one. We agreed to meet once each week he was at Penn to discuss the many issues involved. Three weeks of the month we would continue to meet without him. And so we began.

Although we had an agenda for each meeting, we brought to our meetings anything we thought relevant—life experiences, novels, philosophical ideas, historical sources, biological and physical analogies, anthropology, linguistics, religion, psychoanalysis, and not least, sociological findings.

Over the weeks and months and years that followed, we also consulted with several experts. We each also developed analyses of specific topics.

A. Hunter Dupree, the historian of biology and Darwinism, was invited to speak to us. One of Parsons' former students, James Olds, with whom he had continued to correspond, had become a notable neurobiologist and sent him a long letter describing the discovery of pleasure centers in the brain, for which he had become famous two decades earlier. This was a finding indeed germane to the human condition. Olds was a gifted man who died in an automobile accident shortly after Parsons received this letter. We went to Princeton twice for wonderful long evenings of discussion with the anthropologist Clifford Geertz on the founding myths of several religions, including, of course, the myths of the Balinese. Willy worked out a representation of the different orders of the Catholic Church in the telic terms of the human condition paradigm. Victor and I, also using telic distinctions, developed an analysis of the worldwide variations in Marxist thought, from Mao to Marcuse. We discussed the psychoanalytic theory of family relations in telic terms, of medical practices worldwide, and many other topics. The discussions were wide-ranging and intense, each session often lasting for several hours.

The *piece de resistance* of our meetings, however, occurred quite by accident in the second year. The sociologist of religion, Robert Bellah, whom Parsons had kept informed of what we had been doing for the past almost two years, joined us for an evening session in one of his visits to Philadelphia. At the close of that three-hour session, we all knew we were on to something but were too tired to continue. We agreed to meet again the next morning. That next morning Bellah asked whether we could go to a room with several blackboards. He was excited and said he'd been up all night. In that classroom, he set down on the blackboards that stretched around the room from front to sides a comparative schematic analysis of the major world religions in terms of the human condition paradigm. This was the culminating moment of the seminar. In an inspired burst, he took what we had so far done and extended it over an immense historical and cultural range. This showed us that what we had been working on was genuinely a human-condition issue, not just an American- or Western-condition issue. His breakthrough was, as Talcott quaintly put it, a brainstorm. All of our work in the year following that meeting was spent on consolidating what we had so far done. Parsons recounted much of this as well as aspects of the more general scheme we had worked on in the last book he published, *Action Theory and the Human Condition*.[9]

In 1976, Mark Gould, a friend and colleague at Haverford College, told us there was a chance to bring Jürgen Habermas to Philadelphia for a semester. He had studied with Parsons and Kenneth Arrow at Harvard, and knew Victor, Willy, and Reneé well. He had met and become quite good friends with Habermas while doing research in Europe.

Habermas was at the time perhaps the best internationally known social philosopher among the younger generation of scholars in Germany. He was an intellectual descendent of the Frankfurt-school philosophers, and like them a scholar of considerable learning and intelligence who was not averse to reading and taking "bourgeois" thinkers seriously. To bring him to Philadelphia and have him teach at Penn and Haverford would be stimulating for students and faculty. The problem, of course, was money.

We persuaded our respective deans to share the costs of Habermas' salary. Habermas accepted our invitation, but alas, neither Parsons nor Marković would be at Penn during the semester of Habermas' residence.

Habermas had been critical of Parsons' work. He did not see the dynamic elements in the normative functional theory—a serious misreading that discussions with Victor Lidz in ensuing years corrected. I did not know whether Parsons had read any of Habermas' work, but I was fairly sure that if he had, he would be tone deaf to some of the phenomenological notes that were in it. Discussions between the two scholars might have been rewarding and productive.

Habermas' course at Penn was well attended by undergraduate as well as graduate students and a few faculty. This was the period in which he was embarking on his theory of communicative action, and the materials of the course reflected this interest. Fairly soon after the course began, however, many students grumbled that the course was too difficult and the readings too many. Would this complaint have been made by German students who were expected to read and study many pages of difficult books and articles? Perhaps, but I doubted it.

Habermas had a wide range, going back to Emile Durkheim, Max Weber, and Georg Lukács and continuing through Theodore Adorno, Alfred Schutz, and John Searles, among many others. Much of this material was difficult, or at least unfamiliar, to most of the students and perhaps also to the faculty. I myself, for example, had not read anything of Searles' work up to that time and found Searles' discussions of types of speech acts thought-provoking.

It was clear that Habermas was highly intelligent and learned. Not least, his informality and openness and the workmanlike manner in which he dug into the materials were most attractive. Yet everything that was appealing about Habermas' work, his insights and passion, was also, in my view, animated and skewed by the illusion of perfection, by a belief in an ultimate true communication among human beings that could be achieved once the fetters of a repressive society and a concomitantly faulty understanding were broken. I, who have experienced the rigors of self-examination and understanding through several years of counseling, hardly have achieved, nor do I believe can ever achieve, the perfect self-communication that Habermas desires and thinks possible. Communication and understanding are endless pursuits. Fetters of one sort or another, barriers, defenses, will always exist. They may be lessened, and some may be penetrated, but they

Der Alter Goy

cannot all be eliminated without undoing the human personality. This, I believe, is part of the human condition. Habermas came for a semester and left. I liked him personally. With one or two exceptions, the students at Penn did not refer to him again.

Victor or I would sometimes go to lunch with Parsons during the week he was at Penn. More often the three of us would go together. Mainly, we went to Kelly & Cohen, a corner deli near our building to which the fictitious "Kelly" had been added to the fictitious "Cohen" years earlier to attract a larger clientele. ("Cohen," I found out, was far simpler than the many syllables of the actual owners' Eastern European surname, and thus got the message across quickly.) There one could get anemic corned beef, chopped liver, and pastrami sandwiches on fairly good rye bread, and also a variety of other foods most of better quality than the fare at the faculty club. During the Passover season, K & C also offered matzos and even matzo brie as well as their usual sandwiches, soups, and salads. Many of the faculty in nearby buildings, Jews as well as non-Jews, ate lunch there regularly.

I had gotten to know the owners fairly well, a grandfather, father, uncle, and son. The spirit moved me seldom, but when it did I would say a word or two in Yiddish to the grandfather or one of the older black waiters who was quite fluent in the language. If the weather was warm I would hold one of my midafternoon seminars at K & C when there were few customers, and we could push three or four tables together, sip coffee or Cokes, and talk. After going many times over several weeks to K & C, Parsons had become identified as a "regular." One time in late fall when he was not in attendance at Penn, I went alone to K & C for lunch. The grandfather came over to me and asked, somewhat anxiously, I thought, "Wie is der alter goy?" (Where is the old gentile?) The grandfather had never before addressed me in this much Yiddish—or English, for that matter—and the question startled and also amused me. My wife's aunt had a reproduction of a Franz Hals painting of a jolly, plump, red-faced, white-haired peasant man that she was fond of and referred to as "der alter goy." It had never occurred to me to characterize Parsons this way, and to my surprise I answered the grandfather in a more full-blown Yiddish than I knew I was capable of. "Der alter goy," I answered, "sitzt jetst in sein haim" (now sits in his home) in Boston un shreibt" (and writes). "Er is ein groysn Gelernter" (he is a famous scholar). "Zorg sich nisht" (don't worry). "Er vil tzu Philadelphia in a pur vochen tsurkik kummin" (he'll be back in Philadelphia in a couple of weeks). This information seemed to satisfy the grandfather; he nodded and went back to his station behind the cash register. Parsons had clearly made an impression.

I ate lunch with Parsons alone many times, as did Victor and Willy and Renee. At some point, perhaps the second or third time just the two of us ate together, we began to talk more personally. We told each other things about ourselves, our parents and upbringings, our early and abiding interests, our love of music, some of the things that gave us pleasure or that we didn't much care for. We chatted about the work of colleagues both of us knew and even a few times of their personal habits and foibles. This latter was a kind of gossiping, but on his part, if not always mine, done in good humor and with tolerance and affection. And of course we talked about the ongoing issues of the Human Condition seminar. He told me he had read Malraux's *La Condition humaine* (translated as *Man's Fate*[10]) when it first came out and was much impressed by it—as I was when I read it in English. We both thought Malraux was an extraordinary man and a great writer. The memory of the book and its title were among the sources that inspired the work we were now doing.

During these lunches we developed a kind of intimacy and a sharing of interests I had never expected to find with someone this much older, certainly not with Talcott Parsons, of all people. Despite the enormous differences in our lives and generations—he, old enough to be my father (and in some ways soon became my intellectual father), a New England Wasp, a drinker of bourbon whose family went back to Jonathan Edwards; I, the son of Jewish Russian immigrants, on intimate terms with bagels (then a rarity outside of Eastern European Jewish circles), whose family came out of the common shtetl grass—despite these differences, we became close friends. It was a wonderful, life-enhancing experience, intellectually and personally.

The Human Condition Group also had many dinners together in restaurants and in our homes. Helen Parsons, Talcott's wife, was included in the dinners, and she also gave several dinners for us in the apartment in which she and Talcott stayed while in Philadelphia. She became a good friend as well.

In 1979, Talcott went to Heidelberg. He was the guest of honor at a conference to celebrate the fiftieth anniversary of receiving his doctorate from that venerable and great university. Many eminent German sociologists would be there. Speeches and seminars were planned. At the end of the conference he went to Munich to give more seminars. In the evening of his second day in Munich he became ill. On May 8, the morning of his third day in Munich, he was dead. He was seventy-six years old.

We heard within hours. It was shattering. We had planned to meet with Talcott again after he returned from the conference. Our grief sapped our energy for months. Yes, we understood something of the human condition. Helen Parsons spoke to each of us after Talcott's memorial service in Cambridge. To me she said, "Talcott would have wanted you to cultivate your own garden."

Notes

1. The Free Press, Glencoe, IL, 1959.
2. The Free Press/Macmillan, New York, 1964.
3. University of Chicago Press, Chicago, 1978.
4. Harvard University Press, Cambridge, MA, 1979.
5. International Publishers, New York, 1972.
6. The Noonday Press, New York, 1962.
7. Viking Press, New York, 1964.
8. The Free Press/Macmillan, New York, 1977.
9. The Free Press/Macmillan, New York, 1978.
10. Vintage Books, New York, 1990.

14

The More Things Change...

Reneé stepped down from the chair in 1978. A power vacuum followed into which several contenders, some of whom had never before shown interest in anything beyond their own affairs, were eagerly drawn. Had the events of the next two years not been so painful to so many members of the department, the scrabbling of the contenders for support, the wheeling and dealing, the suspicions and accusations would merit a parody along the lines of Lenin's *Toward the Seizure of Power*,[1] in which power can't be seized because it has been scattered beyond anyone's grasp. None of the contenders could get much support from the other members of the department, many of whom remained on the sidelines, bemused and neutral. The dean was called in to find a way out of the impasse. With an adroit mix of sternness and stroking he gained the consent of the department to bring in a chairman from the outside. A distinguished sociologist in the medical school who previously had not had much to do with the department agreed to serve as interim chair until a new chair was found. Everyone tried, with varying success, to shield the students from it all, much the way warring parents sometimes attempt to protect their children from their madness.

By 1980 a new chair was installed. Also by 1980 there had been a shift in students' political attitudes. Some opposition was mounted to Ronald Reagan's presidential candidacy, but it was pallid by comparison to the protests of the war years. A few small rallies were held and some speeches given, but little else. The war was over, and the politics of protest no longer seemed to have much point. All this would change by 1984, when students were again moved to assemble and urge in speeches and on T-shirts and placards "Let's Not Be Slimed Again"—adopting the phrase from the movie *Ghostbusters*. But In 1980 undergraduate and graduate students had more pressing concerns.

In the late 1960s a few coed communes were put together in houses surrounding the campus. The number of such communes grew rapidly in the 1970s, until at least a tenth of the juniors and seniors lived in them. By the 1980s, however, student interest in communes had fallen. Part of the reason was the attractive and convenient new campus housing. The more salient reason was a cooling of countercultural concerns.

The communes at the University of Pennsylvania were an abbreviated and diluted version of the communes more commonly portrayed as having formed in the countryside. Virtually all students were supported by their parents and knew they would leave their communes when they graduated. Certain practices associated with the communal side of the counterculture were followed, however. There was sharing of costs and duties in maintaining living quarters and in buying and preparing food; there was unanimous agreement required in accepting or rejecting potential members; and far from least, there was a somewhat fractiously achieved latitude in sharing one's bed with anyone who agreed to do so, whether of the same or opposite sex.

As many students straightforwardly said, pot in these communal settings was in plentiful use both by individual members and through frequent late-evening sharing of, as they put it, the "peace pipe." In addition to the obvious reference to the peacemaking practice of some American Indian tribes, the timing and ritualized character of peace-pipe smoking suggested other sources of inspiration. There was something of the quality of a "nightcap" in this ritual that may have been modeled after the practice of some of their parents, for whom the late-evening alcoholic drink was common. In this apparently unlikely respect (as well as in others), the generational gap, which was indeed real, was not quite as wide and deep as it has often been made out to be. Students were turning on, but by 1980 no longer dropping out.

Betty Flower of the philosophy department and I were invited over the years, both separately and together, to dinner at several undergraduate communes. The students were for the most part second-semester juniors and seniors. Most communes were clean, the students were welcoming, and the amount of food served was mountainous and generally good. A few of the communes favored pillows in place of chairs, which was charming but also became over the years increasingly challenging.

The students asked questions about our respective specialties. But more often than Betty or I had anticipated, especially as the 1970s drew to a close, they asked what kinds of jobs one could get or what kinds of careers one could pursue with an undergraduate major in philosophy or sociology. This was not only a sign of economic anxiety. True, the economy was not doing that well in the late 1970s. And the "voodoo economics," as George H. W. Bush had earlier characterized the economic agenda of the ever-smiling Ronald Reagan, was not yet installed and trickling. Their concern now was not only with jobs but with their *careers*, a concern that had taken second or third place for the Vietnam War generation but was asserting itself as primary for this postwar generation as they saw the close of their university years draw near. The counterculture experience was for the great majority of them an interlude whose effects might linger but would for the most part pass away as the demands and routines of work and perhaps marriage took hold. Law, business, and medicine were beckoning.

The graduate students in sociology, who were no longer as numerous as they had been a decade earlier, were four to six years older than the undergraduates. They were already in a professional program studying either to become university teachers or researchers for government agencies or private firms. Several of the older ones had been active in opposing the war. A few also lived in communes, some lived together as couples, but most rented private apartments or rooms. There were, for some, still bits of a "marxistoid" vocabulary (as Parsons might say) in their speech, learned when they were undergraduates and such terms as ruling class, imperialism, domination, class consciousness, fascism were in vogue. But except for a few whose language had remained uncontaminated by ideological clichés, most had adopted the language of the civil rights and women's movements, in which such social science terms as culture, role, sexist, oppression, male dominance, and equality had become common. The lingo of bourgeois sociology had clearly won the day.

On a sunny, mild, late-October afternoon in 1980 as I was walking unnoticed behind two of the new sociology graduate students, one turned to the other and said in hissing anger, "Baltzell is a fascist." I very nearly dropped my book bag. I don't think I had ever heard anything quite as bizarre. Digby Baltzell was among the most popular teachers at the university. He had taught thousands of students and won several teaching awards. One of his earlier books, *The Protestant Establishment*,[2] had been hailed nationally as a trenchant critique of the upper class, and he was for a time one of the minor darlings of the left. His most recent book, *Puritan Boston and Quaker Philadelphia*[3] (1979), was considered by the critics to be a masterwork. Baltzell a fascist? At worst, he was a Kennedy Democrat, which was bad enough for some.

Not trusting my ears, and hoping to hear more, I clutched my book bag tightly and continued walking behind the two students. "Baltzell," the student went on in teeth-clenched exclamations, "thinks the upper class should rule! He comes from the upper class! He's a WASP! He looks like a fascist and dresses like one too!"

The student was clearly very upset and anxious, and her companion nodded in what looked like unquestioning and also concerned appreciation for this bit of information on one of the important professors in the department. (Baltzell at the time was chair of the graduate program in sociology.) She did not ask her friend to describe how a fascist dresses or looks, either because she was simply permitting her friend to let off steam or accepting her friend's views as being true ones. In the latter case, this would be a sign of a lack of critical inquisitiveness that did not bode well for a future in sociological research. (In fact, Baltzell dressed the way most academics of his generation and mine on the East Coast generally dressed: tweed jacket, flannel trousers, Oxford cloth shirt and, in his case, a bow tie. Not even fascistoid.)

The student doing the talking was obviously taking a course from Baltzell and misreading him. She likely didn't know he had popularized the term WASP when he used it as part of a set of research categories without intending the term to become a derogatory acronym. I did not attempt to correct this student then and there, which in retrospect I probably should have done. This might have saved both from months of confusion and groundless anxiety. They would, in any event, both be in my theory seminar next semester, alas, and I would try my best to instruct them. But I did decide then and there to use some of Baltzell's work in my seminar. His study of the rise of a self-conscious national upper class in the United States after the Civil War was the *only* study of the formation of class-consciousness that I knew of. I'm not quite sure why Marxists had not looked into this, probably because Baltzell was not a Marxist. In any event, his early study *Philadelphia Gentlemen*[4] also clarified why the other "classes," middle and working, were not classes in Marx's sense and would likely never be.

Baltzell concentrated mainly on Philadelphia, but he and his students found similar patterns in many other American cities. The American upper class grew after the Civil War as alliances were formed between pre–Civil War "old money" establishments and new commercial, mining, railroad, banking, and industrial elites. New business alliances, however, were but part of the story of the growing upper class. An enlarged, energized set of business circles was soon strengthened by marriages among many of its members. And with marriage came a shared religion, Episcopalian, and for the children local private as well as national boarding schools, mainly Episcopalian in culture, and private universities that soon drew upper-class students from all parts of the country. Within two to three generations the upper class was made up of a many-stranded network of relationships whose members knew one another in their boardrooms and in their living rooms, prayed together in their churches, met one another and played together in their schools and parties, on their vacations, and in their clubs.

As the children of the upper class began to marry one another, take up the reins of their fathers' businesses, and move on to other cities, a growing inter-city commercial class formed whose members were soon a few generations removed from their founders. But with increasing geographical mobility family, religious, school, and club affiliations became less visible and therefore less adequate as a means of identifying class members. In the 1880s *The Social Register* was invented, and within a few decades was published in over twenty-six American cities. Yearly editions of the *Register* include such information as family names and addresses, membership in clubs and societies, academic affiliations, and notices of births, marriages, and deaths of those listed. A later summer edition whimsically lists such seasonal information as "Dilatory Domiciles" and the names of yachts and their owners. Thus, in whatever city they happened to visit or live, class members became easily identifiable to each other, and their social status as belonging to the upper class was validated. By the end of the nineteenth century, the American upper class consisted of nationwide business and political leaders, many of whom were tied to each other in several distinctive ways and could, if need be, locate one another anywhere in the country through *The Social Register*.

This is not to say that all was sweetness and light within the upper class. Intense business rivalries were waged among its members. Although the title is more ideological and pejorative than descriptive, the "robber barons" J.P. Morgan, Carnegie, Rockefeller, Fisk, Astor, Harriman—in sum, everybody in banking, railroads, and industry—were not given that dark name without reason. Yet there is nothing remotely equivalent for the other classes to the social bonds that have formed the American upper class. Families, unions, political parties, churches, neighborhoods, public schools, and not least income are for all other groupings in American society essentially varied and local. Although later in developing, professional associations are an exception—many indeed have a nationwide reach—but they are of many kinds, and whether taken singly or combined, they hardly constitute a social class. The middle class, into which the professions have been lumped, and working class are described by demographers as aggregates distinguished by differences in occupation and income. Good enough for census purposes. But to this description we may add the further sociological notes that the professions are also distinguished by differences in occupational autonomy, by their fiduciary responsibility to patients, clients, and students, and to an increasingly lesser degree, by differences in lifestyle.

There are at least two parts to Baltzell's thesis, one analytical and descriptive, the other quasi-analytical, prescriptive, and moral. The latter is not directly concerned with class but with the place of class in democratic processes. I decided also to spend a session on this second part since it was an antithesis to Marx and in so being served to illustrate the point that political views are one thing, descriptive analysis is another. Although the two are related, they are not bound together hand and foot. The same descriptive analysis can serve different political purposes. One can accept aspects of Marx's analysis without becoming a Marxist, as Baltzell did, just as one can accept aspects of Baltzell's analysis without becoming a Baltzelliist (if there is such a thing).

The great fault of the American upper class, as Baltzell saw it, is that its members began to close ranks against newcomers. This was already apparent in the mere emergence of *The Social Register.* New men of talent, new elites who were not white, or of Anglo-Saxon heritage, or a kin member, or at least Protestant were shut out from all things commandeered by the upper class—neighborhoods, schools, businesses, professions, occupations, clubs. This many-sided exclusivity was not limited to Boston, "the home of the bean and the cod/ where the Cabots speak only to the Lowells/ and the Lowells speak only to God." By late nineteenth century, snobbish and sometimes cruel acts of exclusion by upper-class men and women had become in the land of equality a subject of ridicule and were morally disturbing, if not yet illegal. Edith Wharton wrote of such practices in New York City; they have continued to occupy novelists, playwrights, moviemakers, and not least limerick writers ever since. The latest example of this in Baltzell's experience was the outrageous treatment of the Catholic new-money Kennedys by the Boston upper class.

The students in my graduate theory seminar grasped Baltzell's analysis of the formation of the American upper class quickly. It made good sociological sense. A few observed that Baltzell was analyzing only the American upper class, not the English or the French or that of any other European nation. One of the obvious differences is that the European upper classes were and to some extent still are composed of hereditary aristocracies; the American upper class is not. Indeed, although a modern bourgeois nation, England continues to bestow a knighthood and other aristocratic titles upon persons of extraordinary accomplishment. These titles confer status upon the holder and sometimes their descendants. In this way, the ranks of the aristocracy in England are recurrently augmented. But some decline the honor. Bertrand Russell, for example, refused a knighthood that would expire upon his death, preferring to retain his inherited title as Lord Russell. In America, however, where by constitutional proscription there are no titles and there is no aristocracy, kinship alone does not necessarily grant status, at least not for long.

The American upper class is shaped by a distinctive Protestant culture, Puritan in origin and unofficial, whereas England is also largely Protestant but officially Anglican. Lacking hereditary titles and girded to its nation's culture, the members of the American upper class cannot rest in their status for long but must continually prove their worth by work and accomplishment. Tocqueville observed this in *Democracy in America*[5] as early as 1835. There are social hierarchies in America too, but they are not cast in stone. High positions have not only to be achieved but also maintained, and for this reason are always threatened with being surpassed. However high the status achieved in America, Tocqueville observed, its holder is always tinged with anxiety. An American of inherited wealth able to live a life of ease and leisure without work of any kind—as a beachcomber or a playboy, say—will soon turn from being an object of fantasy to one of disrespect and even derision. (The late Louis Auchncloss, a member of the New York City upper class, has written of these things from the inside, both in his novels and in his 2010 memoir *A Voice from Old New York*.[6])

All the more reason the American upper class has erected barriers to its ranks. When something becomes more common, its value declines. The result of these barriers, in Baltzell's view, has been a weakening of upper-class vitality, a slow but sure desiccation of their talents and vigor, and with this a decline in their moral strength. A fictional portrait of this process as it occurs over three generations is in Auchncloss' novel *The Rector of Justin*.[7] This has left the door open, Baltzell argued, for elites of every kind—Huey Long and Joseph McCarthy are examples—to attempt to gain power by any means often with little effective opposition from what was once a morally strong and socially secure leadership.

Like everyone else, Baltzell grew up in a particular time and place. He was born into an upper-class Philadelphia family that lost its fortune during the Great Depression of the 1930s. He saw the Nazis march when, as a young man, he visited Germany in the mid-1930s. He fought in the Second World War as a navy pilot. What had happened in Germany was a horror to him, as it was to so many others, and he feared signs of its occurrence in the United States. He studied sociology, political science, and history at Columbia University and then turned his professional and indeed lifelong attention to understanding the role of class in American democracy.

Although he read widely on Nazi Germany, Baltzell never wrote anything on the subject—probably because Nazi Germany was primarily his foil, the stark contrast to his real subject, American democracy and freedom. In Nazi Germany, he would say with disbelief, the freedoms of Germans were willingly given up or taken from them with relatively little opposition. There were no independent groups in German society strong enough to oppose the Nazi Party, he would stress, other than some of the landed aristocracy, who were isolated and without influence, and the once influential Social Democratic Party, the SDP, which could have provided considerable opposition to the Nazis had they not lost decisively to Hitler in the election of 1933. A large segment of the working class as well as many intellectuals were in the SDP, but after winning power the Nazis quickly disabled opposition the SDP might still be able to mount by jailing or killing its leaders. The working class, left rudderless by the decimation of the SDP, was not only poorly organized but also suffering so deeply from the Depression that they began to join the Nazi Party in droves, believing that Hitler's promises to restore the nation would save them. The urban aristocracy, many of whom were industrialists like Thyssen, Krupp, Stinnes, Voegler, Kirdorf, and von Schroder, were only too glad to go along with Hitler, whose policies were beneficial to them. Many of the bourgeoisie at all levels, professors, lawyers, and schoolteachers among them, were tied to the state as civil servants, and as with a great many other civil servants remained loyal to the state when the Nazi Party gained parliamentary control. Opposition to the Nazis arose, of course, but it was quickly and ruthlessly crushed. Could this possibly happen here? Sinclair Lewis' popular, partly satirical novel, *It Can't Happen Here*,[8] published in 1935, suggested that it could.

For more than a decade following the Second World War the fear that Western nations might become, or were already becoming "mass societies" like Nazi Germany or Soviet Russia, in which all formerly distinctive groups were leveled and made featureless except for the leader, was common among many American and émigré political sociologists both of the right and the left. Nazi Germany had been defeated, but Soviet Russia now loomed. Ortega y Gasset had sounded the aristocratic alarm early with *The Revolt of the Masses*[9] *(*1930). But it was not merely the revolt of the masses that was the principal political issue. The revolt of the masses alone is never enough. It was, rather, the ways a single group could capture power, and then by reducing all others into an undifferentiated mass be unimpeded in its rule. Franz Neumann in *Behemoth*[10] (1944), Hannah Arendt in *The Origins of Totalitarianism*[11] (1951), C. Wright Mills in *The Power Elite*[12] (1956), William Kornhauser in *The Politics of Mass Society*[13] (1959) were among the many that analyzed the forming of mass societies and the dangers they posed.

Baltzell was familiar with this literature. However, a perhaps greater influence on his thinking that provided him with an analogy of sorts to the American situation was Alexis de Tocqueville's analysis in *The Old Regime and the French Revolution*.[14] Tocqueville described changing relations between two groups that took place over several generations, the French royalty centered in Paris, and the French aristocracy that lived and ruled in the provinces. As the aristocracy began to exchange its authority over the provinces for a place in the royal court in Paris, the administration of the provinces was given over to the king and his ministers. The protections once provided by the now enfeebled aristocracy against excess royal taxes and incursions from other provinces were inevitably eroded. Not least, distant overseers in Paris unfamiliar with the localities began to determine what was appropriate for them. The growing Parisian bureaucracy was not only removed from the provinces geographically but also in awareness of the needs and concerns of their inhabitants. The press of these needs and concerns, which went unrecognized and in any case unanswered by the king and his administrators ("let them eat cake") grew and finally erupted in the rage of 1789.

Tocqueville did not use the term "mass society," but he was essentially describing one and certain of its possible outcomes. We do not have a mass society, nor do we have guillotines. But a mass society for us might require an assassin's bullet to stop a homegrown dictator, as in fact such had succeeded in doing to Huey Long. A far more dangerous scenario might have been played out when President Richard Nixon in 1974, on the very eve of what was believed to be his impeachment, was thought to be ready to call out the army to protect him. As events unfolded, his chief of staff, Alexander Haig, intervened to prevent the army from receiving direct orders from Nixon. Had Nixon called out the army, this would have resulted in a constitutional crisis and could have left the army running the show. In either case, to have to rely on such means as an assassin or the army would be the end of our democracy. Elites of one sort or another will always rule. The questions are which sort of elite will they be, and how will they rule?

The two students whom I had overheard excoriating Baltzell a few months earlier seemed somewhat mollified by this explication of his work. But the one who had been doing most of the talking on that earlier occasion asked to see me in my office. Yes, she said, she understood and appreciated Baltzell's analysis of how the upper class was formed. But why, she asked, turn to the upper class to help guard our democracy? Why should we trust them? There is no reason to believe any of them will do the right thing. And Baltzell, she went on, as a member of the upper class is more or less—she hesitated to say this—tooting its horn. I urged this young woman to make an appointment with Baltzell and argue the point with him directly but perhaps not quite so colloquially. However, there was more than intellectual puzzlement in her comments. As I had done many years earlier and still sometimes caught myself doing, she was looking at persons as though they were categories. Baltzell wasn't a person, he was a WASP, period. I wasn't a person, I was a Jew, period. She wasn't a person; she was a female, period. This is a kind of sociology-think run amok. It is a common failing and has sometimes had harmful consequences. Categories are necessary for many things, certainly for scholarly and scientific research, but they are essentially abstractions, and their misuse often obscures the individual person to whom they are applied. In that case, they inhibit empathy. And without empathy there cannot be a personal relationship or indeed any genuine communication. I pointed this out gently, but also directly, and I think she began to see the point. But she had asked me serious questions, and I felt obliged to answer them.

In Baltzell's view, there are several characteristics possessed by a vigorous American upper class. First, their members will have achieved high status, which means there is greater likelihood their words and actions are influential. Second, should one or more of them "blow the whistle" on political or legal wrongdoing, they will be far more able to weather reprisals. Their money, strong kin network, and professional and social affiliations will support them. Archibald Cox and Eliot Richardson, two members of the Boston upper class, are examples. Cox stood up to President Nixon's illegal maneuvers, and Nixon could do little but fire him, whereupon Richardson resigned in protest. The reprisal and resignation had little effect on the careers of either of the two men but called national attention to the arbitrariness and willfulness of Nixon's actions. The upper class, argued Baltzell, can afford to be financially and socially independent and less fearful in exercising critical judgment. And not least, the American upper class is committed to the nation's democratic values. They also partake of these values, and many have served and continue to serve as the nation's stewards. When these values are threatened, they are threatened personally. Harvard did not permit Joseph McCarthy with his irresponsible accusations to enter its precincts; less confident and less secure universities did. (To set the record straight: although the university in general was steadfast, some administrators within Harvard waffled in the face of McCarthy's accusations. See *The New York Review of Books*, "'Veritas' at Harvard," July 14, 1977, Volume 24, Number 12.)

Baltzell did not claim the upper class would always come to the rescue, only that its members were favorably positioned and more inclined to do so, when the need arose. The support for his argument, I pointed out to the student, was based on a number of sociological and psychological assumptions as well as historical evidence. But whether the argument was sound depended on the worth of its assumptions, its consistency, and the range of the evidence marshaled for its support. These are matters she might want to consider exploring. And with this our meeting ended.

As to my own views: much though I loved and respected Baltzell, I did not agree with him. The upper class is no longer what it once was, as he himself clearly recognized in his *Protestant Establishment in America*. And while not yet defunct, the old WASP American upper class is anemic. To attempt to revitalize the upper class seems to me to be hopeless. Family ownership of banks, brokerages, and industrial corporations no longer provides the foundation for the upper class that it did in the era the class was first established. But even if the class is strengthened, its members will always eventually close their doors to newcomers, and the enfeeblement process will begin again. In any case, this is quite the wrong tack to take in safeguarding American democracy. American democracy will stand or fall through adherence to its constitution and laws. These are our bulwarks, and these are what need to be protected and strengthened continually. And these are where I put my efforts, as all Americans should put theirs as well.

In some respects, Baltzell himself recognized all this. He shook his head in disgust and resignation when he read of upper-class persons who had done politically foolish or cowardly things. He constantly encouraged his minority students who had the ability, but were certainly not of the upper class, to consider going on to study law and then, perhaps, to enter politics. They had a chance of becoming elites. But even if they succeeded, as he well recognized, it might take a couple of generations before any of their descendants had gained a sufficient economic and political foothold to place them at the threshold of the upper class. Whether they would then be invited to come in was, of course, another question. Exceptions do occur, but they cannot be counted on.

In the meantime, however, we cannot wait for a resuscitated upper class to step up. New elites, not of the upper class, have indeed arisen from all parts of the nation. They have gained wealth from new industries and inserted themselves into the business and political mainstream of American life. Some, not all, have given false information to investors and been caught out. They have hurt many people, and some of them are now in prison. None of the whistle-blowers was of the upper class, but so far our morality and laws still hold.

This passionate student who was wrestling with Baltzell's ideas went on in sociology and did well. She worked hard, learned to evaluate people and ideas with less partiality, and got a PhD. I believe she is still teaching in a fine, small women's college in New England, and I am confidant that she looks upon her WASP students as individual human beings.

In 1982, within months of each other, my father-in-law and father died. I mourned them both for several months. My father-in-law, Henry Kottek, was a small man with a big heart and an open mind. He was playful, passionate, and highly intelligent. Like my father, he was a Jew and an immigrant. He had come to the United States in 1904 from Warsaw, alone, when he was a twelve-year-old boy, and settled with his mother's brother and family in New York City. He was largely self-taught, a socialist, admired some of the views of Scott Nearing and Norman Thomas, despised the Soviet Union, loved the plays and writings of George Bernard Shaw and Bertrand Russell, was an avid reader of detective stories and children's poetry, and was a fierce Scrabble player. He had a demanding moral sense and was courageous in standing up to argue for and defend what he believed was the right thing. His selfless passion was beguiling, and he was much loved. He and I had become close friends.

My father was my first teacher, and from him I leaned many things that continue to inform what I do today. I reflected on the odysseys of my parents' and in-laws' lives and thought of my son. I had been the bridge between the older and the younger generations, introducing and helping to explain each to the other, so to speak, and sometimes facilitating communication between them. And now my son might take that place (which in a few years he did) and extend that caring line of life to the next generation. It was a line made up of oppositions at each connecting point, but also one in which the oppositions are joined. Max Weber observed in his great lecture on "Science as a Vocation" that unlike some peasant of the past like Abraham, who at the end of his days knew what was to be known and could die "satiated with life," we in the modern age know that our life is incomplete, that within twenty to thirty years the knowledge of the next generation will have exceeded ours. However great the gap between the generations, it is in the bridges between them, bridges that we all eventually become, that we find ourselves. In that complex mix of oppositions and joinings, of gaps and bridges, there are no final terminal points, only movement. After commiserating with me, a friend said, "So Hershl, now you're on the front lines." Not exactly a cheering observation, but a true one. We all belong to a generation. We all move from the back lines to the front lines. We are all being taught both by the generations that preceded ours and those that immediately follow. And we learn and teach and play our part in this endless process. This is part of our experience of being human. And this is why the destruction of part of a generation through war or plagues or natural disasters is so enormously devastating. All the generations, not only the ones killed, are lessened.

In 1983 Baltzell was almost seventy years old. He had once said of Parsons after he had retied from Harvard, "He's a giant." He was, of course, speaking metaphorically of Parsons' intellectual achievement, but given Parsons' munchkin-like height, it was quite funny. Now Baltzell would soon retire. His entire career had been spent at Penn, and he had given unstintingly of his talents and friendship in service to the sociology department and the university. His work was perhaps better known nationally than that of any other sociologist at the university except Erving Goffman. In his own right he was a giant too. Victor and I decided to organize a colloquium series in his honor. Everyone in the department was asked, and most agreed, to give a talk. Two of his advanced graduate students, Richard A. Farnum and James P. Abbott, were also included, as was Judge A. Leon Higginbotham, who had for years taught a course in the department. At the end of the yearlong series of talks (which some of the faculty said they wished would continue!) the papers were gathered together into a book, which I edited: *Social Class and Democratic Leadership, Essays in Honor of E. Digby Baltzell*,[15] published in 1989 by the University of Pennsylvania Press.

At the end of the spring semester of 1983, after three years of service, our "outside" chairman moved on to become an associate dean in the School of Arts and Sciences. Despite his Rotarian-like ministrations and the beneficial effects of the Baltzell colloquium series, the department's equilibrium was still a bit uncertain, and another outside chairman was quickly brought in. In 1985 Victor left Penn and began teaching at another university nearby. Baltzell retired in 1986 but continued to teach one course every other semester. With four exceptions, the senior faculty who had been in the department when I first arrived had retired or died. I would soon be in the rank they had vacated. Three demographers were hired. The criminologists left the department en masse and moved back to the Wharton School of Business and Finance, where they would doubtless enjoy an increase in their salaries. Despite the obvious jokes from the covertly envious about the need to combat shady business practices, this move was an administrative decision. The department began to use more part-time faculty to teach undergraduate courses. Enrollments continued to decline. The intellectual effervescence of the late 1960s and 1970s was over.

In the late 1980s, our second outside chairman stepped "down" to become provost of the university. The sociology department was clearly a stepping-stone to higher things. Under his somnolent guidance, the department had been lulled into stability for a few years. One of the younger sociologists who had joined the department in the mid-1970s and was now a full professor was elected over two of the demographers to take on the chairmanship. He was intelligent. He was also a radical. Some years earlier, I had challenged another colleague, also a radical, as being an ideologue who would let any student pass who spouted the right political line. Both of these radical colleagues came from upper-bourgeois backgrounds. But as Baltzell used to say, he never met a Communist who wasn't a millionaire. (Neither of these colleagues was a Communist or a millionaire; they had merely both been trained at Berkeley during its period of left-political effervescence in the 1960s and 1970s.) Although the new chair never said or intimated anything of the sort, I wondered whether he and the colleague I had challenged might view me as being a turncoat. But in fact, he treated me and others fairly and even-handedly and proved to be an excellent, thoughtful chairman. I grew to like and respect him.

Within three years this excellent chairman left the department to take a post at a university on the West Coast. A demographer was finally installed as chair, and with only one slight exception, each new chair in the department has since been held by a demographer.

Notes

1. Kessinger Publishing, LLC, Whitefish, MT, 2005 (facsimile edition).
2. Vintage Books, New York, 1966.
3. The Free Press, New York, 1979.
4. The Free Press, Glencoe, IL, 1958.
5. University of Chicago Press, Chicago, 2000.
6. Houghton Mifflin Harcourt, Boston, 2010.
7. Houghton Mifflin, Boston, 1964.
8. Doubleday, Doran & Co., Inc., Garden City, NY, 1935.
9. W. W. Norton & Co., New York, 1932.
10. Octagon Books, New York, 1963.
11. Harcourt, Brace & World, New York, 1966.
12. Oxford University Press, New York, 1956.
13. The Free Press, Glencoe, IL, 1959.
14. Anchor Books, New York, 1955.
15. University of Pennsylvania Press, Philadelphia, 1989.

15

We Happy Few

In late 1991, a few of the second-year sociology graduate students approached me with an unexpected request. Would I give a seminar on the sociologists of the Frankfurt School? There were, they said, other students in the anthropology, philosophy, and political science departments who were also interested, perhaps a total of about seventeen students in all.

I was much surprised by this. With a few notable exceptions, student interest in Marxist thought and in sociological theory in general, which had never been great to begin with, had for the past several years been waning. I doubt whether the kind of courses Victor and I gave a decade earlier would now have been well attended or well received. Interest now was in the assemblage of notions in Pierre Bourdieu's work, which seemed to hold out the promise of easier comprehension than the dialectical analyses of the more obvious neo-Marxists. This turned out to be shorter lived than anticipated. Unlike Sartre, who at least had the odor of the streets about his work, and Levi-Strauss, from whom one got wisps of the jungle, Bourdieu's potpourri of concepts, despite or perhaps because of the claim to their synthesizing, publically directed radicalism, gave off the dusty air of the library bookshelves from which they were culled. There is just so much one can do with the statuary of such terms as cultural, social, and symbolic capital and the recondite, apparently summary notion of "habitas." Erving Goffman's more flexible work would soon move toward the center and be even sooner replaced by network theory. But these developments take us beyond the temporal scope of this book. Lest I be misunderstood, I am not saying all fads are foibles.

At the undergraduate level, interest in theory had become virtually nonexistent. Indeed, my graduate assistant, a young, able English student, once scolded the students in one of my undergraduate theory courses for not having read their assignments! I did not think this was appropriate; the students, after all, were not babies—or at least they weren't supposed to be. Yet I was delighted he had done this. My classes and seminars were required; students liked me personally, but few went on to take additional seminars or reading courses in theoretical subjects. Perhaps the request of the graduate students was an expression of nostalgia for the intellectual excitements of the preceding student generation that they wanted to recapture for themselves. The past sometimes looks rosy when the present is drab. After a couple of weeks pondering whether I would be acting out of nostalgia too, I agreed to give the seminar in the spring semester.

The subject matter of "the Frankfurt School" is difficult and far ranging, involves many philosophical, cultural, political, and historical perspectives as well as those of psychoanalysis and esthetic theory, and is grounded in German sociology, principally that of Marx and Max Weber. It would not be possible to examine more than a very small part of this material in one semester. It was also doubtful the students knew what they would be getting into. What was required was a kind of foundation course, a course that clarified certain of the key ideas that supported the wide range of more specialized developments. Kant, Hegel, Marx, and Lukács again! Ernst Block should be put into the mix as well. And not least, Freud. All this to be followed by selections from Fromm, Benjamin, Adorno, Horkheimer, Marcuse, Lowenthal, and Neumann. Then a short bibliography of other, not-quite-as-well-known Frankfurt School members. And of course Martin Jay's history of the Frankfurt School, *The Dialectical Imagination*.[1] I wrote up a five-page syllabus that covered what I considered the basic issues and the appropriate readings, distributed this to the students who had approached me, and recommended they dip into some of this material over the next few months before the spring semester began.

In reading the new translations of books by Benjamin and Adorno as they came out, I had not thought much about the original members of the Frankfurt School for several years. I had continued to read Marcuse and Habermas also, but the latter's interests drew on more recent philosophical and social scientific discussions and would require separate treatment. I decided to cite but not include Habermas' work in the seminar.

In preparing this material, I began to mull over what I knew about the extraordinary group of men who had produced it and to consider again what the nature of their appeal was. First and foremost, the philosophical and cultural subject matters of their work attracted me. They were dealing with issues of meaning, of the domain defined by

Marxists as "superstructure," which is by and large where my interests lay. They were showing how our feelings, social position, generation, religion influence everything we do—all the things we make or think. Second, their analyses centered on the many obvious as well as subtle ways in which we are estranged from others as well as ourselves, from our bodies and minds, our pasts and loves, our pleasures, imaginations, sorrows, expressivity—that is to say, all the ways that "late"-bourgeois culture separates us from our humanity.

At one time, in my early twenties, this material spoke to me, to my sense of being distant from almost all things, and to the belief that bourgeois culture threw up barriers blocking my desire to reach fully into the world. I thought of myself as akin to Harry Haller, the protagonist of Herman Hesse's novel *Steppenwolf*, the intellectual doomed in the bourgeois age to be forever isolated and alone. But now in my sixties, I was more connected to life, more reflective, and a bit less romantic than I had been as a twenty-three-year-old. And although I was well aware that modern culture is quite thoroughly bourgeois, it did not seem to me obvious how or to what degree the love I have for my wife and son, for my parents and family and friends, for my teachers and colleagues and students, for ideas and music and literature and art (and the World Series) was distorted or compromised or lessened by that culture. Marx once said that the great productive powers of the bourgeois age bring for the first time in human history the cultural riches of the world within everyone's reach—an appreciation of the bourgeois age rarely noted by commentators of the right or the left. I would underscore that one does not need wealth to appreciate these riches. I am neither poor nor rich, but the libraries and museums and concert halls are open to me and to anyone interested in their contents for little and many times for no cost. My *Steppenwolf* fantasy was a conceit expressing other-than-bourgeois dilemmas.

In rereading Adorno, Horkheimer, Benjamin, and Marcuse, I saw that, with the partial exception of Benjamin, these thinkers were extraordinarily tendentious. In his delicate unfolding of what he considered to be the fullness in the European literature and life of the past, accompanied by a faint, barely intimated leitmotif of a future redemption, Benjamin aimed to reveal the poverty in the literature and life of the present. His image of the angel of history forever rushing forward but with head always turned to peer at the receding past is the figure at once emblematic and expressing the tragedy of his life and work.

Adorno's work, on the other hand, is mixed, marred in equal measure by arrogance, great learning, and dismay in apprising the modern age—qualities, I now saw, that distort or obscure the object he is examining. *The Authoritarian Personality*[2] (1950), a massive study of which he was the major author, is an example. The study purports to show that those who have authoritarian personalities—that is, are rigid, uncomfortable with ambiguity, intolerant of differences, moralistic, controlling, punitive, among other characteristics—are more inclined to be attracted to conservative, reactionary, even fascist ideologies. The study ignores the vast array of authoritarian personalities in the ranks of the left of which he, two of my fellow John Reed Club members, and one or two of my left-wing teachers are examples. The study is also remarkably reductive, making political ideology dependent on personality traits while ignoring such things as opinion leaders, life experiences, place in the life cycle, and the constraints of normative values. Perhaps as a refugee from Nazi Germany he had been so shaken by his experiences that he wanted to expose and combat inclinations toward fascism and anti-Semitism in America. Or what is more likely, he wasn't a good social scientist. Whatever may have been the reason, this deeply flawed study is now largely and fortunately forgotten. Almost two decades after it was published, Habermas dubbed the actions of the Marxist slogan–shouting rowdies of 1968 as "linke fascizmus"—left-wing fascism. Exactly right. The right wing does not own this kind of personality.

Another, more sustained example of a kind of erudite deafness in Adorno's work is in his writings on music. After having studied composition with Alban Berg, written a fascinating but somewhat hair-raising book on Berg's music and preoccupation with death, *Alban Berg: Master of the Smallest Link*[3] (1991), and continuing to compose chamber music and art songs, one would expect him to be knowledgeable of a great variety of musical idioms and forms. Yet his commentaries on American jazz are astonishing in their ignorance and wrongheadedness. It is not required that he like jazz, only that he hear what is happening in the music, understand before publishing his views something of the music's origins, the continual and varied sources of its inspiration, and its evolving tonal and atonal structures. But no, as a self-proclaimed arbiter of musical taste and value, he dismisses jazz as repetitious and static, much the way he characterizes and dismisses popular music. In his view, the static quality of jazz and popular music, their seemingly endless fetish-like repetitions, have a lulling effect, which leaves the hearer semi-tranquilized and less capable of being critical of society.

(See his essay "On the Fetish-Character in Music and the Regression of Listening" in *The Essential Frankfurt School Reader*,[4] edited by Andrew Arato and Eike Gebhardt, 1982). He is not speaking of elevator "muzak," for which his remarks would have relevance and make sense. But he had no comprehension of the pleasures to be had in jazz or in popular music, of the communal excitement and joy that both kinds of music can generate, or of the sorrow that they often express. He not only lacked empathy for people's responses to these kinds of music but also seemed unaware of the shoddiness of his scholarship. Just as in his earlier study of the authoritarian personality, he did not bother to consider negative instances to his thesis. "Los Cuatro Generales," to cite but one example of a song more associated with revolt than bourgeois soporifics, was a popular song of the left during and after the civil war in Spain. It is as repetitious and fetishistic as a song can get, but it hardly lulled anyone into inaction. Many other examples can be given. However, he wanted the revolution within music that Schoenberg and Berg had initiated to inspire a political effect. But when did this ever happen? Even the consternation evoked by Stravinsky's innovative "Rites of Spring" when it was first performed in Paris had no other effects than many boos and an emptying of the concert hall. Not exactly a revolution. But Stravinsky was not a composer Adorno much cared for.

Max Weber was essentially self-taught in musical matters. Yet it is instructive to compare his sociology of music (*The Rational and Social Foundations of Music*,[5] 1958) with that of the formally trained and far more technically sophisticated Adorno (*Introduction to the Sociology of Music*,[6] 1976). Unlike Adorno, Weber does not examine what are presumed to be the influences of national character (a concept most sociologists, including Weber, consider to be empirically unsupported and thus sociologically useless) on the internal harmonic developments and moods in the works of the composers of particular nations. Rather, his socio-historical analysis clarifies in a way that we do not find in Adorno the growing rationalization that is singular to modern Western, as apposed to Eastern, music, whether of Germany, France, England, Italy, Russia, or America. Adorno's musical erudition becomes a kind of hyper-intellectual gossip, an ethnocentricity of view in which a salvo of condemnation is directed to aspects of this or that composer (and therefore of this or that nation) that does more to obscure than illuminate. Traditions, national folk materials of rhythm, melody, and mode that virtually all modern composers draw on, are either given little attention or evaluated on irrelevant, largely negative, standards. My understanding in 1991 of Adorno's often skewed musical analyses was later amplified by the comments of musicologist and Beethoven expert Charles Rosen. (See Charles Rosen, "Should We Adore Adorno?" *New York Review of Books*, October 24, 2002, and the discussion between Rosen and his critics, *New York Review of Books*, Feb 13, 2003.) I decided to ignore Adorno's musical analyses in the seminar unless one or more of the students knew enough about music to understand them.

I had never met Adorno but assumed that, like his writing, his attitude in person would be one of disdainful superiority. But even Marcuse, with whom I had spent an evening several years earlier discussing American and European developments and found personally affable and not at all superior in attitude, was, like Adorno and all the other Frankfurt scholars, negative toward the modern. There is indeed a great deal in the modern age that is abominable and deserves to be actively criticized and above all changed. The political repression of vast numbers of persons in countries of the Middle East and East, the continual poverty of billions of people, the ignorance and disease that continue to be the lot of millions of children in the United States and elsewhere, the destructive injustices that many women, blacks, and various ethnic populations continue to experience, the mendacity of many of our political and business leaders that has provoked and accelerated the financial crises plaguing the West in recent decades, and much more, not least, on the cultural front, the misplaced feeling that is intrinsic to the sentimentality of a great many films, stories, novels, paintings, and music that falsifies and confuses our emotional lives. Because their criticism is so blanket and unrelenting, the analyses of the Frankfurt scholars do nothing to correct these dilemmas. As a group, the distinctive quality of their overall intellectual output remains, as my mother used to say of my aunt Celia, "farbissen"—their writings are cranky and bite at everything. (Aunt Celia was a refugee from Paris who lived with us for a time in the late 1930s. Everything my mother cooked or did for her was, as Celia put it, "besser vie a crank"—better than an affliction. But Celia was comparing my mother's efforts with what she had experienced in Paris. So too, the Frankfurt scholars were comparing the modern age to the perfection they envisioned in the future. Who wouldn't be farbissen?)

The ubiquity of alienation as a major theme among the Frankfurt scholars is unique among neo-Marxist thinkers. There is little or none of this in the writings of the French, Italian, English, Russian, Chinese, Indian, African, American, and South American Marxists.

This obsessive emphasis was, and to some extent still is, a puzzle that I tried to unravel (not fully satisfactorily) over the next few months. The thought that anyone who, like Adorno, felt superior to and therefore above most things would by definition feel distant from most things occurred to me, but I quickly discarded the idea since others in this group did not seem to have this attitude to the same degree. Rather, I began with the assumption that the emphasis on alienation might be attributable, in part, to their German-Jewish upbringing as well as to the growing tensions in Germany after the First World War. With the exception of one or two, most of the members of the Frankfurt School were Jews. In addition to several standard texts on the political and religious history of Germany, a few studies by George Mosse, my former teacher, were useful: *The Crisis of German Ideology: Intellectual Origins of the Third Reich*[7] (1964); *Germans and Jews: The Right, the Left, and the Search for a "Third Force" in Pre-Nazi Germany*[8] (1970); *German Jews beyond Judaism*[9] (1985). A few other studies, mentioned below, were also useful. What I found was interesting, but I did not uncover the whole story. In a few paragraphs, the hundreds of pages I had read revealed the following.

As Germans, the Frankfurt scholars were exemplary, occupying the upper reaches of the cultural elite. The range of their learning and the sweep of their concerns fulfilled the highest tenets of the ideal of "Bildung"—cultivation. This ideal, which has its source in the Greek conception of Paideia, was originally concerned with the education of the young. Paideia entered Christian thought early (see Werner Jaeger *Early Christianity and Greek Paideia*,[10] 1969), and in the sixteenth century was generalized by German Pietism into the ideal of Bildung. Bildung was not directed to the young alone; all were enjoined to develop their talents in order to bring out resemblances to the features of God that lie within. To develop one's talents thus not only links one to the divine but also to others who have the same, or potentially the same, features. Gradually, however, Bildung was further generalized by philosophical and political thinkers into a humanistic and Enlightenment ideal that by mid-nineteenth century had become established as one of the highest standards of secular culture. It was through Bildung that one could relate to all of humankind and all that was highest in human culture. By the twentieth century, the religious roots of Bildung had become obscured. But something of the earlier linkage of this ideal to the sacred likely contributed to the honor and status that continued to be conferred upon Germans who were considered to exemplify

Bildung. And the Frankfurt School scholars were such Germans. But they were also Jews.

In late eighteenth-century Germany, Moses Mendelssohn, a Jew, won a philosopher's prize over no less an eminence than Immanuel Kant, and Rahel Varnhagen, also a Jew, entertained the greatest of German poets, Goethe (see Hannah Arendt, *Rachel Varnhagen, the Life of a Jewish Woman*,[11] 1974). Jews, however, were still often excluded from much of German society. Marx's father, for example, could not practice law as a Jew in late eighteenth century until he had converted to Protestantism. But by the early nineteenth century, the Enlightenment and its accompanying ideal of Bildung had taken hold and nourished the hope among many Jews and non-Jews alike that a universal relationship of human beings to one another would be fostered. For Jews, the realization of this hope would put an end to their pariah status and exclusion from civil society. And indeed, over the first decades of the nineteenth century in Prussia and in several cities in other parts of Germany, Jews were granted full citizenship and with this the right to pursue a variety of careers, including the holding of government offices. Anti-Jewish sentiment, however, was never fully stilled. Richard Wagner's 1850 fulminations against Jewish composers, repeated in more elaborate form in 1868, as well as the brothers Grimm's popular portrayals of evil Jewish spirits stoked the anti-Jewish fires. By the 1870s, eruptions of what was for the first time called "anti-Semitism" occurred in Germany, and however assimilated or intermarried they had become, Jews were characterized by some as a distinct race. Despite the extraordinary contributions of Jews in Germany to science, mathematics, medicine, philosophy, art, music, literature, and government, anti-Semitic attitudes and acts of exclusion of Jews began to mount. Georg Simmel, for example, the social philosopher, a generation older than the Frankfurt scholars but known by most of them, was blocked from promotion at the University of Berlin because of what was considered his "desiccating [that is, Jewish] mentality." The facts that Simmel's father had converted to Catholicism and his mother to Lutheranism, and that as a child he had been baptized as a Lutheran, meant nothing. For the racists, once a Jew, always a Jew.

By the early 1920s anti-Semitism was sharply on the rise. Gangs of Nazi hooligans had begun roaming the streets of many cities shouting anti-Jewish slogans and smashing Jewish stores and properties. It was not long before a Jew was killed. Walter Rathenau, a Jew and the foreign minister of the Weimar Republic, was shot to death in 1922.

Gerhard (later Gershom) Scholem, a close friend of Walter Benjamin, who later became one of the great historians of Jewish mysticism, left Germany. With the advice of Martin Buber, he settled in the British protectorate of Palestine in 1923. There he wrote to Benjamin to join him, but Benjamin never did.

All the members of the Frankfurt School except for Benjamin left Germany in the mid-1930s for America. They had achieved the highest cultural standards of their nation yet had to flee for their lives because they were Jews. The fact they were thoroughly secularized mattered not at all; to be a Jew was no longer an overtly religious attribute but a biologically inherited one. Given these experiences, It would be understandable were they to turn against their country. But in fact the global condemnation of the modern bourgeois age, already present in their writings while they were in Germany, continued unabated after they left. Other German Jews, equally accomplished, who were honored for their achievements and denigrated in Germany for being Jews—among many hundreds of such, Ernst Cassirer, Fritz Kaufmann, Hannah Arendt, Alfred Schutz (who was Austrian), and Karl Mannheim (who was Hungarian) are examples—were not "farbissen," did not condemn the entire modern age; they condemned the Nazis and their racist ideas and fascist practices. Being a Jew in Germany, therefore, could not have been the sole reason for their global negativity. But their experiences in Germany surely gave them further reason to continue being negative: in the Marxist view, fascism was the grotesque spawn of capitalism. Reason enough to be critical of the entire age that produced this late horror. This conclusion could have served to further rationalize the alienation they already experienced, their sense of being marooned in the age in which they had no other choice to live. Adorno was the only one of the Frankfurt scholars to return to Germany after the war ended.

I was not satisfied with this analysis. I knew how easy it was for me to slip into the "half empty" as opposed to the "half full" evaluation of things. But I had no way of tapping into what I was sure was also important, namely, the psychological dimension of the Frankfurt scholar's negativity. I decided that in the seminar I would be an expositor of their work, try my best to clarify issues and hold my evaluations to myself unless asked.

At the beginning of the semester five students showed up to enroll in the seminar. A few of the several other students who had expressed interest sent notes of regret referring to scheduling conflicts. Perhaps my five-page syllabus had frightened them off. In some ways, I was relieved and decided, given the few students, the seminar could meet comfortably in my office. Two of the students turned out to be quite good, grasped the arguments well and were creative in discussing their implications. The remaining three were having difficulty, which required that I do more translation and exposition of the materials than anticipated.

Teaching does not require much energy, but it does require some. There were weeks when, after three late-afternoon hours of fairly intensive discussion, I would leave for home quite tired. The days were only slowly getting longer, and it was for many weeks of the semester still dark by the time I left the campus. Sometime in early March, about midway through the semester, I had an odd and troubling experience that has stayed with me ever since. Soon after boarding the train for my ride home, I fell into a light sleep in which my thoughts were a mix of remembrance and fantasy. Earlier that afternoon, as I well remember, we had been having a lively discussion of Marcuse's *Eros and Civilization*[12] and relating his notion of surplus repression to Marx's *Capital* and early *Economic and Philosophical Manuscripts*[13] as well as to Freud's *Civilization and its Discontents*.[14] Alienation overcome and freedom gained was, as usual, the theme of the discussion. One of the students pressed the analysis farther than it seemed to me Marcuse had taken it. He thought the idea of freedom in Marcuse was conjoined implicitly to the idea of the completion of society, a kind of perfection in its makeup that did not yet exist. Once achieved, this student believed Marcuse was saying, the truly complete society would make free everything that human beings do, their thoughts, loves, friendships, work, art, science—everything. Another student, a young married woman who had a child, observed that raising a child is never free and unrepressed. And on the discussion went until it was narrowed down to issues of determining what Marcuse meant by surplus repression as opposed to the more limited repression of the free society. As the rocking of the train continued to lull me, parts of the afternoon discussion became mixed in my thoughts with a strange fantasy-dream. In one of the buildings in a city in which all the buildings were of marble, I dreamed that an immensely large book in front of me was being closed. "Now we have finished," I either concluded or heard a voice say. And as one sometimes does in dreams that are not deep, I began to associate in a distorted way to comments in the seminar, to the idea of the completion of society. But these became mixed with another set of associations. As the very large book was being closed I heard a rumbling. I went to the window and there saw vines and vegetation beginning to move toward the buildings of the city. They began to embrace all the buildings, including the one where I was. Slowly the marble slabs began to fall and crumble from the fronts of the buildings as the vines grew larger and tightened their hold about the outer walls, and then the buildings began to crash down. I probably had heard the screeching of the brakes of the train, but I think I was frightened into waking up—luckily, since my stop was approaching. I kept thinking of the dream while walking the few blocks home through the now dark and quiet streets. Had I associated to some of the images in Gabriel Marquez's *One Hundred Years of Solitude*[15]? I had read this magnificent book over twenty yeas ago and hadn't thought much about it since. I could see, however, the associated analogies from Marquez's book. Just as the protagonist of the story is finally able to decipher everything in the parchment and finally gain all the knowledge of his family, the family and the city in which he lives come to an end. I stopped walking as the other associations became clearer to me. Just as in the completions of my dream and in Marquez's story, so too does the completion of society lead to an end. In the former it is the end of families and cities, in the latter it is the end of society itself.

Perfection and completion are final. There is nothing better, nothing more. This is essentially the Hegelian notion when, in the final synthesis and completion of knowledge in which all historical contraries are reconciled, the end of history is reached. Then humankind is no longer alienated from God but becomes synthesized with the eternal. The standards against which the degree of our alienation is measured, both for Hegel and the Frankfurt neo-Marxists, are standards of completion. In this final standard, as Lukács put it, subject and object are no longer separated but become one. And if that indeed occurs, then there is no longer a subject or an object. I knew that Marx differed from Hegel. Hegel's "end of history," he said, was the end of human prehistory. But he was never clear, nor indeed could he be, given his anti-mysticism, as to what would follow. These comments were in his youthful writings. In his mature works, he concentrated on issues of exploitation and immiseration but did not speak of alienation again. Indeed, without Hegel's eternal God or some equivalent, the total overcoming of alienation in the merger of subject and object in this world would mean their annihilation, their death. Did Marx see this and therefore replace some of his youthful formulations?

Dinner was waiting and it was chilly, but I needed to walk and think. I couldn't put out of my mind the question whether there might be in the utopias of the Frankfurt scholars an unexamined, tacit yearning for death. Completion and perfection are final things; there is nothing more. Was it this, the end of history, the end of humankind, for which these utopian scholars were reaching? I have not been able to answer this question. Perhaps I do not want to. It seems bizarre and mad. But it remains, and it is troubling.

In the courses on sociological theory I taught until I retired twelve years later, there were practically no students that showed interest in Marx, Marxism, or in any kind of sustained theory. A few concepts here and there is what students wanted, ideas that would help them organize a study that dealt with a social problem or a social phenomenon that seemed to be gaining public attention. And there were, I hasten to say, some very good and interesting studies that students continued to do—more interesting in some ways than what many students had done before. One student, for example, did a fascinating study of an Ayurvedic medical institution in western Massachusetts and the social composition of its largely American clients. Another student did a study of friendship patterns of women as compared to friendship patterns of men. (I hope this study is published because it puts an end to the simple-minded, and I think destructive, clichés of both men and women about their so-called profound social differences.) Yet another student explored an odd and unexpected change in definitions of virginity that had begun to occur among middle-class teenagers in the early 1990s. Still another fascinating and revelatory study was done of family patterns among poor African Americans. Another student carefully explored the way middle-class single mothers who had turned to welfare to support themselves were managing to maintain and project their middle-class identity. Many other fine studies were done while I was teaching, but in none was Marxian theory of much or indeed of any use. A bit here from Goffman, another bit from Weber, something of a network concept, and the usual array of sociological ideas such as role, status, gender, group, norms, and so on. By 1995, Marxism had quietly slipped away from the interest of sociology students at the University of Pennsylvania without leaving a trace. Perhaps Marxism will matter again someday, but I have my doubts.

Notes

1. Little Brown, Boston, 1973.
2. Harper, New York, 1950.
3. Cambridge University Press, New York, 1999.
4. Bloomsbury Academic, New York, 1982.
5. Southern Illinois University Press, Carbondale, IL, 1958.
6. Continuum Publishing, New York, London, 1988.
7. Grosset & Dunlap, New York, 1964.
8. H. Fertig, New York, 1970.
9. Hebrew Union College Press, Cincinnati, OH, 1997.
10. Belknap Press of Harvard University Press, Cambridge, MA, 1961.
11. Harcourt, New York, 1974.
12. Beacon Press, Boston, 1955.
13. International Publishers, New York, 1964.
14. Norton, New York, 2005.
15. Harper Collins, New York, 2003.

Afterword

Among the extraordinary occurrences of the twentieth century—the two world wars, the political revolutions, the spectacular advances in weapons of mass destruction, the decline of centuries-old world powers and the rise of new ones, the emergence of new nations, new classes, new kinds of national leaders, the development of a global economy, the great and ever growing numbers of technological, industrial, scientific and medical triumphs, the beginning exploration of space, among many, many others—one occurrence has extended throughout the entire century and, until recently, been the subject of a great deal of controversy and comment. That occurrence is Marxism, both as an ideology and a political agenda. Throughout the twentieth century, Marxism was the vehicle adopted by many groups, especially, but not only, in economically backward countries, to accomplish their political and social aspirations. Marxisms of various kinds have arisen around the world, in the nations of the East as well as the West, in Africa as well as in South America. Marxism has been not only, or not so much, a supra-mundane "religion" as an ideal adopted and refashioned by peoples to gain fulfillment, as they understand it, in *this* world.

The success of Marxism among the many competing doctrines of earthly hope and salvation produced in the nineteenth century was due in part to the example, in the beginning of the twentieth century, of the uprisings in Russia, followed, at the conclusion of the First World War, by the successful Soviet revolution. The rapid, worldwide dissemination of the news of these uprisings and revolution, and with it elements of a Marxist vocabulary as well as Marxist ideas, secured for Marxism a place in the consciousness of people that no other doctrine was able to achieve. However many doctrinal differences among Marxists soon appeared, and however deep they became, there is little doubt that Marxism, at least early in the twentieth century, was strongly linked to the example of the Soviet Union. This link has—perhaps—proved to be fatal. For this was also a century in which the massive Soviet Russian attempt to realize a version of Marxism failed. And with that failure, occurring less than a decade before the beginning of the twenty-first century, Marx's ideas, which had seemed so well entrenched and growing, have been almost completely dismissed (with, of course, a few lingering but fast-diminishing holdouts), both in Russia and the West. There is movement in this direction as well in the East, especially in China.

The worldwide spread of Marxism as well as its sudden collapse are, at the very least, puzzling. How did either of these events, affecting so many billions of people, happen? What is the nature of the appeal that Marxism had in the West and the East? Why Marxism? How did Marxism's hold loosen? These are questions whose answers await the studies of future historians when the ideological passions that still linger over Marxism will have cooled. For the moment it seems safe to say that Marx's theory, if not his ideology, is seen in the West as an ambitious nineteenth-century intellectual effort that has been largely superseded by later developments. But not Marxism as an ideology, as a projection of the hope of rescue and betterment of oppressed peoples, which is another matter.

To speak of Marxism in the West and East, moreover, is not merely to distinguish two kinds of Marxisms, one European, the other Asian. It has been clear for some time that, even from its inception, Marxism was not, and never did become, of one kind either in the West or in the East. Despite many of its adherents' claims that Marxism is a "science," Marxism is not equivalent to any physical science. The laws of physics do not change from nation to nation; there are not national "Newtonianisms." There has been much contention, political as well as ideological, among Marxist thinkers. There have been many Marxist groups, many different Marxisms, much effort to define the authentic Marxist way. Nevertheless, despite internal disputes of occasionally grave import, the chief Marxist ideas that emerged in the twentieth century were all nationally framed.

Marxism is as various as there are nations. There are, or have been, the Russian, the Chinese, the Korean, the Japanese, the German, the French, the Polish, the Austrian, the English, the American, the Latin American, the Italian, the Indian, the Islamic Marxisms, among others. Moreover, Marxist intellectuals and ideologues of each of these areas and nations were well aware of their often deep differences. Marx's ideas and political programs have been shaped and redefined as they passed through these different national and political cultures.

Afterword

Although its reach is no longer global, Marxism continues to inspire and move people who have found in elements of Marxist thought and language a way to express their hopes for rescue from many sufferings. It is not hunger and endless toil alone that move people, however. Nor is it the arbitrary rule of leaders who throttle the freedoms of the people they rule and place enormous economic and social burdens upon them. It is hope of deliverance from their oppressions generated and expressed by those in whom they give their trust, whether mistakenly or justifiably—in a Mao Zedong, or a Fidel Castro, a Hugo Chavez or a Nelson Mandela—these are what move people. Marxism has declined in the West and has become a weak voice, but its world import is not yet spent. As a way to give words to what many people desperately need and hope for in this world, Marxism still matters and will continue to matter until other, better words are found, other voices heard. This is the remaining legacy of Marxism.

Acknowledgments

I wish to thank several friends and colleagues who have read portions of or the entire book in manuscript and given me support and helpful advice: Matthew Bershady, Stuart Bogom, Michael Brodie, Michael Ciliberti, Valerie Ciliberti, Robert C. Cohen, Richard Farnum, Reneé C. Fox, Allen Glicksman, Robin Wagner Pacifici, Peter Simmons, and Diane Sjolander. Howard Schneiderman's excellent judgment was especially helpful in guiding the book into publication. Norman Miller read the entire manuscript, made valuable suggestions, cheered me on, and corrected my idiosyncratic versions of Yiddish. Harriet Lefley and Samuel Z. Klausner also read parts of the manuscript, corrected several errors, and made many useful suggestions. Above all, I thank Victor M. Lidz for serving as an unstinting sounding board and loyal friend, correcting faulty interpretations and encouraging me to continue when I faltered.

Index

A
Aaron, Raymond, 118
A Contribution to the Critique of Political Economy, 113
Action Theory and the Human Condition, 211
adolescent novels, 33
Adorno, Theodore. 95, 117, 119, 122, 235
  erudite deafness, 236
Agnew, Spiro, 198
Alban Berg: Master of the Smallest Link, 236
Albrecht, Milton, 67
Alcott, Louisa May, 11
Alechem, Scholem, 207
Ali, Muhammad, 162, 163
alienation, 18, 146, 238–241
Allen, Fred, 6
Allen, Woody, 6, 38
A Mask for Privilege, 42
American Indians, 11ff.
  Iroqruois, Navaho, 11
American Youth for Democracy (AYD), 44–75
analysis versus morality, 222
Anderson, Elijah, 200ff.
accomplishments, 200
  racism in Sociology Department at Penn, `196, 200ff.
Americanicity, 193
anger and flight, 79–80
Anscombe, G. E., 151, 153
A Place on the Corner, 201
Arato, Andrew, 237
Arendt, Hannah, 131, 168, 240ff.
Aristotle, 44, 78
Arrow, Kenneth, 217
assembly line work, 95–99

Auchncloss, Louis, 223
Aulinsky, Saul, 135
A View from Old New York, 223

B
Baltzell, E. Digby, 145, 168–9, 185, 219ff.
  class consciousness, 71–72, 138, 219ff.
  Tocqueville, Alexis De, 222, 225
"back to Kant," 95
Bananas, 58
bandits, 3–6
bar mitzvah, 16ff.
Barnard, Chester I., 100
Barnouw, Victor, 50
  primitive communism, 50
  private property, 48ff.
Baron von Reventlow, 123
Becker, Howard, 123, 125, 201
Behemoth, 225
Being and Nothingness, 94
Bellah, Robert, 151, 241
Bellow, Saul, 207
Benjamin, Walter, 224, 235, 240
Benny, Jack, 6
Berkeley, 29, 134, 139
Bilbo, Theodore, 69–70
"Bildung," 239–240
Black church and Hasidic synagogue, 204ff.
Black Philosopher; White Academy: the Career of William Fontane, 150
Black Worker in the Deep South: a Personal Record, 205
  Hosea Hudson, 204
  Nell Painter 204, 205
Block, Ernst, 124, 224
blue books, 181
Bourdieu, Pierre, 233

253

Bourgeois versus socialist art, 56ff.
Bread and Wine, 56, 192
   Silone, Ignazio, 56
Brecht, Berthold, 122
   Weimar, 122ff.
British Museum, 112, 181
Brodie, Michael, 157, 163
Bucharest, 2
Buddenbrooks, 95, 159
Buffalo, New York, 2–50
   bohemian section, 44
   early years, 2ff.
   ethnic populations, 11
   petty bourgeois, 49–50
   winters, 10
Buhle, Paul, 134
Bulgakov, Mikhail, 65
Burning Daylight, 28
   Jack London, 28

C

Caesar, Sid, 120
Call of the Wild, 28
Cantor, Nathaniel, 67
   Sociology Department, 67ff.
   University of Buffalo, 35–48
Capen, Samuel P. 41ff.
   Liberal standards, *12, 70*
   University of Buffalo, 35–48
Capital, 25, 31, 98, 126, 155, 181, 242
Capitalism, Socialism and Democracy, 69
capitalist victims, 25
Caruso, 7
Cassirer, Ernst, 120, 208, 241
Castro Fidel, 132, 133, 249
categories, 111, 194
Catholic Church, 14
Catholic Workers Movement, 56
Cemeteries, 189
   Marx's grave, 189
Character and Social Structure, 128
   C. Wright Mills, 121, 133
   Gerth, Hans H. 120–129
Chavez, Hugo, 249
Che Guevara, 132
Chomsky, Noam, 95, 178
Chopin, 46
Christ, 13
Christians and Jews, 14ff.
Cioran, Emil, 87
civil rights, 96, 107, 130, 134, 148, 154, 156–7, 167, 2–9, 219

   march, 152
   movement, 149
class and ethnicity, 187ff.
class consciousness, 71ff., 138, 219ff.
cold war, 77, 94ff., 130, 164
communes, 45, 217, 218
   kibbutzim, 47
   Twin Oaks, 117
   University of Pennsylvania, 218
Communist party, 46ff.
   Buffalo, 47ff.
   Italy, 153–4
   joining, 47ff.
   ideology, 48
   leaving, 75
   SLP, 46
   Soviet Union, 41
   students' role 31
Cooperstock, Henry and Ruth, 182
Coulanges, Fustel de, 55
Court Jester, 58
Cox, Archibald, 227
Cronkite, Walter, 168
Cuba, 130ff.
   Castro, 132, 133, 249
   Che Guevara, 133
   cult of personality, 131
   Mills, C. Wright, 133
   paradise, 132
   Sartre, Jean Paul, 133

D

daily prayer book (Siddur), 6
Darkness at Noon, 66
Darwin, Charles, 35
Das Capital, 126
Dawes Plan, 122
De Leon, Daniel, 28, 31, 168
Death on the Installment Plan, 38
DeCraemer, Willy, 200, 205, 210
Democracy in America, 223
Democratic Centralism, 152
Descartes, 74
Deutscher, Isaac, 112
Dewey, John, 91ff.
   Trotsky, 71
   Whitman, Mary, 78, 91–93
dialectics of death, 242–244
Dialectics of Nature, 105
Dilthey, Wilhelm, 95, 113
Dostoyevsky, 22
draft counseling, 163

Index

drug use, 163ff.
Dubois, W. E. B., 141, 203
Dupree, A. Hunter, 210
Durkheim, Emile, 68, 95, 155, 158

E
Eagleton, Terry, 34
Early Christianity and Greek Paideia, 239
early doubts, 52
Economic and Philosophical Manuscripts, 242
Edel, Abraham, 150
Einstein, Albert, 39
Eisenhower, Dwight D., 89, 93, 96, 128–9
Elder, Joseph, 125, 128, 173, 179
Eliot, T.S., 57–8, 199
Elman, Mischa, 7, 36
Engels, Frederick, 43, 44, 54, 73, 185 189
England, 184ff.
   British Museum, 112
   cemeteries, 189
   class and ethnicity, 187ff.
   class and understatement, 188
   personal discovery, 193
   Sherwood forest, 186
   textile mills, 190
entering middle class, 79ff.
equality, 46, 87, 222
   kinds, 48ff.
Eros and Civilization, 242
evil eye, 10
Experiment Perilous, 196
   Fox, Reneé, 169
exploitation, 85, 111, 243

F
Fackenheim, Emil, 127
factory owner, 12
factory workers, 10–13
Farber, Marvin, 41, 78, 85, 90, 116, 117, 149, 151, 183
father and father in law's deaths, 228, 229
Father Coughlin, 6
father's bible stories, 5
father's business, 18, 20, 31–34
   attempt to unionize, 41–48
father's experience in Bolshevik army, 63ff.
Faulkner, William, 57
F.B.I. in Madison, 136
Fitzgerald, Ella, 35
Fleisher, Leon, 52
Flower, Elizabeth, 150, 153, 218

Fontane, William, 150
Ford, Gerald, 198
forms of knowledge, 90
   necessary reason, 175
Foundations of the Critique of Political Economy, 126
Fox, Reneé, 169, 195ff., 210ff., 217
Frankfurt School, 53, 91, 117, 153, 234
freedom undefined, 178
Freud, Sigmund, 123
Freud: the Mind of the Moralist, 137
From Max Weber: Essays in Sociology, 121
   Gerth, Hans H., 124
   Mills, C. Wright, 124
from student to teacher, 144, 154
Fromm, Erich, 89
Functions of the Executive, 106

G
Galli Curci, 7
Gasset, Ortega De, 225
Gay, Peter, 124
Gebhardt, Eike, 237
Geertz, Clifton, 210
General Mark Clark, 27
generation, 63, 66, 71–93, 103, 113–119, 129 133–5, 143–4, 156, 160, 184, 191, 202–3, 211, 214, 218–222, 225, 229, 237, 240
genius, 80
German Bund, 113–114
German Jews Beyond Judaism, 239
German Jews, 237
Gerth, Hans H., 118, 124, 124ff.
   adviser, 135
   hydraulic Marxism, 125
   reaction to Parsons, 127–8
   return to Germany, 128
   teacher, *122*
   Weber, 121
   Weimar, 122, 127
   writer, 127
Gillespie, Dizzy, 35
Ginsberg, Ralph, 144
God, 17–22
   prayer, 70–72
Goodbye to All That, 101
Gould, Mark, 211
Gouldner, Alvin W., 57–8, 101, 176ff.
grade inflation, 154–5
Graduate studies, 81
Gramsci, Antonio, 152, 168

Grandfather's study, 207
Grandmother's stories, 2–4
Graves, Robert, 101
Grey, Zane, 11
Gross, Llewellyn, 67
Grosz, Georg, 124
Growth of the Soil, 57

H
Habermas, Jürgen, 211
Haig, Alexander, 226
Haitian uprising, 26
   Tousant L'Ouverture, 26
Hammet Dashiel, 60, 66, 67, 108
Hamsun, Knut, 57
Harvard, 39, 41, 81, 116, 125, 141, 178, 181, 196, 200, 207–8, 211, 227
Hegel, 125–6, 243
Heidegger, Martin, 85, 116, 125
Hemingway, Ernest, 57
Herzog, 207
Hess, Moses, 82
Hesse, Herman, 235
Higginbotham, A. Leon, 230
Hillel at Penn, 142
History and Class Consciousness, 117
History and the New Left: Madison Wisconsin 1956–1970, 134
Hook, Sidney, 92
Horkheimer, Max, 235
Horowitz, Vladimir, 173
Hosea Hudson: His Life as a Negro Communist in the South, 205
Hume, David, 94
Hunger, 57
Husserl, Edmund, 78, 85, 94
hydraulic Marxism, 125

I
Ideology and Social Knowledge, 179
ideology and sociology of knowledge, 179
Ideology and Utopia, 112
ideology, 47, 49, 178–9, 225, 247
   anomaly in Marx, 53, 113
"idiocy of rural life," 46
imitations, 93ff.
intelligent managers, 99ff.
Intention, 151
intermarriage, 36
International Publishers' bookstore, 31
Introduction to the Sociology of Music, 237

J
Jaeger, Ellsworth, A., 112
Jaeger, Werner, 239
James, Henry, 42
James, William, 42 91
Janowitz, Morris, 131ff.
Jaspers, Karl, 122, 127
Jay, Martin, 191, 234
Jazz, 126ff.
Jew hatred, 5, 15, 240–1
Jew or Gentile, 37
Jewish students at Penn, 143
Jews, American and European, 191
   attitudes at Penn, 143ff.
   Orthodox and Reform, 13
John Dewey, Philosopher of Science and Freedom, 52
John Reed Club, 41, 51ff., 56–8, 61
Johnson, Lyndon Baines, 124, 162, 167
Journey to the End of the Night, 58
Joyce, James, 57
Junior faculty, 170–171
Just So Stories, 133

K
Kafka, Franz, 57
Kamenka, Eugene, 89
Kant, Immanuel, 85
   Concept of history, 128
   Critiques, 94
   ethical precepts, 85
   utilitarianism, 86
Kaplan, Norman, 115, 199
Karl Marx: Pre-Capitalist Economic Formations, 52
Kaufmann, Fritz, 78, 93, 94, 117, 120, 241
Kaye, Danny, 58
Kelland, Clarence Buddington, 11
Kennedy, John, 128, 154,
   assassination, 154
   Civil rights, 154
   Cuba, 147
Kenton, Stan, 35
Kierkegaard, Soren, 87
Kiev, 1, 3
King, Martin Lither, jr., 152, 167
Koestler, Arthur, 65
Korean War, 89
Kornhauser, William, 225
Korsch, Karl, 118
Ku Klux Klan, 70
Kuklick, Bruce, 150

Index

L
Lackawanna, New York, 30
Lang, Fritz, 124
Lavin, David, 141, 144, 172
Lavin, Marguerite, 182
leaving Madison, 135
Lenin, 33, 47, 119, 153, 168, 217
Leventman, Seymour, 144
Levi-Strauss, Claude, 233
Lewis, Sinclair, 224
liberal integrity, 70
Lidz, Victor, 104, 105, 127, 186, 197, 198, 211
"linke fascizmus," 226
Lipset, Seymour Martin, 182
London School of Economics, 182
London, 186
   England, 184ff.
London, Jack, 28
Long, Huey, 225
"Los Cuatro Generales," 237
Lowenthal, Leo, 117, 234
Lukács, Georg, 85, 113, 117, 182ff., 123, 243

M
Madison, Wisconsin, 123ff.
   population and ethnicity 1959, 128ff.
Malraux, André, 215
Man's Fate, 215
Man's Place in Nature, 207
Mandela, Nelson, 249
Mann, Thomas, 95, 117, 123, 159
Mannheim, Karl, 85, 112–114 121–123,
Manzù, Giacomo, 192
Mao Zedong, 249
Marcuse, Herbert, 117, 238
Marković, Mikhailo, 150ff., 172, 178
Marquez, Gabriel Garcia, 243
Martin Eden, 28,
Martins, Herminio, 179, 182
Marx and Judaism, 83ff.
Marx, Karl, 24, 25, 44ff., 60ff., 80ff., 90ff., 114ff., 124ff., 157ff., 179ff., 198ff., 242–244
Marx's grave, 189
Marxism and Christianity, 84
Marxism and Philosophy, 118
Marxism and Poetry, 34
Masses and Mainstream, 57
Mead, George Herbert, 91, 95
Mendelssohn, Moses, 240

Merton, Robert K., 177
messianism of Jews, 84
Meyerson, Martin, 143
Miller, Henry, 55
Mills, C. Wright, 121, 131, 133, 225
M. I. T., 158, 178
modern poetry manuscripts collection at University of Buffalo, 42
Monroe Doctrine, 25
Morgan, 189
Moser, Shia, 78, 117
Moses identification,
Moses stories, 5,
Mosse, George, `19ff.
Mother and music, 7
Mother and police, 107
Mother's death, 173

N
Naptha, Felix and Georg Lukács, 124
Native Americans, 10–12
Natural History Museum in Buffalo, 11
Nausea, 133
Nazis, 6, 7, 13, 14, 224
necessary reason, 175
   Parsons, 175
Negative Dialectics, 125
neo Marxists and utopian thought, 119
Neumann, Franz, 117, 225
New Left Review, 34
New York Review of Books, 227, 238
Newton, Isaac, 176
Nixon, Richard M., 128, 167, 225–6

O
Odessa, 2, 88
Olds, James, 210
"On the Jewish Question," 83ff.
One Hundred Years of Solitude, 213
organic view of society, 164
organicist metaphysics, 183ff.
Oriental Despotism, 54
Origin of Species, 57

P
Paideia, 129
Painter, Nell, 204ff.
Pap, Arthur, 175
Paradigm of the Human Condition, 205ff.
Parry, William Tuthill, 78, 81–82
Parsons, Helen, 214, 215

257

Parsons, Talcott, 67, 79, 95, 127–128, 175–179, 182, 187, 199, 205–217, 229
    Whitehead, 127, 183
Peirce, Charles, 91
Pentagon Papers, 195
phenomenology, 74
    Husserl, 78
Philadelphia Gentlemen, 220
Philadelphia in 1962 and 2012, 138ff.
Philosophy Department at University of Buffalo in 1950, 77ff.
Philosophy Department at University of Pennsylvania, 1962, 149ff.
philosophy of science, 90ff.
    Social Sciences, 91
Piano playing, 20, 35
Pinchik, 7
Plekhanov, 34
police, 106
    custodians, 108
    others, 106
Pollak, Otto, 192
Pope John XXIII, 192
Pound, Ezra, 57–8
Pragmatists, 91ff.
prayer, 12, 18
Presidential campaign of 1952, 88
Presidential campaign of 1960, 128
primitive communism, 51
private property, 49ff.
    Simone Weil,
promised land, 7
    utopia, 5
Protocols of the Elders of Zion, 49
Psychology Department at University of Buffalo in 1950, 78

Q
Quixote, Don, 22

R
rabbis, 55
Rachel Varnhagen: the life of a Jewish Woman, 240
Rachmaninoff, Sergei, 46
racism in sociology department at Penn, 196, 200ff.
radical critics, 56ff.
radical intentions, reactionary views, 99
radicalism in 1950s

Radio Days, 6
radio shows, 6
relativism, 87
religion, 16ff., 22, 35–6
    Marx's view, 55
    response to Gouldner, 176ff.
Reveille for Radicals, 135
Richardson, Eliot, 227
Richler, Mordechai, 184
Rieff, Philip, 137, 144
riots in United States and Europe, 164
Rizzo, Frank, 166
Robertson, Roland, 183
Robeson, Paul, 47, 48, 65, 75
Roosevelt, Franklin D., 39
Rosen, Charles, 238
Rosenberg, Ethel and Julius, 96
Rosenblatt, Yoselle, 7
Rubenstein, Jonathan, 109

S
Safire, William, 198
Saint Matthew Passion, 55
Salmon, Joseph E., 25, 34, 35
Samuelson, Paul, 159
Sartre, Jean Paul, 81, 91, 93, 117, 233
Scheler, Max, 83, 85, 96, 117, 177
Schumpeter, Joseph, 70
Schutz, Alfred, 241
Schwartz, Maurice, 7, 29
Searles, John, 212
secret research, 164ff.
Seghers, Anna, 123
Settembrini, 126
    The Magic Mountain, 126
Shachtman, Max, 70ff.
Shawnee leadership conference, 156ff.
Shostakovich, Dimitri, 65
Silone, Ignazio, 56
Simmel, Georg, 95, 113, 157, 207, 240
Simpson's Department Store, 12
Singer, Isaac Bashevis, 10, 36
Skinner, B. F., 91, 119
Sklair, Leslie, 182
snobbery, 9
Social Class and Democratic Leadership, 230
social democracy, 154
Social Democratic Party (SDP), 225
Socialist Labor Party (SLP), 29–31
Socialist Workers Party (SWP), 71

258

Index

Sociology and the Military Establishment, 131ff.
Sociology at University of Buffalo, 1946, 67ff.
Sociology at University of Wisconsin, 1960, 121ff.
sociology of knowledge, 112ff., 1176ff.
Sokolifke, 3
Solzenitsin, Alexander, 88
sour grapes nastiness, 79
Soviet Union, 23, 117, 123, 129, 134, 153–4, 183, 204, 228, 247, 335
Spencer, Herbert, 127, 189
Stalin, Joseph, 35, 189
Steppenwolf, 235
Stern, Isaac, 88
Stevens, Wallace, 101
Stravinsky, 237
Stevenson, Adlai, 89
subject-object relations, 95, 240
   Lukács, Georg, 85, 113
synagogues, 17, 18, 108

T
Tarski, 78
teaching sociology, 146ff., 151–155, 158–9
textile mills, 190
The Ancient City, 55
The Ancient Regime and the French Revolution, 225ff.
The Apriori in Physical Theory, 175
The Apriori in Talcott Parsons' Social Theory, 175
The Authoritarian Personality, 236
The Coming Crisis of Western Sociology, 176
The Crisis of German Ideology, 239
"The Criticism of Everything," 129
The Descent of Man, 57
The Dialectical Imagination, 234
The Essential Frankfurt School Reader, 237
The German Ideology, 53
The God that Failed, 56
The Modern Prince and Other Writings, 152
The Need for Roots, 51
The Origins of Totalitarianism, 32, 225
The People, 29
The Philadelphia Negro, 141

The Politics of Mass Society, 255
The Power Elite, 131, 225
The Protestant Establishment, 219
The Rational and Social Foundations of Music, 237
The Rector of Justin, 228
The Revolt of the Masses, 225
The Sea Wolf, 28
The Slave, 31
The Structure of Social Action, 126ff., 175
The Vanishing American, 11
Theses on Feuerbach, 72, 94
Thomas Mann: The World as Will and Representation, 95
Thomas, Dorothy, 169–170
Thomson, George, 39
Three Penny Opera, 124
Tillich, Paul, 87
Tocqueville, Alexis De, 228ff.
Tokugawa Religion, 151
Toronto, 1, 4
translating Lukács, 124
Trotsky, 58, 65, 92, 93, 112, 168
Twin Oaks, 119

U
Ukraine, 1
Ulysses, 57
Unamuno, Miguel de, 143
uncles, 21, 23
undergraduate chair, Sociology Department, 168ff.
University of Buffalo, 39ff.
University of Pennsylvania, 137ff.
University of Toronto, 182
Utopias, 3, 54, 60, 112, 119–120, 149, 132–156, 244

V
vaues seminar at University of Buffalo, 87ff.
veterans of World War II in university classes, 1946
Vietnam war and protests, 162ff.

W
Walden Two, 119
warehouse apartment, 19
Weber, Alfred, 113, 155
Weber, Max, 68, 95, 126, 229, 237
Weil, Simone, 57

Weimar Republic and culture, 122ff.
Wharton School, 130ff.
Whitehead, Alfred North, 127, 183ff.
Whitman, Mary, 78, 91, 98
Wiley-Halsted Press, 182
Williams, William Appelman, 125
Windelband, Wilhelm, 40
Wisconsin radicals in 1960
    comparison to veteran radicals, 134
    view of socialism, 134
Wittvogel, Karl, 124
Wolfers, William, 78
Wolpert, Jeremiah, 67

work experiences, 97–110
    auto assembly line, 97
    junior executive, 99ff.
    social work, 102ff.
    police and foremen as fellow workers, 106–107
world libraries, 80

Y
Yevgeny Yevtushenko. 85

Z
Zinoviev, Grigory, 117, 118